SOUTHERN LITERARY STUDIES

FRED HOBSON, EDITOR

FAITHFUL VISION

TREATMENTS OF THE SACRED,

SPIRITUAL, AND SUPERNATURAL

IN TWENTIETH-CENTURY

AFRICAN AMERICAN FICTION

JAMES W. COLEMAN

LOUISIANA STATE UNIVERSITY PRESS

BATON ROUGE

Designer: Andrew Shurtz
Typeface: Minion
Typesetter: G&S Typesetters, Inc.
Printer and binder: Edwards Brothers, Inc.

LIBRARY OF CONGRESS
CATALOGING-IN-PUBLICATION DATA:
Coleman, James W. (James Wilmouth), 1946–
Faithful vision : treatments of the sacred, spiritual, and supernatural in
twentieth-century African American fiction / James W. Coleman.
p. cm.—(Southern literary studies)
Includes bibliographical references and index.
ISBN 0-8071-3091-5 (cloth : alk. paper)
1. American fiction—African American authors—History and criticism.   2. Religion
and literature—United States—History—20th century.   3. American fiction—
20th century—History and criticism.   4. Religious fiction, American—History
and criticism.   5. African Americans in literature.   6. Spiritual life in literature.
7. Supernatural in literature.   8. Spiritualism in literature.   9. Holy, The, in literature.
10. Faith in literature.   I. Title.   II. Series
PS374.N4C643 2005
813'.509382—dc22
2005007354

CONTENTS

FAITHFUL
VISION

Faithful Vision

Its Definition and Significance in

African American Culture and Fiction

RELIGIOUS AND BIBLICAL TRADITIONS that engender faith are arguably the most important cultural feature to African Americans, and therefore also to African American writers who write about black culture. However, despite the large amount of recent theoretical and philosophical work that addresses religion, critics who write about black novels seldom deal with religious and biblical traditions in fiction. It is interesting, for example, how often commentators have denied the seriousness of the treatment of the Bible and Christian faith in James Baldwin's *Go Tell It on the Mountain* (1953) and how many others just ignore it and write about different aspects of the text.[1] Perhaps not all black writers incorporate the Bible in some important way into their fiction, following the cultural pattern in which black people make it an integral part of life communally and individually, but black novels reveal that most writers with a significant opus explore the Bible as a dominant part of some text. Yet no study of African American fiction deeply examines how religious tradition based on faith and centrally bound in the Bible manifests itself in a significant number of novels from the late twentieth century, when black writers had the freedom and formal resources to portray the tradition as complexly as possible. Perhaps critics of African American fiction are too insulated and concerned largely with the critical discourses holding sway in the academy, reminiscent of how mid-twentieth-century writers like Richard Wright and Ralph Ellison focused on mainstream literary traditions to establish themselves. These academic discourses do not necessarily preclude a cultural analysis showing that faith stemming from the biblical and religious is a primary rather than secondary or symbolic reality in black life and oftentimes in black writing, which is what my analysis reveals. However, it is not popular practice to apply academic discourses to investigate the aspects of black novels that I analyze in this study.

I would argue that many—perhaps most—African Americans have faith in the sacred, spiritual, and supernatural because belief is the only thing possible, in the final analysis, in the context of the African cultural background and black American culture and history. Particularly in light of a history of oppression, only faith can contain the unfathomable evil of the past and present and project future deliverance from it. In *Go Tell It on the Mountain*, the black slave woman Rachel is illiterate, but she knows the story of God's liberation of his people in the Bible. She says, "When the Word has gone forth from the mouth of God nothing can turn it back" (71), and she thus has faith in the coming of the freedom of black people. W. E. B. DuBois in "Of the Faith of the Fathers" in *The Souls of Black Folk* (1903) talks about a similar faithful "religious feeling of the slave" (190). This belief is a large part of what sustained black people through slavery with "souls" that represent the essential expression of American humanity. Thinking about oppression historically, black people look at the range of human possibility and explanation and what is beyond. The African American past shows the intentions of white people with power to destroy the humanity of powerless blacks through the process of making them chattel. From this perspective, what I call "faithful vision" represents reality because it is beyond comprehension that African Americans could emerge from the destructive past as complex human beings without the agency of the sacred, spiritual, and supernatural that subverted the plans of people with power. Faithful vision also emphasizes a daily individual struggle related to the group experience, just as the Bible does, and encompasses the personal need to do what is necessary—good, bad, and indeterminate—to survive and accomplish goals. Biblical grace is a practical doctrine relating to personal and individual action because it enables forgiveness and salvation through faith. In neither *Go Tell It on the Mountain, The Souls of Black Folk*, nor in life is faithful vision simplistic and otherworldly; oftentimes, it is a self-serving but powerful religious belief that relates to actions in this world.[2] The Bible is the main text in cultural tradition that supports a generally faithful vision—expressed in ritual, song, and saying—of collective and individual worldly endurance, success, and divine salvation in African American culture. However, with regard to faithful vision, the African worldview of the shadowy voodoo religion has a strong influence and a relationship with the Bible and the associated Judeo-Christian ethic.

Traditionally, an appropriated story of faith is more substantively influential than biblical moral statute. Faith overarches the philosophical, social, and political concerns of the secular world, and grace saves the soul through faith, grace—the unmerited love and forgiveness of God that is always available—having important implications for saving the individual self. Among its vast complexities, the Bible presents the Old Testament story of God's plan that allows human perfidy, oppression, and suffering; the New Testament story of Christ and the doctrine of saving grace; and prescriptions of moral law. In Romans 9:13-26 of the King James Bible, Paul refers specifically and generally to the Old Testament; the text tries to resolve the unknowable mystery and apparent oppressive arbitrariness of God's purpose as it is revealed throughout the Bible. Verse 26 says, "And it shall come to pass, that in the place where it was said unto them, ye are not my people; there shall they be called the children of the living God." From one possible position, the point is not so much that it is important to adhere to religious law as that those oppressed as part of God's inscrutable plan will finally be embraced by God. Philosophical questions and social and political problems only have resolution in faith in ultimate moral purpose. Individually, grace negates sin and saves. Paul says in 1 Timothy, verses 14–15, "And the grace of our Lord was exceeding abundant with faith and love which is in Christ Jesus. This is a faithful saying, and worthy of all acceptation, that Christ Jesus came into the world to save sinners; of whom I am chief." For the most part, African Americans do not share the clarity of Paul's biblical vision, and they have countless responses to and interpretations of the Bible, including different ideas about the limits and meaning of grace. But it is still arguable that an appropriated biblical story has been the dominant source of a faith that has evolved historically with racial experience in African American culture. As my analysis shows, voodoo "faith" has potentially innumerable connections to the biblical and is inseparable from it, in spite of voodoo's relative obfuscation.

The African American imagination is conceived in the individual struggle and the historical travail created by the horror of the past of slavery and racism. The core of this past is, as Toni Morrison's novel *Beloved* (1987) calls it, "unspeakable thoughts, unspoken" (198–99). It is atrocity, pain, and suffering seared indelibly on the collective racial being by its unfathomable brutality, evil purpose, and intended perpetuity. The result is that it exists minimally in language and profoundly in a region of feeling beneath language, which is where the "unspeakable thoughts, unspoken" reside in *Beloved*. African American imaginative projection is concrete and abstract. It is outwardly directed toward secular causes and solutions, and more importantly, inwardly focused on a defining vision of religious and spiritual faithfulness with regard to African American life. This vision, like the Bible, Christianity, and the African worldview of voodoo that inspire it, looks beyond the limits of the secular world. Faithful vision is a powerful counter-structure in the imagination of the "unspeakable." It sees sacred, spiritual, and supernatural agency that accounts for African American suffering and oppression, that aids individual and collective survival and salvation, or that justifies what is beyond the scope of human understanding. Most broadly, faithful vision is the saving, sustaining belief that African Americans find collectively and individually in biblically based Christianity in the face of historically determined racial oppression and the hardships of an American experience directly and indirectly connected to the racial. Yet in voodoo/hoodoo culture it is the belief in African-derived gods and spirits that relate syncretically to Christianity and to oppression and life in similar direct and indirect ways. Stated differently, faithful vision is a belief in sacred, spiritual, and supernatural agency that saves the race and furthers the purposes of individuals who adhere to this agency; it is culturally inscribed as a primal-type racial symbol diversely accessed by people in terms of gender and individuality and by religious denominations and communities that sometimes syncretize Christianity and voodoo/hoodoo.

Due to its importance to black people and culture, most black writers at some time substantively portray African American faithful vision and concomitant African and Western religiocosmic influences. Sometimes novels directly or indirectly explore the agency of God in life, but African American women writers often write in opposition to the patriarchal macrocosmic Christian perspective of God and locate the sacred and spiritual in the womanist self that engages in personal, individual relationships. These depictions still portray traditional, less womanist faithful vision as the characters' or the black community's vision rather than the writer's or the text's, and the text's own critical perspective may be conflicted and ironic. In other cases, texts imply such vision because they reveal and do not negate the sacred, spiritual,

4

and supernatural, leaving open the possibility that faith in power beyond the mundane and the rational mind is all that there can be. Reflecting black cultural need and investment from a more controversial perspective related to African tradition, writers also construct alternative theological, spiritual, and supernatural perspectives against oppression and hardship based on the voodoo or hoodoo religion.[3] These narratives engage Christianity in relationships of syncretism and revise the Bible and Christian theology, and voodoo/hoodoo may be a construction that opposes them. In these texts, faithful vision invests the writers in the cultural tradition that they depict, producing a variety of critical and adversarial treatments that seldom reveal the writers' ability to reject their characters' cultural belief.

The novels in this study, most of which are canonical and postmodern, and were written in the last fifty or so years, reveal that the African American fictional tradition has turned back to affirming faithful vision after moving away from it at midcentury. In *The Negro's God as Reflected in His Literature* (1938), Benjamin Mays shows that black literature and religious expression before midcentury portray a traditional biblical God who has relevance in the social life of black people. Mays traces the conceptions of God in "mass" literature—spirituals, sermons, prayers, and Sunday school literature—and "classical" literature—poems, novels, slave narratives, autobiographies, biographies, orations, and social science writing—from 1760 to 1937. His general conclusion is that both focus predominantly on God's intercession in black people's social lives.

> The most outstanding revelation of this study is the fact that the Negro's idea of God grows out of his social situation. The cosmological and teleological conceptions of God are conspicuous by their absence in Negro literature . . . The moral, traditional approach is the one "classical" Negro writers have used. They have apparently been indifferent to modern expressions of God . . . The Negro is not interested in any fine theological or philosophical discussions about God. He is interested in a God who is able to help him bridge the chasm that exists between the actual and ideal. The Negro's life has been too unstable, too precarious, too uncertain, and his needs have been too great for him to become sufficiently objective to theologize or philosophize about God. (254–55)

Talking about writers' indifference to "modern expressions" of God and black people's lack of sufficient objectivity to theologize and philosophize about God, Mays implicitly takes a critical stance toward black writers and black culture that I am not taking. However, he also indicates that in pre-1937 literature and cultural expression, there is a pattern that is the precursor to the later in-depth treatment of faithful vision. God is a practical part of black people's everyday lives. He reveals himself in this world in a "moral struggle against sin and evil" (18) in the broad historical scope of black experience and in individuals' attempts to fulfill their needs. Black writers before 1937 seldom deny the existence or importance of God: "It is tremendously revealing to note that Negro 'classical' writers have, for the most part, adhered rather closely to the orthodox, traditional views of God. In fact, there are to be found only a few astonishing ideas of God in the whole survey. Where there has been a radical departure from orthodoxy, it has been a departure toward atheism as expressed in Humanism or Communism" (253).[4] I would say that black people who are nonwriters deny this existence or importance even less frequently. The significance of the Bible is unstated but implied in what Mays says, and so is faithful vision as a larger, dominant aspect of the culture that earlier writers did not have the freedom and formal resources to display to the extent that contemporary writers can. Obviously, African American literature has changed a lot since 1937. However, more recent black fiction writers have included Christianity among diverse perspectives of the sacred, spiritual, and supernatural and have greatly extended what black writers did before Richard Wright and Ralph Ellison.

Faith is not a word that most associate with hoodoo/voodoo because it is popularly considered "superstitious" and "evil," and it is necessary to establish that faithful vision is an aspect of the religion's syncretism with Christianity in various forms. Theophus H. Smith's Conjuring Culture: Biblical Formations of Black America (1994) is a scholarly text that makes the point about voodoo/hoodoo as a serious, substantive religion that amalgamates with Christianity. (Smith distinguishes the term voodoo from hoodoo, and uses hoodoo and conjure, or conjuration, as parallel terms (48–49, note 27) that denote the North American variant of voodoo. I am not choosing hoodoo over voodoo as the preferred term, but instead conflating the two to indicate an evolution of belief and practice from Africa throughout the diaspora. For me, conjure is synonymous with voodoo and hoodoo.) Smith states that "the sacred text of Western culture, the Bible, comes to view as a magic formulary for African Americans; a book of ritual prescriptions for reenvisioning and, therein, transforming history and culture . . . African spirituality [is] a potent source of black North American religious experience" (3). African American religion is "the interplay of African-derived practices with Euro-Christian sources and traditions" (3–4). Biblical belief becomes transformed to a sustaining faithful vision that is as much constituted by the magic and ritual of voodoo/hoodoo inspired by African culture as it is by the Christian. Smith's analysis demonstrates that voodoo/hoodoo is such an integral part of African American Christian belief and practice as to be inseparable from it.

Certainly in eighteenth-, nineteenth-, and early twentieth-century black communities there was sometimes a clear individual and group awareness of this interplay, but it is unclear to what extent individuals and communities since then have retained voodoo/hoodoo influence unconsciously while being consciously Christian and implicitly and explicitly rejecting voodoo/hoodoo as evil, superstitious belief. In the novels that I treat, faithful vision is a substantive aspect of African American life in instances where people are aware as well as unaware of voodoo/hoodoo, with it always being possible that some black communities could be unaffected. A syncretism with the biblical and Christian, or an oppositional relationship to them, is always there when voodoo/hoodoo is present.[5]

Ellease Southerland's novel *Let the Lion Eat Straw* (1979) affirms faith in the sacred, spiritual, and supernatural as *the* central intention and theme of its narrative and the black communities that it depicts; it represents hoodoo's fusion with Christianity and the Bible and a syncretized faithful vision as a scholarly text can rarely do.[6] Thematically, *Let the Lion Eat Straw* is as much about African American religious faith related to the Bible as are black texts about African Americans who strongly avow Christianity; it is one of the few black novels that so clearly foregrounds religion and related biblical textuality. If anything, the title of the novel gives it a clearer connection to the Bible than the titles of *Go Tell It on the Mountain* and Randall Kenan's *A Visitation of Spirits* (1989), which are about the African American Christian faithful vision that I analyze in chapter 2. *Let the Lion Eat Straw* anticipates the hybrid forms of the sacred, spiritual, and supernatural in many black postmodern novels and perhaps suggests the understated, unknown, or unacknowledged elements of hoodoo in the cultural milieus of novels like *A Visitation of Spirits*. It is not possible to separate hoodoo from its Christian host in the ensuing explanation of faithful vision in this deceptively complex novel.

Let the Lion Eat Straw is partly a celebration of life based on Judeo-Christian faith, but more generally it affirms faith in God that incorporates the characters' good-and-evil-related hoodoo practices and rituals. The Bible projects a substantive aspect of the novel's faith in God's benevolent but inscrutable plan, of which the main character's life and the experience of black people generally are a part. The epigraph is from Isaiah 11:6–7: "The wolf also shall dwell with the lamb, and the leopard shall lie down with the kid . . . and the lion shall eat straw like the ox." The entire last page of the novel reads "And the lion shall eat straw like the ox" (181). In spite of the biblical implications of God's inescapable will, the power that the characters draw upon and that the novel affirms is more than Judeo-Christian. The hoodoo, nature-influenced agency of the "half Indian, half African" Mamma Habblesham (5) and the clairvoyant resources of her evil-spirited mother Angela strongly affect the life of Abeba, the main character. The dominant perspective grafts the African past and ambience onto the biblical and weaves it together with the supernatural that is generally associated with Africa and voodoo and the natural force of the hoodoo-infused environment of the American South, accessed primarily by the hoodoo woman Mamma Habblesham. Before and after her death Mamma is a spiritual, mystic presence that balances Angela's meanness and potential evil.

Angela's distinctly evil acts generated partly by hoodoo supernatural powers are necessary to Abeba's divinely planned life. Angela combines Christian belief grounded in churchgoing, hoodoo divination, and ideals of upward mobility and social uplift in a murky, ambiguous character that is shaded toward an evil that manifests itself in the things that she does to her daughter. She inexplicably will not intervene when Abeba tells her that her uncle is raping her at age fifteen (65–66), keeps the knowledge until Abeba is married and pregnant with her first child, and then threatens to tell Abeba's husband Daniel if she has more children (100–101). This leads to Abeba informing Daniel herself and his subsequent mental breakdown and lifelong psychological instability (102–4). Angela has taken Abeba to a spiritualist who, unknown to Abeba, has predicted that she will have between twelve and twenty children (90–91), and Angela wants to defeat this prophecy that does not fit her plan for her daughter to go to Juilliard and be a great musician. This reasoning does not explain why she lets her daughter be raped approximately fifty times, however (102–3). Angela resents the illegitimate Abeba, whom she blames for all her problems (14–15), but her actions are still always inexplicably mean and evil-spirited. In *Go Tell It on the Mountain* John is the promised great son that his stepfather Gabriel does not want, yet he nevertheless fulfills God's promise in spite of what Gabriel does; similarly, despite her intentions, Angela's actions contribute to Abeba's divinely planned life.

The novel's view (which is ultimately its own faithful vision that is literally contained at beginning and end by the quotations from Isaiah 11:6–7) accepts evil and the efficacy of the acts of individuals whose faithful belief incorporates evil; the breadth and inclusiveness of faithful vision is characteristic of hoodoo's connection to Christianity.[7] *Let the Lion Eat Straw* depicts Abeba's life in which evil perpetrated against her by someone who lives by faith is a significant factor, and concludes that "God has plans which mortals don't understand. He rests in the womb when the new baby forms. Whispers the life-dream to infinitesimal cells. It is God who lies under the thoughts of man. He is cartilage. Memory. The spinning of this earth and a thousand other earths" (176). Mamma's faithful vision is a life-supporting Christian/hoodoo one grounded in the natural practice of hoodoo. Mamma, a midwife, "could look up in the sky on a bright day and tell new life on the way. She start down the road and come across some [pregnant] nervous somebody beating a path to her house" (5). Angela's Christian/hoodoo vision highly influenced by materialism contributes to Abeba's meaningful life, her mother's vindictiveness, abusiveness, and apparently evil intentions notwithstanding. As the novel ends after the forty-five-year-old Abeba's death from cancer, at the funeral Angela says with a "loud voice . . . 'sleep on. Sleep on'"; Mamma "said ever so quietly, 'Hush your mouth'" (180). The voices of Mamma and Angela symbolize the broadness of hoodoo-motivated faithful vision as shown through the characters and also as affirmed by the text.

Let the Lion Eat Straw suggests the overall syncretism of African American faithful belief in the sacred, spiritual, and supernatural that entails personal, individual struggle and coping with and transcending unimaginable racial oppression. The novel's faithful vision is not otherworldly; it addresses good and evil in this world in terms of the individual—mainly Abeba's life—and the historical, which is the unfathomable evil represented by the "hundred million [killed] in the ocean" during the Middle Passage (161). African Americans use different aspects of faithful vision to strive and struggle. Through faith they accept and give thanks for what is good, and remember and accept evil and give praise for its transcendence.

My analysis of *Let the Lion Eat Straw* reveals the similarity and equality of faithful vision in African American novels and communities that see themselves as Christian and hoodoo, their syncretism defining the construction of the latter in the diaspora. Faithful vision has different traits in novels in which black people confess Christianity than it has in works like *Let the Lion Eat Straw* in which the community, and the text itself in this case, more markedly bring together hoodoo and Christianity. The novel *Louisiana* (1994) has a different but similarly strong expression of faithful vision that is hoodoo. *Mama Day* (1988) has a more ambiguous system of belief; its characters verbally reject hoodoo at the same time that they practice and avow it on a deeper psychic level. However, the novel compares well to *Let the Lion Eat Straw* as a text in which the characters combine Christianity and hoodoo in their faithful vision, which is developed in terms of the history of family and community in *Mama Day*. *Let the Lion Eat Straw* has commonalities with most, if not all, of the works chosen, and probably with most that foreground the centrality of African American religious and biblical traditions.

It is clear that faithful vision is essential to African American culture and to many black texts, and its negation or effacement can create a substantive void, even in canonical works. This void sometimes exists in the texts of earlier twentieth-century African American writers working in the realist or naturalist mode or trying to position themselves as modernists. Realism, naturalism, and modernism are obviously different, but each limited writers' exploration of the sacred, spiritual, and supernatural in black culture, in some instances precluding in-depth portrayal and artistic exploration.

Chapter 1 shows how the three literary movements constrained the portrayal of cultural tradition, and also reveals that writers sometimes evolve toward more substantive depictions of black tradition in which faithful vision is important. A survey of eight works demonstrates, among other important points, how the novels' approaches superficially treat an aspect of black cultural tradition instead of delineating it in depth, as the works in the subsequent chapters do. The texts covered are Paul Laurence Dunbar's *The Sport of the Gods* (1902), Richard Wright's *Native Son* (1940), Ralph Ellison's *Invisible Man* (1952) and *Juneteenth* (1999), and John Edgar Wideman's *A Glance Away* (1967), *Hurry Home* (1970), *The Lynchers* (1973), and *Hiding Place* (1981). In chapters 2 through 5, I analyze James Baldwin's *Go Tell It on the Mountain* and Randall Kenan's *A Visitation of Spirits,* Toni Morrison's *Beloved* and John Edgar Wideman's *The Cattle Killing* (1996), Alice Walker's *The Color Purple* (1982) and Gloria Naylor's *Mama Day,* and Erna Brodber's *Louisiana* and Ishmael Reed's *Mumbo Jumbo* (1972).

These novels present an engaging overall textual perspective and an interesting cultural portrayal of faithful vision among African American characters. Textual perspectives include ironic stances toward and affirmation of Christian belief, parody and subversion of it, and apparent affirmation of hoodoo faithful vision. The characters' beliefs within the texts range from traditional Christian faith to untraditional hoodoo faith.

Go Tell It on the Mountain and *A Visitation of Spirits* typify the diverse textual representations of faithful vision in the lives of people and communities that express it differently because of individual and gender experience and the peculiarities of communal experience and history. These novels also fit the overall textual pattern in which faith in the sacred, spiritual, and supernatural with its foundation in the Bible is African American culture's common, salient feature that the text fails to reject, in spite of subjecting it to analysis and negative criticism. *Go Tell It on the Mountain* is probably the foremost canonical novel with regard to foregrounding the black church life, reliance on the Bible, and the historical importance of religious faith, and therefore is particularly important in my study. Kenan's novel does not make religion and the church as central as Baldwin's does, but from the former work's own unique perspective, the tradition of faithful belief that entails the Christian and biblical is a dominant part of theme and structure to almost the same extent that it is in *Go Tell It on the Mountain.* The texts' stances toward the characters' religious tradition are sometimes critically ironic, but just as often the narratives leave open the way for acceptance of traditional faithful belief.

A Visitation of Spirits is postmodern because of its thematization of its own writing and textuality and because it emphasizes the power of the Bible as *writing;* my analysis of it is a transition to my critique in later chapters of novels that are postmodern in narrative technique or according to narrative theory implied or stated in the text itself. Generally speaking, the postmodern is a practical mode to use in writing about the sacred, spiritual, and supernatural in black culture because it broadens the range of the conceptualization of reality so that writers can be more innovative formally and thematically. It also gives writers access to the complex imaginative dimensions of the sacred, spiritual, and supernatural in African American culture that are intangible.

Toni Morrison's *Beloved* and John Edgar Wideman's *The Cattle Killing* are postmodern novels that explore, among other things, the role of the biblical and religious tradition and the concept of God as they are "written" into black culture and thus influence the narrative about the culture. Each novel shows a different textual approach to portraying the sacred, spiritual, and supernatural in a unique community and in individual lives that all share the same general view of African American oppression and are commonly sustained by religious faith grounded in God and the Bible and/or African-derived voodoo. *Beloved* may initially seem to have little to do with religion, but under closer scrutiny, it reveals a rich treasure of references on this topic, and its characters solidly base their lives in faithful belief. *Beloved*'s approach to Christianity and particularly the Bible is a subtle, powerful parody unlike any other in African American fiction. The main target of the parody is the *text* of the Bible itself rather the belief of the characters, which is set in the Bible and also partakes highly of folk and African sources that connect more clearly to the African American experience of oppression. It sounds like African American belief is ultimately influenced by hoodoo, but the text does not state this, leaving the final classification ambiguous. *Cattle Killing* is very much about the oppressiveness of God as inscribed in the Bible. However, unlike *Beloved*, its narrative opposition does not break free from the influence of the Bible, and the characters recourse seems to be the retention of faithful vision that binds them to an oppressive God who can still, paradoxically, reveal his saving power at the instance of greatest oppression. Along with *Beloved*'s, *Cattle Killing*'s treatment of faithful vision is one of the most interesting in African American literature.

The text that is most intentionally subversive of African American traditional belief in God and biblical and contemporary patriarchy is Alice Walker's *The Color Purple*. It and Naylor's *Mama Day* thematize writing. *The Color Purple* does so from the perspective of achieving female voice, and *Mama Day* from the perspective of telling a story that is passed down in words and is also subconscious myth. Thus both fall into the postmodern pattern that allows writers to innovate and to delineate the complexity of the African American imagination. Naylor's novel is perhaps less critical of the patriarchy, but both pose female spirituality as an alternative to that tradition. Walker's text presents a uniquely direct attack on God and Christianity, and also ironically formulates a counternarrative to the dominant one in which a much more traditional faithful vision is implied. I stress that although the text does not affirm faithful vision, it parallels its loud polemic with an understated formal and thematic structure that validates faith and the Christian tradition, which suggests the inability of the narrative perspective to separate itself from cultural belief. This is a different exposition of faithful vision that is adversarial and yet at the same time reflective of its power and centrality for African Americans. Naylor's work is a comprehensive cultural exposé of the African American sacred, spiritual, and supernatural instead of a parody of religious tradition. Its depiction of hoodoo's syncretic relationship to Christianity is a crossover to the treatment of the greater depths of the diasporan cultural tradition in *Louisiana* and *Mumbo Jumbo*.

Brodber's *Louisiana* and Reed's *Mumbo Jumbo* define African American hoodoo in terms of its conflation with the diasporan. Most consider *Mumbo Jumbo* to be an African American novel because Reed was born in America, and some may question the inclusion of Brodber's work in a study that is primarily about African American novels because she is Jamaican. *Louisiana* has its primary setting in New Orleans and defines African American hoodoo in terms of its link to the diasporic. The writers' nationalities notwithstanding, there are no substantive differences between the general subject matter of the novels as it relates to hoodoo as a diasporic religion with qualitatively similar beliefs and practices that transcend national boundaries and typify the African American. *Mumbo Jumbo* is an African American novel that yokes the African American and Haitian, and *Louisiana* is an African American novel that joins the African American with the Jamaican.

Further, it is important to include *Louisiana* because it is explicitly a strong treatment of hoodoo that compares well with Reed's novel. *Let the Lion Eat Straw* provides an example of hoodoo faithful vision, but although it is deceptively complex, does not work in a balanced comparison to *Mumbo Jumbo*. Also, like *Mumbo Jumbo* and unlike *Mama Day*, the entire narrative of *Louisiana* is a specific, unambiguous avowal of hoodoo, which it makes clear is not a peripheral occult practice. It is a serious African American religion based in faithful vision that is similar to the Christian in *Louisiana* and dissimilar but equally strong in *Mumbo Jumbo*.

Brodber's and Reed's novels describe hoodoo in representative specific instances of its almost endless variations, and continue along the lines of the broad pattern of novels with postmodern approaches that are well suited to the exploration of black culture. *Louisiana* revises the biblical and Christian with a strong emphasis on the centrality of black women, which makes it generally similar to *Beloved*, *The Color Purple*, and *Mama Day*, and in theory this revision is embedded in the novel's postmodern narrative through a hoodoo aesthetic that accounts for the text's production. There is a corresponding hoodoo aesthetic in *Mumbo Jumbo*, which is much more oppositional to the Bible and Christianity than *Louisiana*. With the possible exception of *The Color Purple*, its faithful vision is the most radically different conception of black religious faith in the tradition, and among the novels I examine it is probably the most oppositional to Western religious values.

Mama Day, Mumbo Jumbo, and *Louisiana* highlight how much voodoo/hoodoo practice and belief have inflected and, in the last two novels, overridden African American Christianity. Considered as a whole, these texts and the others that I examine display an African American Christianity that is significantly different from the mainstream as a result of hoodoo influence, and the characters often are unaware or refuse to notice it. In the conclusion, I talk about the difference between the textual and cultural viewpoints, and use the former to support the overall judgment that African American faithful vision is still Christian, although it is more universal because of inflection by elements of hoodoo, which is broad, inclusive, and harmonic. In this context, there are latent and minor implications of hoodoo in several texts that I note in the summation.

This analysis is mostly about African American postmodern novels since 1970 when African American writers have had the wherewithal to explore the tradition of the sacred, spiritual, and supernatural insightfully and imaginatively. In connection with this, Jean Toomer's *Cane* (1923) is an early work that deserves mention. In his unclassifiable thematic and formal medley, the racially ambiguous and undetermined Toomer, who was not committed to African American culture for very long, did not produce portrayals of Christianity and faith that have the depth of those depicted in the texts studied here. Like Toomer, the protagonist is not close to black people, and at the end of *Cane*, he runs away from African American culture because it is significantly grounded in the legacy of slavery and the attendant folk tradition, which includes the Christian religion that has fostered the faith to endure. Still, the text thematically leaves open the possibility that the tradition and its religion have meaning for African Americans, particularly those in the rural South where *Cane* is set. Although *Cane* has a distanced perspective that does not penetrate as deeply as it could into the culture, Toomer does not negate African American culture from the textual viewpoint, and in the overall process manages to create one of the best presentations of African American faithful vision before the contemporary works dealt with here. His work is a significant forerunner of the later treatments that I investigate. Charles Chesnutt published the stories of *The Conjure Woman* (1899) much earlier, but *Cane,* which also has suggestions and implications of hoodoo, is a more substantive portrayal of African American religious belief than Chesnutt's. Zora Neale Hurston's *Jonah's Gourd Vine* (1934) is another notable early work. Besides using the dominant symbol of the story of Jonah in its title, the novel thematically parallels the allegory of the biblical book, and it gives serious credence to Christianity and hoodoo as aspects of the culture in the African American community.

In *Jubilee* (1966), Margaret Walker recreates the history of African Americans from slavery to Reconstruction through the character Vyry Ware, who overcomes oppression throughout the years because of traditional Christian faith and strength. However, as evidenced by her actions during the dangerous Reconstruction period, there are hints in the novel that Vyry has ways of seeing and understanding that are hoodoo vestiges of the African past.[8] Finally, over the last four decades, Ernest Gaines's novels broadly chronicle African American life and, in the process, the centrality of Christianity in the cultural tradition.

CHAPTER 1

African American Faithful Belief

Imposing Social Determinism, Naturalism, and Modernism

AFTER THE LITERARY BREAKTHROUGHS of Richard Wright and Ralph Ellison in the mid-twentieth century, African American writers were able to focus on black cultural traditions, such as the religious, from their individual artistic perspectives with fewer pressures from the literary mainstream in which Wright and Ellison had to establish themselves. In James Baldwin's *Go Tell It on the Mountain* (1953), the sophisticated portrayal of the biblical and religious tradition unconstrained by the modernist concerns paramount in Ellison's work is well ahead of its time. Most African American writers did not deal with the unique African American cultural perspective shaped by the Bible, Judeo-Christian tradition, and the African-derived voodoo religious tradition in great complexity until the 1970s. The works covered in this chapter are pre-1970 and largely do not focus on the biblical and religious tradition in the same depth as works discussed in later chapters. To show the predominant background to the post-1970s novels, this chapter briefly surveys novels that treat the biblical and Christian in the prevailing contexts of naturalism, realism, and modernism.

Naturalism, realism, and modernism are literary worldviews that are largely antithetical to the African American religious tradition, and black writers like Ellison and John Edgar Wideman move away from these literary creeds toward artistic forms and thematic approaches that foreground the African American ethos deeply set in faithful vision. The evolution of Wideman's work is the best example of an African American writer being ineluctably pulled away from modernism to a positive portrayal of the sacred, spiritual, and supernatural as he integrated the black cultural view into his own artistic perspective. In Wideman's fiction from the late 1960s to the early 1980s, a black survival response of which faithful vision is an integral part displaces the modernist pessimism of the first three novels; the change in perspective becomes clear in *Hiding Place* (1981). Ellison's fiction also seems to develop similarly from the 1950s to the 1990s. Using John F. Callahan's edited text of *Juneteenth* (1999), one can only speculate on Ellison's direction after the highly modernist depiction of *Invisible Man* (1952); however, it seems clear in Ellison's edited work that African American religious ritual that symbolizes faithful vision also figuratively represents the potential achievement of American freedom and equality. From this general standpoint, Wright's writing opposes Ellison and Wideman's. His negative personal and literary viewpoint, grounded in naturalism and social realism, controls his narratives, and his thematic approach flattens and stereotypes his portrayal of African American culture and character.

Generally speaking, African American novels portray some potential of people to struggle against the oppressive social and political realities of black life, and although the texts themselves often do not affirm it, they show the creative potential and effect of faithful vision in some aspect of individual characters' lives or in the life of the community as part of the struggle. *Native Son* (1940) is atypical in the African American tradition because it is one of the few novels that minimizes and virtually negates the agency of the sacred, spiritual, and supernatural while also limiting the human potential of African Americans. Richard Wright is by no means the only black writer who is atheist or agnostic, but he is one of the few who limits the black cosmos with his own bleak view. Paul Laurence Dunbar's *The Sport of the Gods* (1902) (a novel that is forward-looking for its time, like *Go Tell It on the Mountain*) anticipates *Native Son*'s naturalism and also portrays African American culture as limited in the fashion of Wright's text.

Although there are no "gods" in *Native Son* and Wright would never envision any, his and Dunbar's novels are remarkably alike in worldview; *The Sport of the Gods* is an incidental thematic predecessor of *Native Son*'s dead-end faithlessness if not a directly influential literary ancestor. *The Sport of the Gods* is not as politically provocative as *Native Son*, but Dunbar lived in a time when he did not have Wright's freedom to express himself as a writer. As critics generally say, he only learned about black culture from the stories his parents told him and not from experience as Wright did, and further, he did not have available to him the complex portrayals of black culture from W. E. B. DuBois's *The Souls of Black Folk* (1903) or the literary works and pronouncements of the Harlem Renaissance. In this context, his superficial portrayals of black people and culture are more understandable. Nevertheless, Dunbar breaks the established fictional pattern to show the destructive forces affecting black people from a different perspective, which is like Wright's bold innovation in *Native Son*. From the primary view of their comparison, however, I find it remarkable that, in spite of social, personal, and literary constraints, Dunbar in *The Sport of the Gods* presented a portrayal of African Americans that anticipates so much *Native Son*'s depiction of them as having no sustaining cultural tradition of faithful vision. The realities of life, although imposed by the "gods" instead of nonsupernatural forces, easily dehumanize his characters because they, like the characters in *Native Son*, have no beliefs to support them. If one removes the "gods" and invests their power more purely in the human, Dunbar's narrative reality is substantively Wright's.

Although it seems paradoxical and confusing, *The Sport of the Gods* shows by the end that the characters once had a faithful belief in God; implicitly then, it must be the text's narrative viewpoint that negates the effect of faithful vision and imposes its own faith in the malevolent power of the "gods." Most of the novel focuses on the cruel play of unspecified and unexplained "gods" who use racism and the realities of urban life to doom both black and white characters. But the ultimate revelation that the black characters had faith in a Christian God at one time apparently means nothing in terms of their ability to struggle against the so-called gods and the social and political realities that they utilize in their destructive sport. Abruptly, the text asserts in chapter 18 that Berry Hamilton has lost his faith, but Fannie Hamilton has not: "'Don't Be'y, don't say dat [you used to pray to God but will not any longer]. Maybe we don't un'erstan' [God's plan, apparently]'" (145). "Her faith still hung by a slender thread, but his had given way in that moment." Berry seems to have his faith briefly rekindled when someone else kills Fannie's new husband and saves him from doing it, and he loudly thanks God (147). The destruction of the Hamiltons is almost complete, though, because they are "powerless against some Will [of the gods] infinitely stronger than their own" (148). The text attests to the powerful will of the gods manifested in the tangible reality in which the reader should believe, but these characters have no meaningful traditional Christian faith that would make a difference. This is strange in the context of the depiction of the African American cultural tradition in the majority of black novels and, just as importantly, with respect to the dominant expression of the tradition's own cultural voice in the past and in the evolving present. If the text itself did not mention the characters' faith, then the distortion of faithful vision's potential and the black cultural ethos generally would not be as explicit, but it would still be implicit.

Native Son's main character Bigger Thomas is set apart from the mass by an accidental murder, but he very much represents its social and cultural conditioning. He trivializes and rejects the tradition of faithful vision and tries to find faith in similar feelings of men in the physical world around him, and by the end his own acceptance of his rebellious acts of murder and consequent death are all the meaning that he can find. African American folkways offer nothing important to Bigger; black life is solely a product of degrading naturalistic forces, including slavery that lasted three centuries (360), which are oppressive but not even necessarily immoral. In the words of lawyer Max, who articulates the textual viewpoint, African Americans are a mass of twelve million that is "stunted, stripped, and held captive" (364), a bestialized "new form of life" (361). Beneath the almost total dehumanization of black people historically and in the present is a great distortion of faithful vision. Wright cannot see that the black people whom he portrays in the novel would most certainly be historically grounded in sacred and spiritual belief that makes the sum of their humanity much more than the product of the oppression of race and class.

Bigger tells an amazingly flat, simplistic, and stereotypical story of Christianity: he shows no signs of being part of a culture in which the Christian story has historically had a meaningful impact on daily life, and the black people he describes have no real grounding in Christianity that sustains. From creation to the crucifixion, Bigger presents Christianity in completely mystical terms (262–66), and black Christians do not effectively relate religious belief to their lives. In the tradition, however, the mysticism of the story is not the main point as the text implies; the point is the substantive effect of the story on black people's lives. Bigger's account totally ignores the necessary engagement of belief with reality, and this is what makes his portrayal and the portrayal of black life in *Native Son* superficial. The text's lack of faithful vision reveals its own failure of cultural discernment.

The tradition of faithful vision empowers black people through the accurate recognition that the plans and intentions of human beings in power often have the desired tangible results in the short term, but historical developments over time deny people the ability to plan and control the destiny of others, especially with regard to white Westerners' plans to enslave black people perpetually and essentially to destroy their humanity. Before he killed Mary Dalton, Bigger's first "murder" had been the story of creation and what follows, which the preacher tells him in his jail cell. Bigger killed this story and his hope because "to those who wanted to kill him he was not human, not included in the picture of Creation; and that was why he had killed it. To live, he had created a new world for himself, and for that he was to die" (264). It is true that white people who hate him refuse to see Bigger's humanity, and this generates a hard existence for him and black people generally. Yet the tradition of faithful vision in African American culture shows that reality is more than the hard existence created by white people at any particular time, and even the sum of a dehumanizing history of oppression for black people is their humanity. Bigger, however, only looks at the present and recognizes the power of whites because they have the ability to impose their hatred on him. An individual such as Bigger might certainly feel this way under his personal circumstances, but the text misrepresents the black cultural tradition by denying the effect of Christianity. If it were true that black people did not have a practical belief in the agency of the sacred, spiritual, and supernatural and rather believed in the ultimate power of men as Bigger does, then long centuries of oppression would have made African Americans collectively bestial, and the situation would be as bleak as the novel shows.

In the scene with the black Reverend Hammond and the white communist Jan, the text further misunderstands faithful vision in the African American tradition by privileging whiteness and trivializing black Christian belief. Earlier, Bigger denies any constructive agency of a creative spiritual force beyond his own body and thus denies any faith that is not totally organic (255). Bigger wants to feel something beyond his own black body, though, and in this scene, he looks toward the white man for faith. Bigger rejects the Christian view as projected by the black preacher, and the "word become[s] flesh" (268) only when Jan shows sympathy for him. This makes sense in the text because the preacher's faith is a kind of blissful ignorance that makes him incapable of comprehending and dealing with the mundane. The preacher talks in simple terms of opposition between love and hate (269), whereas the vision that is an integral part of African American tradition incorporates all human emotions and actions, good, evil, and indeterminate. The preacher's view is not representative of the complex African American awareness that encompasses all that human rationality can and then looks beyond that to faith; the preacher's belief has none of the depth of traditional African American faith.

The text's description of Bigger's mother emphasizes her simplistic otherworldliness and ignores the potential depth of her religious belief. The mother actually describes what would be a practical faith that sustains; Christianity has enabled her to endure a life of drudgery in which she worked for and maintained hope for her children (277–78). Bigger disregards her earthliness, though, and only sees significance in an otherworldly vacancy in his mother's eyes: "Her face was lifted to his; her eyes were empty, eyes that looked upward when the last hope of earth had failed" (277). At the end of their encounter, "he stood up and lifted his hands and tried to touch his mother's face and tell her yes [he would pray]; and as he did so something screamed deep down in him that it was a lie, that seeing her after they killed him would never be. But his mother believed; it was her last hope; it was what had kept her going through the years" (278). The power of belief that supports his mother means nothing to him; he only responds to her apparently substanceless plea that he pray and believe that he will see her in the afterlife. The shortsightedness lies in Bigger's vision that separates the mundane and the spiritual rather than in his mother's potential effective integration of them.

The novel's final words on faith are the "white" view of Max, which essentially shows potential in the actions of white men and, paradoxically, the basically hopeless vision of Bigger. Both perspectives belie an African American tradition that was empowering in the face of white hatred that denied the being of black people. Max tries to convince Bigger of the "belief of men" that builds and holds together the city's concrete structures, and he tries to tell Bigger that "what you felt, what you wanted, is what keeps those buildings standing there" (389–91). Bigger should believe in men who have created the physical things of the world and thereby revealed their power; the capacity of men to assert their will and make things be is important. Bigger gleans from Max's words that he should accept his act of murder as meaningful and die because the murder is what life made him feel and murder is what it made him want to do. Bigger's experience has so degraded him that he cannot possibly relate to feeling what white men feel and having their power; the only thing real is his act that leads to his own destruction. Obviously, if faith in the African American tradition did not empower black people to overcome spiritually the impositions of white people, then they would collectively be as dehumanized as Bigger and at the point of making his hopeless choice.

Wright's explanation and analysis of his negative perception of black people and black culture in *Black Boy* (1945) does not change the fact that his depiction of the otherworldly and impractical belief in the sacred in both books was a distortion of black cultural tradition. Perhaps a lot of what Wright felt about the role of Christianity in black life came from his bad experience with the Seventh Day Adventist religion of his grandmother. According to *Black Boy*, the Christian story told by the Adventist church was "a cosmic tale that began before time and ended with the clouds of the sky rolling away at the Second Coming of Christ; chronicles that concluded with the Armageddon; dramas thronged with all the billions of human beings who had ever lived or died as God judged the quick and the dead" (113). One has to wonder how someone with Wright's great creative ability, a writer who knew the power of stories, could not see how even this kind of mystical story could be practical by imaginatively strengthening people in life as well as pointing them to the afterlife. But Wright can find nothing effective in black religious belief, and this is one of the main reasons that he limits black life to an "essential bleakness" (45–46), finding that black culture lacks all the important human qualities such as love, honor, and loyalty. Wright certainly strongly believes this, but it is also clear that he misrepresented the broader cultural tradition and experience that he purported to portray in such an important African American novel as well as in a famous autobiography.

Native Son specifically shows Wright's knowledge of the Bible through Bigger's account of Christianity in Book Three and in the novel's epigraph from Job, but Wright captures none of the Bible's great social, political, and philosophical depth and complexity and none of the relationship of its emphasis on the everyday to African American life. Maybe one can only attribute Wright's choice to ignore the Bible's richness and complexity to his strong desire to simplify and trivialize, and to distance himself from black people and black culture, but the difference between Wright's implied interpretation of the Bible and its richness and complexity as a "living" text for black people is great nevertheless. For example, the book from which Wright takes *Native Son*'s epigraph is a fantastic story of Job's faith. God inexplicably afflicts Job for being good and righteous, and only restores everything after Job endures such psychological suffering and physical pain that he first curses the day of his birth and then accepts his reality. Wright seems to utilize the epigraph from Job—"Even today is my complaint rebellious, My stroke is heavier than my groaning"—as a counterpoint to the dead-end suffering in his own book.[1] Wright's use limits interpretation, however, one interpretation being that Job teaches that the most unbearable pain and suffering, which may seem arbitrary and unexplainable, is part of a larger test of faith in which righteousness is rewarded. Whatever the interpretation, it would seem to take a strongly negative attitude toward black culture for Wright to appropriate the book of Job in the context of his novel. Contrary to the implied meaning of the epigraph, black people in everyday life draw upon the story of Job to deal with unexplainable and seemingly unbearable affliction. The story of Job is indeed powerful when applied to individual lives or more broadly and figuratively to racial history in America.[2]

Richard Wright is an important African American writer and *Native Son* a significant novel, but one must conclude that his cold universe of inefficacious faith, while being true to his belief and the belief of many other individuals, does not represent the deeper complexity and substance of the cultural ethos.[3] I certainly do not want to diminish the great achievement of *Native Son*. This graphic novel accomplished what no African American novel had; it painted an unflinching picture of African American life that had a great impact on critics and readers and that began to lay the foundation for African American fiction's moving to the forefront of American literature. However, James Baldwin is correct in "Everybody's Protest Novel" when he says Bigger's tragedy is that "he admits the possibility of his being sub-human and feels constrained, therefore, to battle for his humanity according to those criteria bequeathed him at his birth" (22). Ironically, the first black novel to have such a large audience and effect presents the "white" perspective that African Americans had no spiritually uplifting beliefs that were central to a humanizing, sustaining cultural ethos.[4] It was hard for readers to romanticize Bigger and feel good about him, but perhaps his lack of humanity and the novel's evisceration of black culture is part of why white critics such as Irving Howe may have unconsciously liked

Native Son while also consciously praising it for its creative power (Howe 100–101).[5]

Invisible Man, the next African American novel that got a lot of attention from Howe and other white critics, is different from *Native Son* in some ways but generally similar in its negation of the importance of African American culture. Throughout its twenty-five chapters, the text reveals more awareness of the full complexity of black life and tradition than does *Native Son*. Although it was more critically successful than *Native Son*, *Invisible Man* concludes by ultimately subverting the black tradition that it defines against the backdrop of its own protagonist's naïve denial and ignorance of it.

Many would strongly question the claim that there is a "negation" of African American culture. After all, the hypothetical solution proposed at the end is the narrator's and not Ellison's, and although he does not talk about the black cultural tradition, the narrator does not specifically say that it will have no place in the new way of life. Also, particularly in the early chapters where the narrator learns important lessons, the exposé of the wide range of black cultural formations, approaches, and responses, which include faithful vision grounded in the biblical and Judeo-Christian, is a large part of what is vivid and memorable about the text. Still, however, the epilogue is shocking in its conclusions that, at best, ambiguously imply the inclusion of the African American cultural tradition. The epilogue obviously constitutes the last words of the narrator in the novel, and I would say that his failure clearly to include black culture is at least symbolically a negation of the *importance* of the tradition.

My main point about *Invisible Man* is that imposing modernist themes and ultimately a modernist cosmos over faithful vision and the black ethos generally makes them secondary and diminishes the novel's otherwise rich vision. Christian practice manifesting faithful vision reveals the crass, superficial, and hypocritical about black people in some situations in *Invisible Man*, but in positive contexts, its ritual manifestation transports them to the deepest expression of their reality and truth, providing their greatest sustenance. Throughout most of the novel, African Americans use faithful vision in all their endeavors; true to African American life, it is an empowering part of existence inseparable from the secular world. In the prologue, the narrator relates events that have already happened, bringing him to his conclusions about modernist reality and black life and the centrality of religious rituals in expressing its indefinable complexity. After he tells the story, how-ever, the outcome in the epilogue virtually ignores the African American. The narrator seems almost to portray himself as the only African American alive while he stresses the idea of individuality in a hypothetically ideal world, and does not apply the specific insights about African American cul-ture that the text shows throughout his conscious and unconscious narra-tive. He alludes to his enigmatic, folk-oriented grandfather's understanding of the democratic plan's principle of diversity, but except for the grand-father's trickster tactics in the process of realizing the humanity that the principle grants everyone, this is a construction of a white ideal, a hypothet-ically replanned America, with no modernist chaos, that does not include African American cultural forms. Highlighting the need to deal with mod-ernist chaos at the end, Ellison perhaps insured the novel's establishment as part of the American canon, thereby serving the African American literary tradition well in the long run by bringing it into the American canon also. However, the cultural tradition and specific biblical and Judeo-Christian as-pects of it are undercut because of the focus on modernism.

A series of episodes constructed from various parts of the text shows the powerful ambience of faithful vision even as the novel builds the back-ground for its pessimistic conclusions about modernist chaos and African American involvement and complicity in corruption. The narrator is never fully conscious of the truth about either African American or modernist re-ality until the end, but a section from chapter 23 (495–98) dealing with the reverend Rinehart is a starting point. The narrator's relatively high level of consciousness and the development of textual viewpoint converge to show more clearly the relationship between the black cultural and the American modernist tradition that the narrative brings to realization, only to undercut the African American at the end.

He hears a prayer coming from Rinehart's church that implies the con-nection of faithful vision to survival in the secular world. The "voice rose and fell in a rhythmical, dreamlike recital—part enumeration of earthly trials undergone by the congregation, part display of vocal virtuosity, part appeal to God" (496). Rinehart's church is an elaborate deception possible in the chaotic world of invisible, lost people. The text, however, implies more than the narrator says about the importance of spiritual belief. The narrator can-not give the reader the feeling of the spirit within the church, but the overall portrayal of the scene makes it an easily imagined reality. The skilled ritual recital of earthly problems that calls on God evokes a saving spirituality that has brought black people from slavery to freedom to this fraudulent church in New York. The old women the narrator meets (496) and the rest of the congregation are part of this new black corruption that is also American, but in the same way that they have dealt with the hardship and oppression of the black past, they praise God and continue (497). They do not solve problems or change anything, but neither does anyone else, including the narrator. But through faithful vision, they do survive as complex human beings who express their humanity and spirituality, in spite of being deceived and oppressed. Even the narrator shows that faith has influenced him, although he clearly understands little. He partially remembers a biblical passage as he expresses his confusion about blindness and invisibility: "For now we see as through a glass darkly but then—but then—" (491). The words come from Paul in 1 Corinthians 13 and relate to the ultimate greatness of charity. However, faith is also one of the three great virtues, hope being the third, which endures. Other late chapters that portray the narrator as less aware and present a similar textual viewpoint lead up to this chapter.

In chapters 21 and 22, ritual expressing faithful vision more specifically accesses truth, substance, and sustenance that white people and even middle-class black people like the narrator do not understand. At Tod Clifton's funeral in chapter 21, a man sings the spiritual "There's Many a Thousand Gone" (452). Because he is even more obtuse than he is in the Rinehart portrayal in chapter 23, the narrator becomes angry because the song reminds him of church meetings from his past (453). He also implies that there is something he is missing, though. There is a power in the song that goes beyond the "slave-borne words; it was as though he'd changed the emotion beneath the words while yet the old longing, resigned, transcendent emotion still sounded above, now deepened by that something for which the theory of [the white] Brotherhood had given no name." One cannot separate the transcending power from the resignation to oppression, but the power sustains. The narrator speaks with contradictory voices here, condemning African American cultural ritual in one instance and analyzing the positive in the other. In chapter 22, the Brotherhood totally rejects the idea of the people in Harlem coming out for Clifton's funeral. The narrator then speaks again in the positive voice when he tells the white men of the Brotherhood that they totally misunderstand the Negro people (468); he states that the crowd turned out because "we gave them the opportunity to express their feelings, to affirm themselves" (469). He seems to say that there is true sustenance in this expression and affirmation.

Early chapters reveal the pattern of the connection between the black cultural and modernist, too. Chapter 5 implies a similar point about ritual appropriated by powerful white people and middle-class black people to use in the pursuit of power and personal gain, and reveals nuances of the truth and substance of African Americans at the same time. At this point, the novel has not made African American cultural tradition so clearly secondary to its emphasis on the modernist themes of chaos and corruption, but the narrator is also less perceptive about the complex levels of black cultural expression and interaction than he is later. The blind preacher Barbee creating a powerful vision that enthralls the audience, particularly the white trustees, and then falling to the floor shows that his sermon is a negative example of ritual expression. However, shortly after Barbee falls and Dr. Bledsoe, moaning hypocritically, helps him to his chair, the student body sings "sincerely . . . not . . . for the [white] guests, but for themselves; a song of hope and exaltation" (134). The song engenders a brief glimpse of genuine expectation and joy that uplifts and that the narrator observes but does not understand. Yet the narrator does not totally fail to sense the deeper truth and reality of blackness potentially inherent beneath superficial ritual expression. Earlier in the chapter, he seems to feel how he had unsuccessfully tried to use his own empty, preacher-like ritualizing of words in the chapel to touch a deeper, more authentic black reality as represented by Miss Susie Gresham, the matron who is a *"relic of slavery whom the campus loved but did not understand, aged, of slavery, yet bearer of something warm and vital and all-enduring"* (113–14). But as the italics indicate, the narrator is speaking from his subconscious mind; he never fully understands the text's larger implications about black culture.

Overall, the narrator negatively judges black culture, but the text makes no final judgment. Faithful vision is an important part of black cultural tradition that has brought the people to the present, and it helps to move them ahead in their own fashion. The narrator understands the weakness of the two old people being evicted in chapter 13 but not the strength of their faithful vision, symbolized in their Bible and reliance on prayer. He says, "They don't want the world, but only Jesus. They only want Jesus, just fifteen minutes of Jesus on the rug-bare floor . . . You [white people] got the world, can we have our Jesus?" (279). The narrator states, "All we have is the Bible and this [white] Law [standing] here rules that out" (280). In terms of the novel's building modernist theme, the narrator feels confused about what he really means as he speaks, but on one level his words clearly satirize the impracticality of black people's otherworldly Christian focus that prevents them from developing the political wherewithal to deal effectively with situations such as the eviction. The reality of the situation is nevertheless more complex than the narrator's words imply. Black people are perhaps law-abiding and thus politically docile as a result of their religious belief, but because of it they also resist oppression, although not in an organized, politicized way that would solve the problem. The old woman resists when the white evictors try to take her Bible (269–70), and then both the man and woman insist on going back into the apartment with the Bible to pray (273–74), which causes the riot. In these characters, faithful vision is the deepest support of African American life through the generations; black life as lived on this street in Harlem would not be possible without it. The existence of African American life itself is obviously good, and the poverty, continued oppression, and constant danger, as represented in their plunge into the riot, are bad. Everything considered, black people are here, and they continue into the future, to a significant extent because faithful vision sustains the spirit and the will in the real world.

Critics talk about Jim Trueblood's ability to face his truth by singing the blues and gaining a blues perspective, but his attempt to pray and his singing of a church song precede singing the blues and consequently expressing himself intensely and honestly (66). Also a singer in the school chapel of "what the officials called 'primitive spirituals'" (47), Trueblood has appealed to the preacher who rejects him, and thinks that his attempt to pray fails. But his failed prayer is ironically part of a process that is both secular and spiritual. The attempted prayer leads to "some kinda church song" which becomes blues; Trueblood experiences one of the most human moments in the novel through the process. Spiritual rituals initiate Trueblood's confrontation of his action and acceptance of his self and fate; his submission shows a secularized faith that he will make it. I emphasize that for African Americans faithful vision comes from an appropriated biblical story and that it is fully a part of African American secular life. Utilizing the spiritual along with the secular to touch the truth of the self, which could save Trueblood in this world if not in the other, represents the potentially most positive use of faithful vision in the African American cosmos where the spiritual and secular always intersect. Briefly at least, Trueblood transcends to become an authentic human being as no one else in the novel does.

In the most substantive and serious effort to understand African American reality after the narrator realizes his invisibility, the prologue uses the rhythms of the folk sermon to raise questions about the meaning of blackness, and it references the old slave woman singing a spiritual in a setting that examines the meaning of freedom for black people historically and in the present. The spiritual song symbolizes faithful vision at the beginning of the episode conceptualizing ambivalent freedom (9–12), and the secularized sermon preached from the *"lower level"* (9) evokes the ambiguity of blackness. The old slave woman exhorts the narrator to *"Go curse your God, boy, and die"* (10). A painful contradiction drives her bitterness: she hates her master because he lied about setting them free and loves him because she loves her sons that he fathered (10–11). In the larger view, the contradiction of spiritual faith as reflected in her song and contempt for God who allowed slavery for centuries is a problem at the center of African American faithful vision in the context of oppressive black history. The old woman's legacy from slavery is pain and confusion, and since this makes her ambivalent about freedom, she cannot help the narrator define it. He never resolves the contradictions that produce the old woman's ambivalence and realizes that his experience has made him ambivalent too. And blackness itself is a text of ambiguity, as articulated in the preacher's secular phrasings in sermonic rhythms (9–10). Blackness is real although ambiguous and ambivalent, however, and the questions associated with black existence are urgent though unanswerable. Blackness can be expressed although it cannot be defined, and on the deepest levels that the narrator can access, the folk sermon and the spiritual are keys to and beginning points of this expression.

I would argue that Ralph Ellison knew African American culture better and was much more attuned to its depth and complexity than Richard Wright; *Invisible Man* supports this with its complex portrayal of faithful vision and of African American culture, clearly the most complex in the literary tradition at that time and for many years to come. However, there is still a similarity between the overall conclusions of *Native Son* and *Invisible Man*.

The plan of the white founders that engenders belief in the epilogue of *Invisible Man* is like the powerful faith of white men that Max tries to convince Bigger that he must feel in *Native Son;* it obscures the importance of the faith and cultural ways of black people.[6] By the epilogue *Invisible Man* has shown that the substantive and practical in African American life relates directly to surviving in the corrupt American system and therefore is itself part of the corruption. The only way to change this, hypothetically at least, is to go back to the American beginning and institute another plan that imposes order on modernist chaos and establishes true democracy. As is the case at the end of *Native Son,* this plan is very "white" because potential in *Invisible Man* apparently resides solely in white men, the founders of the country who must set the principles of American democracy over chaos. In the final analysis, *Invisible Man* seems to put a lot of faith in the power and human potential of these men while de-emphasizing the African American cultural tradition, a central part of which is faithful vision that brings the sacred, spiritual, and supernatural to bear on life. One has to ask why African American cultural vision and ethos are not an aspect of the hypothetical new beginning. Perhaps there would be no racism and oppression in this ideal new world, and the uniquely African American shaped by these realities would not exist. But still, the African American way of seeing the world, which would hypothetically include faith in the sacred, spiritual, and supernatural influenced by African cultures even before the experiences of Western slavery and oppression, seems totally left out. This worldview may have points of similarity to the Western Christian view, which could somehow be implied in the novel's ideal democracy, but it has a difference that is fundamental to black people and that is important to all people.

Ellison died in 1994 and never published the long-awaited novel that would follow the great achievement of *Invisible Man,* but apparently he wrote fiction throughout his life. John F. Callahan has taken sections from a vast manuscript that Ellison left and edited them, with Ellison's imagined intentions in mind, to produce *Juneteenth* (1999). However, it seems clear from Callahan's account that he tried to structure the edited narrative to make it coherent while not substantively changing the individual parts that he chose, and so although Ellison never completed a novel, the segments that Callahan edits and arranges are still primarily Ellison's work.[7]

Juneteenth could indicate that Ellison intended to make the African American cultural perspective deeply set in sacred and spiritual belief more primary in his later work. One cannot make conclusive judgments about the entire text that Ellison left from Callahan's edited version, but *Juneteenth* clearly puts the emphasis generally on the "principles" of faithful vision and

African American culture instead of on those of the white founders, as *Invisible Man* does. *Juneteenth* moves away from *Invisible Man*'s white modernist perspective emphasizing chaos, and examines the achievement of an American ideal exemplified by African American culture. Both texts depict quests for virtually unattainable ideals (although *Invisible Man* more definitely and clearly affirms the ideal), but significantly in the later text the rituals of faithful vision of the sacred and spiritual are the most substantive quality of black culture and also exempla for American cultural achievement. The pursuit of his modernist agenda in *Invisible Man* had its goals and the reward of making Ellison a canonical writer, but perhaps then instead of portraying white principles as the hope for African Americans and all Americans, he wanted to focus on the essential qualities of the African American ethos as the foundation for America. Maybe this is at least part of what Ellison's later fiction would have revealed.

In *Juneteenth,* a concept of freedom is appropriated from the Bible and presented structurally and thematically. The concept is a hard-to-attain American ideal of freedom that begins with African American faithful vision of divine salvation. Communal performance of and participation in the African American sermon figuratively represent the attainment of the ideal. The folk sermon communally ritualizes the Word in an open-ended process of visual and rhythmic oral imaging that generates emotion that spiritualizes earthly suffering and oppression. Black people confront the reality of earthly life, but their community responds to life by raising the oppression apparently caused by white people and the inscrutable trials and tribulations imposed by God to a spiritual level that accesses God. White people think that they are superior and that they justly subjugate black people, but black experience is really a mysterious divine crucible that all people, including Jesus Christ the man who suffered before returning to the spirit, must pass through to attain freedom and salvation. Black ritual is an earthly spiritual response to God that frees and saves. Interestingly, *Juneteenth* seems to make a mostly different point about African American ethos and Christian belief: The African American view of the world and especially the ritual practices of faithful vision are the beginning points for the potential realization of true American human values.

A central theme in the novel is that the virtuoso voice of the folk preacher initiates a spiritual vision that lifts black people to the realization of a higher humanity; the spiritual continually interacts with the secular and profane in a process that symbolizes American democratic creative possibilities. In their Juneteenth sermon, the main characters Hickman and Bliss rhetorically ask if the African American condition is an act of man or an act of God and tell the congregation that it was an "act of God . . . through . . . an act of cruel ungodly man . . . [a] cruel calamity laced up with a blessing—or maybe a blessing laced up with a calamity . . . It was a blessing, brothers and sisters, because out of all the pain and the suffering, out of the night of storm, we found the Word of God" (118–19). Bliss and Hickman use the Word creatively to spiritualize African American life so as to bring it in line with a higher realization and expression of humanity that can be attained only by humble supplication to God. Belief in the creative spiritual power of the Word follows the description of the Word embodying the flesh of Jesus Christ and Christ being the (en)Light(enment) of the world in John 1–14.

Black people do not become saints but only sinners who retain great human potential as long as they stay in touch with the creative ritual of the Word and all that it entails to humble themselves before God and spiritually transform their lives. The Juneteenth religious communion in the church includes the outside quest of secular desire. Hickman explains secular desires and spiritual communion of the Word coming together. "Sure, [outside] there was always whiskey—and fornicating too. Always. But inside there was the Word and the Communion in the Word, and just as Christ Jesus had to die between two criminals, just so did we have to put up with the whiskey and the fornication. Even the church has to have its outhouse, just as it has to have a back door as well as a front door, a basement as well as a steeple. Because man is always going to be man and there's no true road without sides to it, and gulleys too, no true cross without arms that point away in two directions from the true way" (139–40). The ritual creativity of the Word raises human beings to the perception of both the spirituality and the commonality of Jesus Christ and thus the commonality and the potential for subjugated spirituality of all people, including white people.

This can be a model for Americans to achieve democracy and never stray too far from spiritually inspired ideas that humanize and save. The words of Jesus Christ as invoked in Hickman's ritual—"Lord, why hast thou [forsaken me]?"—keep Americans grounded by the knowledge of God's harsh testing of all and the common need for at least saving human understanding and compassion, if not intercession for divine salvation. However, this is still very much an ideal whose attainment is problematized by the reality of the

American secular world beyond the African American church ritual that begins with the Word.

For Bliss in *Juneteenth*, the problems are his ability to escape blackness after he clearly understands the political weakness of black people, and also the magic lure of the Word's creative possibilities that take him far from an African American earthly ideal that is almost impossible for "white" people. The white-looking Bliss's racial ambiguity stands for the true ambiguity of American race, but he becomes fascinated with the power of whiteness when the crazy "white" woman calling him her son pulls him from the coffin during the resurrection ritual and scares the black people (153–59). He in turn calls her his mother and sets out to find her in movie figures who look like her, and to pursue a career in movie making, a magic which represents white power.[8] *Juneteenth* does not specify how, but Bliss becomes a "white" senator who uses the Word to denigrate black people and becomes famous by exploiting the gift of black creativity of which Hickman made him aware.

Bliss's characterization brings out the American problem of white people's inability to accept the example of black human struggle as figured in the use of the Word and to stop testing and pursuing the negative potential afforded by a white identity, mainly the exploitation of black people to gain power and profit. In a coma-like reverie after he is shot, Bliss thinks, *"Oh, if only I could have controlled me my she I and the search and have accepted you as the dark daddy of flesh and Word—Hickman? Hickman, you after all"* (264). Bliss could have become an *"ideal symbolized in the concrete form of man"* (278), a black ideal in the body of a "white" man that *"pointed the way for all of us who would be free—yes!"* (280). But once the woman breaks the ritual, she ruptures his chance of pursuing human freedom on the highest plane (265–66). Shallowness, superficiality, and crassness as symbolized in the movie image replace the substantively agonizing and spiritually creative image engendered by the ritual of the Word. The potential for American progress toward human values no longer starts with a ritual of faithful vision but with a shadow lacking sustenance: *"And what is this desire to identify with others, this need to extend myself and test my most far-fetched possibilities with only the agency of shadows? Merely shadows. All shadowy they promised me my mother and denied me solid life"* (266). This could be a problem for everyone, including black people, after the ritual spell of black folk culture is broken by the possibilities of technology and modern life. The implications about modernity thus suggest the modernist themes of *Invisible*

Man, but *Juneteenth* sets the sacred and spiritual of African American culture above the modernist.

In his first three novels, John Edgar Wideman was influenced by Ellison's modernist portrayal in *Invisible Man* and by white modernist writers, but in the fiction that follows, he makes African American culture more prominent and shows that faithful vision is a mainstay of black people.[9] The later development in Wideman's work is not a direct result of Ellison's influence but seems to parallel what occurred in Ellison's writing after *Invisible Man.* Both Ellison and Wideman progress away from modernist forms and themes that restrict the portrayal of the African American worldview. The narrative of a short story from his first collection, written at the end of his transition toward black cultural perspective, makes clear the change that has occurred in the five previous novels. In "The Songs of Reba Love Jackson" from *Damballah* (1981), gospel singer Reba Love testifies that she always sings her first song for her mother, but the first song and all the others are for God too: "Cause that's what Gospel is. Singing praise to God's name. So I'ma sing a praise song and dedicate it to [my mother] the one loved me best on this earth. The one I loved best and still do. What a Friend. Yes, Lawd. What a Friend We Have" (111). God is inseparable from her relationship to her mother, the others she has known in her life, and everything that has happened to her. The African American belief in God and spiritual church ritual have become essential in Wideman's writing and have displaced reliance on modernist intellectualism and human secular agency.

Even Wideman's first novel, *A Glance Away* (1967), however, presents a brief but memorable portrayal of African American faithful vision in a text in which modernism subsumes the black tradition and makes it secondary. *A Glance Away*'s narrative connects the black Eddie Lawson, who is himself a modernist figure alienated from family and psychologically traumatized, with the white professor Robert Thurley, a homosexual modernist figure pursuing spiritual renewal through intellectual analysis and social adaptation in the manner of T. S. Eliot's Prufrock. In the context of its thematic development, a scene in the prologue reveals African American emotional religious expression in the midst of black poverty and sensual pursuit in the secular world beyond the Sunday church services.

The episode describes African American religious ritual performance: The tone is mocking, or at best ambivalent, but the spiritual uplift and sustenance characteristic of the role of faithful vision in African American life still stand out. The scene starts sarcastically describing the congregation before the appearance of the preacher, a charlatan: "Let the King come in—tall and sparkling, heady and sweet—a brown eyed handsome man. Didn't it rain children, didn't it rain. And joy showered down, inundating the crude, crowded room and the bouncing hearts, and the tired, dark faces for a moment reflected the soul's smile" (15). Then Tiny starts his ritual shout.

> Tiny started to sway. Barely perceptively at first, then his broad back rolled from side to side, first to the left then to the right, off time—a rhythm all his own—warming up—shaking his body's chains, palpitating inside each roll of fat, reviving the dead, hanging flesh so it quivered, so it jumped like so many nervous cats and in a moment on his feet, not lumbering as his tremendous bulk should move, but agile and smoothly coordinated like the lithe body of a shake dancer. Tiny up and feeling good. Arms out at either side, bent at elbows so fingers pointed up trembling with joy, his head rolling from side to side, glazed eyes staring as if possessed by some miracle on the ceiling. He switched down the narrow aisle, wide buttocks wagging more supple than swivel hips of brown girls in tight dresses on the avenues. Twitching, shaking, light on his toes and balls of feet Tiny danced. In his world, in that moment he lived for, when the tremendous weight of his soft, spreading flesh would be cast off, and somewhere like a leaf or a gust of music he would be lifted by the wind, borne off lithesome on a cloud of grace.
>
> Tiny's moment was [Eddie's grandfather's] DaddyGene's moment and in a subtle transformation became eternal in small boy wide eyed, excited beside him. (15–16)

Tiny's movements are those of a virtuoso who frees himself spiritually in a church community that shares his faithful affirmation through performance, and he greatly affects the young Eddie, who never liberates himself to live spiritually like this after witnessing Tiny's moment. This Sunday church setting is clearly a place where Tiny feels a liberating joy as the most skilled performer representing the congregation in the spiritual flight that his huge, incongruous body accentuates. For the young Eddie, who watches the scene from outside the church alongside his grandfather DaddyGene, it becomes a legendary family narrative that he tries to pass along to his younger sister

Bette and wants to retell so as to incorporate Tiny's dancing flight into his own life. In telling the story to Bette, Eddie at first seems to capture the musical spirit of the setting: the "piano, trumpet, tambourines, drums, whatever anybody could beat or shake or blow noise through was in their hands and wagged at the devil" (127). Yet he cannot "keep pace with [the rhythm of] Tiny's dance" because apparently his own abstract imagination fails him, and he "gaze[s] thoughtfully and silently at a spectacle his words could no longer describe" (128). Eddie implicitly criticizes people who believe the devil is real and who carry out rituals to keep the spirit free from his influence. But those people are so spiritually alive, and Eddie is dead: "I'm dead Bette, the plain fact of the matter is that Eddie's dead." He is spiritually dead from a black cultural perspective and in the novel's abstract modernist terms, and he expresses a longing to live as people do when they experience the freedom, although momentary, that Tiny and the congregation experience. The death of his mother on Easter Sunday (129–30) just after Eddie arrives home trying to resurrect his own dope-plagued life drives him to the black church once more, but again he cannot access its rhythms for sustenance (138–41). In his desperation, Eddie makes a final disavowal of African American faithful vision in the bar with Thurley and Brother after having tried to return to his naïve boyhood ceremony of prayer; he says that he will pray no more to God, as his mother taught him, because he has lost all faith. Eddie finally looks for support in Brother and particularly Thurley.

The text, however, never negates the image of the uplifting influence of faithful vision that its own careful representation of Tiny creates; the language describing Tiny makes him an exemplum and implies the power of his transcending spirituality in this episode that is also paradoxically negative. The church scene is an emotional spectacle in a superficial black cultural setting—the *Tioga Street Sanctified in the Name of Jesus Christ Church* (13)—that dupes black people in a white world that has oppressed and impoverished them, but the detailed description of Tiny and his movements also celebrates him. Tiny is at first inert and then off-time; then he deftly goes into beautifully expressive agile motion that defies his gigantic bulk, as he lifts himself to grace as though he sees the vision of a miracle. The portrayal of Tiny evokes his momentary transcendence and makes him one of the most compelling characters, in spite of his brief role. Certainly, the language depicts a potent spiritual state just as much as it satirizes black emotional spirituality in a novel that foregrounds the abstract, intellectual modernist tradition. So Eddie cannot imagine the vision of Tiny in a way that allows him to access the spirit of Tiny's life, and he cannot find hope in the church on Easter following his mother's death years later. However, the text's attention to detail in describing Tiny's compelling feat suggests its power and potential despite Eddie's detachment and the novel's final emphasis on solutions grounded in the human connection among the three men, the Prufrockian Thurley chief among them.

Hurry Home (1970) is also a highly modernist novel; the main character Cecil's fantasies and illusions are modernist intellectual "prayers" (a la T. S. Eliot) to reconcile himself to his miscarried son and to his wife Esther.[10] Cecil takes journeys to Europe and Africa in search of self, but just as substantively he undertakes the search in the medium of his own text: "There is no novel. I have a vivid imagination, and countless frustrations. Therefore I retreat to illusion, fantasy. Call my imagining my novel. Journal as close as I get. But not even journal, more like . . . like nothing but fantasy, illusion. My notes to [my son] Simon, my prayers unaddressed and unbelieved even as I pray" (154). Cecil's text directly and indirectly alludes to the journeys in T. S. Eliot's "The Love Song of J. Alfred Prufrock" and *The Waste Land*, and other texts. At the end, Cecil's search is typically inconclusive in modernist fashion. "Cecil dreamed" (185) his life, back home again still in a state of uncertainty if not chaos: "Is he coming or going, is [the door of his home] opening in or out" (184).

If anything, the novel juxtaposes an even stronger portrayal of faithful vision to the main character's modernist perspective than does *A Glance Away;* set against Cecil's satirical view of Christianity is the ritualized prayer of his wife Esther, a more prominent character than Tiny. For Esther, even Cecil's blasphemous disbelief shows God's grace. She does not fear for Cecil's soul because God allows him to blaspheme to reveal the "unfathomable limits of [his] mercy, [his] redemption that can pluck a sinner from the very jaws of Hell's mouth" (127). Cecil has caused Esther great pain, but Cecil's actions are part of God's plan that leads her to salvation and that, ironically, makes Cecil a saint (120).

A Glance Away criticizes Esther as a woman accepting the biblical view of God's chastisement and Cecil's abusive male dominance even as it shows the efficacy of faith in the patriarchal God based in the Bible. When "Cecil raised his hand to [Esther] it was as [God's] instrument . . . if the instrument of [God's] knowledge must blister the flesh, surely it is better received here in earthly fires and in a time that has beginning and end" (126). It is this same objectifying, self-abasing faith in her relationship to God that allows her to withstand social ostracism: "There were those who were affronted when I sat beside them in church. I was called harlot, fool [for living with Cecil and taking care of him before they married]. I did not explain to them. You chose a blind man [Cecil], a whore [Esther], even the dead [Simon] to illuminate your mysteries. My worldly life was public and misunderstood; my life in You was for myself. And Cecil" (127).

Nothing can shake Esther because she has faith that everything, all earthly afflictions, are part of God's mysterious wisdom, and the novel ultimately leaves open the possibility that Esther's faith has sustained her and that her faithfulness will turn out to be the foundation of Cecil's refuge. Esther thinks that Cecil's cruel abandonment of her is an act of God that reveals his grace in her time of need. She prays for forgiveness for her anger and prostration because Cecil walked out on her: "I was a little girl on that floor, Father, till Your infinite, divine mercy lifted me and restored what I did not deserve. Cecil's halo, that better part of him made a brand in my soul" (124). Cecil returns after three years to find Esther dutifully waiting for him, lying naked and asleep on the bed (183). From its negative perspective, *A Glance Away* exposes Esther's worldly vulnerability because she ignorantly accepts Christian doctrine, but her Christian belief has given her the strength to wait for Cecil—who is still lost and confused in his dream of life—to give him a home. Viewed this way, Esther is a rare, Godly, charitable, selfless person; she may be the saint that she thinks Cecil is.[11]

The Lynchers (1973) presents no faithful vision in opposition to modernist dream/fantasy, but reveals a yearning to realize a "Black God" (172) that will "tear a hole in history" (173)—which has been for black people an arbitrary nightmare reality manufactured by white people (116)—to create the possibility to imagine a new history that empowers. History's reality is very much in the imagination, but that conception holds the oppressive, tangible world of the present in place. The characters have lost all "vision beyond a wavering faith in something better than the misery we have lived through" (180); they are truly hopeless without something to combat the dreadful reality of the oppressive American historical tradition. The character Littleman tries to imagine into being a god to serve the purposes of black people. He thinks that the collective will makes possible the creation of a god, that he is the individual in whose mind the god materializes (186–89), and that he has assisted in the "birth of the God" (188). While in the hospital recovering from a police beating that prevents him from taking part, Littleman thinks of the conspiracy he has planned as a human act that manifests the power of his god to determine human life: "The metaphor is almost too obvious. This boy [Anthony the orderly] as a messenger, as youth entrusted with the secrets of the plan. Our link with the generations to come. He will not understand the words, not realize they contain the possibility of death and resurrection" (178–79). But the plan never becomes more than a grotesque fantasy shared by the four conspirators; the novel ends with an image of death amid modernist frustration and chaos (263–64). The plan cannot do the work of a black god who can change historical imagination and thereby create a new life for black people.

Historically, the collective and individual imaginations of African Americans are informed by belief in God and the wisdom of God's plan in light of everything, including oppression; in *The Lynchers,* there is a conspicuous lack of the traditional God in the black imagination. Littleman ironically reveals this in conceptualizing the black god: "A god is created when the will and spirit of the many focus repeatedly on a lack, an emptiness each senses in himself" (187). In African American tradition, the biblical God is already a presence instead of a "lack" in the black imagination that generates the need for Littleman's black god, and although it does not bring about the political revolution that Littleman wants, belief in God does substantively reshape the past and present in black terms. There are shards of supportive religious belief and ritual in the generally nightmarish consciousness of *The Lynchers'* black characters, but no oppositional scene or character stands out in the modernist landscape, as is the case in the first two novels, to manifest faithful vision. It does not seem to be part of *The Lynchers'* thematic intention to show a "lack" of the Christian God, but Littleman's desire for the black god and the negativity of the other black characters' lives show that there is.[12] The larger context of the potential of faithful vision's paradoxically portrayed presence in the first two novels also implies a "lack" of God in *The Lynchers,* and the recognition of the cultural importance of faithful vision in Wideman's later fiction even more clearly implies it.

As Wideman has said in interviews and elsewhere, and as critical assessments have shown, he attempted to portray African American life from a black cultural perspective after *The Lynchers.* Presenting Christian belief from the viewpoint of the black community therefore becomes more important. In this context, *Hiding Place* (1981) depicts God as much more than an implied lack in the imagination or as a paradoxical presence. God and spirituality are individual and community realities that are necessary for life and that both Christians and non-Christians experience through church rituals and intimate associations with others.

For one of the main characters, Mother Bess, a suppressed story is synonymous with an alienated, bitter life; the text is about the restoration of the story as Bess moves back to family and community. Bess's is partly an oral narrative, but its medium is more the open-ended consciousness of associated images and emotions that constitute a positive self-history of relationships with family and community.

During the best time of her life, church singing and the spiritual images and empowerment associated with it are inseparable from her loving relationship with her husband and positive self-identity. In the same way that Eddie Lawson in *A Glance Away* remembers the virtuosity of Tiny's church performance, the animated image of Frank Felder singing "Farther Along" recurs in Bess's consciousness: "That old preacher, dead these many years, singing [her husband's] song [that he would sit on the back step of Homewood A. M. E. Zion Church to listen to]. Black Frank Felder, his big head like a bowling ball above the white collar, his tiny eyes squeezed shut, his mouth pained, busy at the corners like he's trying to talk to himself while he's singing the words of the hymn" (22). Bess's undevout dead husband says Frank Felder is "no better than none them other chicken-stealing holy rollers but that man can chirp, Bess" (22).

Bess must also acknowledge the need for God in her story because God is the only entity she can imagine standing against the changeless, unfathomable senselessness of life. She lost God in her own defiguration of the words "Farther Along." She had thought the words were "*Father* Along" for years before she saw the words written. In seeing them written, she lost her "Father Along, lost his smile, his infinite forgiveness, his dance, strut, glide, stomp, gentle walk, his brown eyes and the tender sweep of his garment. She lost her God" (23). Bess's later loss of her husband and son virtually suppressed the story. Its regeneration begins after her sister's great-grandson Tommy invades Bess's life; the story's gravity point is Tommy's dying baby niece that his sister Shirley brought to Bess. Remembering what happened and telling the story, Bess can only say "Jesus . . . and Good God Almighty because . . . there ain't nothing else to say even though I ain't been a Christian for years, Jesus and Good God Almighty cause what else you gon say when some old woman ninety-nine years old still living and breathing . . . and that little baby's gone" (130). Bess must say "Jesus . . . and Good God Almighty" *because* "ain't no power ever gon change what's gon be. And what's gon be ain't never gon make no sense" (132–33). Bess again calls the name of God in the darkness at the end, before she imagines burning down her shack with the help of an angel child, awakening her sleeping husband, and returning to Homewood with him to tell the truth about Tommy (156–58).

As Tommy tells his story through a process of open-ended consciousness similar to Bess's, he shows that he needs spiritual strength and belief in God in his life, which is full of trouble and mortal danger. The singing of the Commodores and Dells, the exploits of family figures and heroes of street life, and his own sexual prowess and destructive, shameful behavior are all part of the story that Tommy tells in an attempt to define, understand, and thereby control his life. But he also includes in the narrative his own witness of the spirit in religious songs and rituals in the church, and observation of the power of God in family and community.

Tommy is by no means a true Christian, but church images and rituals and references to spirituals and gospels comfort him. He remembers the Rev. Claude Jeter, "lead tenor of the Swan Silvertones . . . [a] voice going places sweet tenor ain't supposed to go" (42). When he sings "My Lord, what a morning," he makes "My Lord . . . a king and a friend and your own jive self walking cross that valley of shadow." The image of Reverend Jeter conflates with scenes from the Homewood A. M. E. Zion Gospel Chorus singing the song, and Tommy witnesses, "Yes, Lawd," attesting to the spirit of the church singing. The music is gospel, but it inspires Tommy to see beyond danger and bondage as the spirituals did: "They want him dead. They want to kill him but he made it through the night. A thousand years of night. Haze was lifting, the sun rising behind him" (42–43).

The immanence of God in others brings to light Tommy's ambivalent faith at the same time that it draws him to substantive belief beyond his being. In the funeral parlor at his grandfather's funeral, Tommy tries to close his eyes and pray, and can only think of old age and death that he associates with people who pray. Simultaneously, however, he thinks that the image of Christ looking down from the wall has none of the power of Christ invoked by the prayer of "Elder Watt knee-walkin cross the bare floor of Tioga Street Sanctified in the Blood of the Lamb Church of God in Christ" (108). (Elder

Watt is another virtuoso like Tiny, "black Frank Felder," and Reverend Jeter.) "Spying on" his mother's face beside him, Tommy realizes that her prayer and song have the transcendent power that allows her to be "two places at once" (111), in the sorrowful funeral parlor and in the church rocking with Elder Watkins at the same time. Tommy ultimately longs to "sing those old songs and dance on the waves" (123). The reality, promise, and potential of faithful vision are prominent in *Hiding Place*, whereas they are secondary in the modernist-dominated milieus of *A Glance Away*, *Hurry Home*, and *The Lynchers*.

CHAPTER 2

The Centrality of Religious Faith

Communal Acceptance, Textual Ambiguity, and Paradox

GO TELL IT ON THE MOUNTAIN (1953) and *A Visitation of Spirits* (1989) reveal the centrality of the Bible and the related African American religious tradition and at the same time significantly oppose them. The tradition of faithful vision based on the Bible is important to black people and an important influence on these narratives, no matter how critical they may be on different narrative levels. *Go Tell It on the Mountain* politically opposes the biblically derived practices and beliefs that privilege the patriarchy. In terms of what is *written*, the Bible is rigidly doctrinaire in its portrayal of patriarchal privilege, which limits the appropriation and use of its creative and cosmic vision, particularly for a writer like Baldwin with such a thorough political consciousness. However, his novel places the power and reality of African American faithful vision based on the Bible in the foreground of its own vision of "truth" as much as it critiques and rejects it. Although homosexual proscription is not as often dealt with as patriarchal privilege, the Bible seems equally rigid in its treatment of homosexuality. *A Visitation of Spirits* implies great ambivalence about the biblical beliefs that condemn Horace to suicide because he so deeply internalizes African American religious tradition. (*Go Tell on the Mountain,* of course, reveals the suppression of John's sexual attraction to males because beliefs based on the Bible influence him.) Kenan's novel has a more postmodern focus on its own textuality and on writing generally, and therefore it emphasizes the potential power of the Bible as *writing,* the ultimate limitations of narratives to convey a substantive or truthful story notwithstanding. However, the novel does not re-

43

strict the Bible's importance to its power as an iconic text that creates un-questioned traditional beliefs that are negative and dangerous. The Bible and the black religious tradition also are potentially positive and saving, just as they are in *Go Tell It on the Mountain*.

James Baldwin's *Go Tell It on the Mountain* is unique in its portrayal of black religious belief, but unlike Richard Wright's *Native Son* (1940), its main dif-ference from most of the novels that I analyze is the depth of its focus on re-ligion and not an underlying general theme that totally undercuts the importance of the African American religious tradition. To a greater extent than any other novel, *Go Tell It on the Mountain* foregrounds the Bible as an intertext, and Christian faith and practice as the main features in the lives and cultural tradition of its characters.[1] There are always multiple perspectives in the novel. There is a general fascination with the potential of the Word of God to evoke the mystery of the underlying design of human existence and inter-action, while the Word is also the potential solace against the mystery. There is also a paradoxical perspective that sees the saving power of the Word of God in the character's lives, and at the same time criticizes the characters' use of the Word because it limits their self-perceptions and self-critique in rela-tionships with others. From the paradoxical perspective, the novel implies that the Bible is full of the law and moral prescription that prevents the char-acters' exploration of humanity through relationships, which is the essence of living for Baldwin, and also so full of that very mystery of human existence, interaction, and motivation that Baldwin believed relationships always re-veal.[2] It is more than just the paradoxical complexity of the Bible as a text, however, that accounts for the power of the Word of God in *Go Tell It on the Mountain*. The novel's own visual perspective shows this power as it affects the lives of people. The novel never negates its multiple, conflicted perspec-tives, but it does not deny the reality of the power of the Word that it sees.[3]

Go Tell It on the Mountain moves inevitably toward the anguished mys-tery of existence, particularly of African American life, and the implication that God must *be* that mystery; the mystery of God *is* the saving Word that one can *know* only by faithfully giving up the self to the spiritual *experience* of the power and benevolence of God. Thus, the mysterious Word of God is the only sure thing that can bring light to a fearful, fathomless darkness. The text shows John's deliverance from the darkness through the self-abnegating threshing floor experience that enables the Word's spiritual habitation of his mind and body. Perhaps Deborah comes closest to describing the unexplainable experience of the mysterious Word of God. She says to Gabriel, "ain't no shelter against the Word of God, is there, Reverend? You is just got to be in it, that's all—'cause every word is true, and the gates of Hell ain't going to be able to stand against it" (100). From the novel's paradoxical perspective, this is a dubious otherworldly view. But it is also where the characters' desperate quest for meaning and salvation takes them, and it seems to be what Baldwin's own angst-filled quest made him see, if not believe.

Baldwin's novel implies epistemological questions that take him beyond the limitations of his own *words* to the teleological possibilities of *the* Word as appropriated by him and his characters. Epistemologically, no human creations, including literary, political, historical, and social portrayals and analyses, seem to account for the complexity of human life. There must be a life-generating final cause that we cannot know behind the mystery.[4] God is the unfathomable final cause that nevertheless speaks powerfully through the Word of the Bible. From a social perspective, Baldwin really believed that unlegislated human interaction was important. He found in it not the characters' desired sure knowledge underlying everything that leads to salvation, but the achievement of all that can be in life, the striving itself.[5] There is an irresolvable conflict here between human limitation and godly possibility that his mind cannot negate; he deals with this by writing the textuality of the Bible throughout *Go Tell It on the Mountain* even as he rejects its Word. His appropriation of the Bible does not reveal the transcendent knowledge of human interaction and all of life behind the Word, but it does show the Word's power to evoke its own mystery and to give the promise of answers. While not eliminating human travail, this potentially gives life greater meaning and purpose through the inscrutable agency of God. Baldwin's intellectual self could not deny, and some part of his human self may also have longed for, the possibility of what his characters found through religious belief enforced by biblical traditions—that satisfactory meaning in life, which feels difficult through sensory experience and is unknowable through our finite minds, can only be found through faith in the goodness of the divine, which is the mysterious, all-powerful Word. The novel strongly opposes this politically while simultaneously rewriting it through the characters' experiences and biblical intertextuality.[6]

Gabriel is, perhaps, *Go Tell It on the Mountain*'s most complex character: His destructive effect on the lives of others and his total inability to look at himself critically parallel the potential saving power of the Word of God in his life. On one hand, Gabriel *experiences* the Word of God in his spirit like King David, the Old Testament "Lords anointed" from whom Gabriel takes his title, and like King David he does destructive things to other people, particularly women. Why is David not only the "Lord's anointed" but the "Lord's anointed" from whom the Lord never takes the title, as he takes it from King Saul in I Samuel? David is a warrior king who literally is responsible for killing thousands upon thousands, but his position as king that contrasts Gabriel's powerlessness is not the question here. In the more domestic realm, in which he can be compared with Gabriel, he has six sons by six different women, thirteen sons by Bathsheba, one daughter, and unspecified children by concubines (I Chronicles 3:1–9).[7] Most importantly for this analysis, he forcibly takes Bathsheba, the wife of Uriah the Hittite, while Uriah is away fighting in David's army. He impregnates her, tries to deceive Uriah and manipulate him into thinking that he impregnated his wife, and then essentially murders Uriah when his lies and deception fail. God punishes David by refusing to hear his prayer for his sick infant son by Bathsheba and by letting the son die, but when David repents for his sins and takes Bathsheba for his wife, God gives him another son by her, Solomon, a great and wise king. The Lord never deserts David in spite of the horrible things that he does, and although the Bible suggests several different reasons for this, the clearest seems to be that despite his terrible acts, David was true to God in his heart, as he asks God to let him be in Psalm 19:14: "Let the words of my mouth, and the meditation of my heart, be acceptable in thy sight, O Lord, my strength, and my redeemer."

In the context of *Go Tell It on the Mountain*'s relationship with the Bible, what Gabriel believes about himself is "true" because it is so indelibly written in the story of David and parts of the New Testament, *and* intertextually in the novel, along with the novel's opposing political and social critique that is grounded in the secular world. (This applies to what the other characters believe about their own lives as well.) Gabriel has as much claim to truth as David, whose goodness we must come to terms with in the biblical context, even if this means finding ways to subvert the Word.[8] As is the case with King David, Gabriel believes that God has punished his sin and that his salvation has grown out of his sin and repentance. No matter what Gabriel and David have done to others, God will forgive and favor them because in their hearts they truly want to do the right thing according to God's Word. Their lives are a part of the unknowable, benevolent plan of God's work and part of the plan for their own individual redemption.

Go Tell It on the Mountain portrays Gabriel's interior life where he contemplates God and his own deeds with a biblical voice that reveals his seriousness about doing God's will and being saved.

> For he desired in his soul, with fear and trembling, all the glories that his mother prayed he should find. Yes, he wanted power—he wanted to know himself to be the Lord's anointed, His well-beloved, and worthy, nearly, of that snow-white dove which had been sent down from heaven to testify that Jesus was the Son of God. He wanted to be master, to speak with that authority which could only come from God. It was later to become his proud testimony that he hated his sins—even as he ran towards sin, even as he sinned. He hated the evil that lived in his body, and he feared it, as he feared and hated the lions of lust and longing that prowled the defenseless city of his mind. He was later to say that this was a gift bequeathed him by his mother, that it was God's hand on him from his earliest beginnings; but then he knew only that when each night came, chaos and fever raged in him; the silence in the cabin between his mother and himself became something that could not be borne; not looking at her, facing the mirror as he put on his jacket, and trying to avoid his face there, he told her that he was going to take a little walk—he would be back soon. (94)

Gabriel always commits sins of the flesh before he returns from his walks. However, it is impossible to deny that he is committed from a biblical perspective because in his heart he acknowledges his sin, although he cannot escape it, and he has his war with the flesh as David perhaps did and as Paul explicitly says that he did. Paul says that sinful lust is the essence of his physical body, and he can only escape through the transcendent spiritual potential of Jesus Christ: "For I delight in the law of God after the inward man: But I see another law in my members, warring against the law of my mind, and bringing me into captivity to the law of sin which is in my members. O wretched man that I am! who shall deliver me from the body of this death? I thank God through Jesus Christ our Lord. So then with the mind I myself serve the law of God; but with the flesh the law of sin" (Romans 7:22–25).

Paul expresses the paradox of God trapping human beings in the lusts of the body that cause sin; in this context, Gabriel wins the war over the body in the only way that it can be won—through transcendent spiritual faith. From this viewpoint, hating sin "even as he ran towards sin, even as he sinned" is not a simple rationalization. We must take Gabriel seriously not only because Baldwin writes the hegemonic textuality of David's example in the Bible so thoroughly into *Go Tell It on the Mountain* but also because Gabriel's predicament, as expressed by Paul, has the "truth" and reality of human limitation. Here the Bible as a text has power because the necessity to have faith in the benevolence of God behind the unknowable mystery is grounded in the knowable physical limitation of human beings.

Given the novel's relationship to the Bible and its own consequent ambiguity, one cannot tell what Gabriel's selfish, destructive actions mean in the larger, unknowable scheme of existence. Perhaps the text is least ambiguous about Gabriel's relationship to Esther; however, this portrayal remains complex and contradictory.[9] Gabriel impregnates Esther while he is married and then rejects her. He constantly prays for Esther and for his illegitimate son Royal, and "to be delivered from blood guiltiness" (138), but Esther dies after he rejects his responsibility to her because it will interfere with his responsibility to God. From the standpoint of society's morality, there is absolutely nothing good or redeeming in this situation. In the biblical context, however, Gabriel never loses faith during the whole episode with Esther, and afterwards "he would not turn his face from God, no matter how deep might grow the darkness in which God hid His face from him. One day God would give him a sign, and the darkness would all be finished—one day God would raise him, who had suffered him to fall so low" (137–38). However, we inevitably return to whether we judge Gabriel by the interior truth of his heart or whether, as his sister Florence says, we "know the tree by its fruit" (213). Clearly, on one hand, Gabriel is the most self-justifying hypocrite, but on the other he is true to the biblical character of the "Lord's anointed." It is difficult to ignore the latter because the textuality of the Bible is so prevalent in *Go Tell It on the Mountain.*

Although the realities of his physical senses and her unattractive body defy him, Gabriel has good and even noble intentions to elevate his first wife Deborah in the process of carrying out his work for God, and this is much harder to judge than Gabriel's relationship with Esther.[10] Gabriel violates Deborah's trust by committing adultery and stealing her money to send the pregnant Esther away (134–35). In contrast to this, he had married Deborah so that she could continue "to help him to stand," "to raise her up, to release her from . . . [the] dishonor [of her rape by white men]," and to have his royal line of children (109). He also thinks of Paul's words: "'It is better to marry than to burn'" (109; 1 Corinthians 7:9). Gabriel "struggled to wear out his visions [of sin with Esther] in the marriage bed, [and] he struggled to awaken Deborah [sexually to have his royal line]," although he grows to hate her in spite of himself. (127–28). Gabriel later replaces the money, which he admits to Deborah that he stole, along with admitting that Royal is his son (147–48). Deborah dies childless, but not because of Gabriel's lack of effort.

Weaknesses of the flesh and his actions to conceal those weaknesses defeat Gabriel in his effort to change his and Deborah's lives positively, and he deals with his failure and makes it right in his heart. But *Go Tell It on the Mountain* complicates our judgment of Gabriel's relationship to Deborah by juxtaposing his view of himself to Deborah's view of him and implicitly to a world beyond his own self-concept.

> "Deborah," he asked, "what you been thinking all this time?"
> She smiled, "I been thinking," she said, "how you better commence to tremble when the Lord, He gives you your heart's desire." She paused. "I'd been wanting you since I wanted anything. And then I got you."
> He walked back to the window, tears rolling down his face.
> "Honey," she said, in another, stronger voice, "you better pray God to forgive you. You better not let go until He make you *know* you been forgiven."
> "Yes," he sighed, "I'm waiting on the Lord."
> Then there was only silence, except for the rain. The rain came down in buckets; it was raining, as they said, pitchforks and nigger babies. Lightning flashed again across the sky and thunder rolled.
> "Listen," said Gabriel, "God is talking." (149)

Earlier, the text seems to show that Gabriel believes in his own sincerity in truly asking God for forgiveness, but here Deborah's apparently more genuine holiness and the novel's profane narrative voice mock him. (As I show later, the text at this point clearly speaks in one voice that satirizes Gabriel's pretensions, but it gives no perspective for analysis of Deborah's faithful belief in God except her actions that support her professed belief, thus leaving us to determine what her steadfast faith means in terms of a life of hardship and abuse.)

Gabriel's deep conviction that God has a plan to raise up a royal line through him controls much of what he does and thinks in his marriage to Elizabeth. Again we cannot separate *Go Tell It on the Mountain* from biblical portrayals, and Gabriel's characterization is complex because his actions have ambiguous and potentially positive results that are beyond his control. In this way the novel implies the possibility of God's mysterious benevolence in which the characters believe. Gabriel rejects and hates Elizabeth's illegitimate son John, whom he initially promised to accept as his own (188). He considers John the son of a "weak, proud woman and some careless boy" and not "the son that God had promised him" in his long-ago dream (115) that prompted him to ask Deborah to marry him (111–13). In "Gabriel's Prayer," which gives access to his interior life, the text does not go far in showing what he thinks about Elizabeth, except to portray his dissatisfaction with her because she is unworthy according to his perception of God's plan for him. Yet his abuse of her as shown from John's perspective is graphic. Pleasing God is an excuse for deceit and cruelty from the novel's secular viewpoint.

The potential of John to be saved by the Word of God because Gabriel intervenes and falsely promises to love him is where Gabriel's relationship to Elizabeth, where John's characterization, and the novel's overall portrayal of the African American religious tradition is especially rich and complicated. Elizabeth thinks that Gabriel's connection to her and John has the effect of raising them up through trials, which shows her faith that Gabriel is part of the plan for salvation that is always achieved by "trials and tribulations" in the Bible. When she meets him, Gabriel's voice and presence make her perceive hope for the first time since the death of John's ungodly father Richard: "*All things work together for good to them that love the Lord*" (185; Romans 8:28). She feels that her life with Richard and her overall past has imposed a "bitterness that only the hand of God could have laid on her, [but] this same hand had brought her through" (176). (Elizabeth is bound by anguish over God's wrath because of her past life, especially her relationship with Richard, and her fear—like Florence's fear because she is sick and dying—may lead her to grace. Although Elizabeth does not understand it, the text clearly shows from one perspective that the human connection of love and respect that she and Richard share is good. But what compels Elizabeth in the present time of the novel is that she would have chosen Richard—who had once said "You can tell that puking bastard [Jesus] to kiss my big black ass"

[163]—above God.) Nevertheless, her hard, unloving marriage to Gabriel bestows a last name upon her illegitimate son and gives her a family that includes three other children and the support of a church community. Through Gabriel, she "who had descended with such joy and pain, had begun her upward climb—upward, with her baby, on the steep, steep side of the mountain" (185). This is an example of the novel's paradoxical disdain for faithful vision and acknowledgement of the inevitability of God's plan and power to save, although there is a lot of pain and suffering in the saving. From the secular viewpoint, Elizabeth may be as self-deluded as Gabriel, but at the same time, the novel's intertextual relationship to the Bible steeps everything in mystery and possibility.

The novel's third-person narrative of John's conversion, which is grounded in the same religious tradition as the other characters but lacks the complication of potentially selfish and self-serving motives generated over a lifetime, makes the mystery and possibility of the biblical Word a potential reality more than anything else.[11] John has a crisis of belief on his fourteenth birthday and experiences a mysterious change. It begins with a fall into darkness like the time before creation at the beginning of Genesis and before the Word brings light in John 1:1–5: "that moment was . . . locked in darkness, was wordless, and would not come forth" (194). John has a yearning for his friend Elisha, which he is incapable of understanding, and a hatred for Gabriel, which he well understands, but the text places "the secret, the turning, the abysmal drop . . . farther back, in darkness" (195), beyond self-delusion created by physical desire and hate.

In his conversion, John sees spiritually the mystery and possibility of the Word, which is also the mystery and possibility of his relationship to Gabriel and of African American oppression. John's vision is influenced by his primal sexual being, white racism, and biblical narrative, but its essence is the mystery of spiritual realization beyond the rational. In his inner darkness, John has a strong conviction that he has sinned because he has looked at and dreaded Gabriel's "slimy," serpentlike male nakedness and then hated him for it (196–97). John's feeling that he has sinned is substanceless from the novel's ironic viewpoint that denies the truth of his experience, but it is ineluctable from the perspective of the biblical idea of original sin conjoined with his suppressed sexuality and of his unconscious influence by white racist social construction of blackness as sin. He associates his sin with that of Ham because he has looked upon his father Gabriel's nakedness as Ham looked upon Noah's (197; Genesis 9:20–27). John cannot make sense of nor can he escape the idea that his sin is the curse of Ham, and in the darkness Gabriel is also a sinful son who tries to expiate the curse by beating it out of John. Desperate to escape from Gabriel, he calls *"Father! Father!"* (199) and encounters the sound of generations of African Americans coming out of the darkness. He wants also to flee from the horribly oppressive fate of these generations that has developed over the centuries seemingly because of the curse that he thinks Ham put on the race and that he himself is perpetuating. The image of the torn, oppressed multitude becomes revelation when someone cries out ritualizing the Word. *"'Sinner, do you love my Lord?'* Then John saw the Lord—for a moment only; and the darkness, for a moment only, was filled with a light he could not bear. Then, in a moment, he was set free; his tears sprang as from a fountain; his heart, like a fountain of waters, burst. Then he cried: 'Oh, blessed Jesus! Oh, Lord Jesus! Take me through!'" (204). The momentary transformation from darkness to light is his salvation and the salvation of the black multitude. This moment is the shining, blinding mystery of God that he cannot stand to contemplate, but the novel reveals that it is also the possibility that all things—including Gabriel's hatred and racial oppression grounded in the socially constructed symbolism of blackness as sin—through faith in the Word of God can lead to the (en)light(enment) that frees. *"All things work together for good to them that love the Lord"* (185; Romans 8:28).

The conversion, which turns out to be a transformation of darkness to light that is lasting spiritual vision, is reminiscent of prophetic vision in the Old Testament and the New Testament.[12] "The light and the darkness had kissed each other, and were married now, forever, in the life and the vision of John's soul. *I, John, saw a city, way in the middle of the air, Waiting, waiting, waiting up there.* He opened his eyes on the morning, and found [the others in the church witnessing the conversion], in the light of the morning, rejoicing for him" (204). The text conflates the "soul" vision of John Grimes with the revelatory vision of the apostle John: "And there came unto me one of the seven angels . . . And he carried me away in the spirit to a great and high mountain, and shewed me that great city, the holy Jerusalem, descending out of heaven from God" (Revelation 21: 9–10).

A profane, doubting voice and a holy, faithful voice oppose each other during the conversion, and the faithful voice empowers John by the end. The negative, ironic voice tells him to rise and flee from the fate of "all the other niggers" (193–94) early in the conversion episode, but after it is over, John's "words came upward, it seemed, of themselves, in the new voice God had given him" (206). John's conviction that he is saved is steadfast after this. At the very end, he faces Gabriel and smiles when Gabriel refuses to smile, and his last words are "I'm ready . . . I'm coming. I'm on my way" (221). John Grimes could possibly "tell his prophecy from the mountain" revealing the Word, which is Jesus Christ, just as the apostle John and John the Baptist did. Shirley S. Allen describes John's great promise at the conclusion: "Because of all the [biblical] allusions, all of which Baldwin reiterates in the course of the novel, the title becomes symbolic of the specific human situation when a costly break with the past has been made and a new road, beset with dangers but promising salvation, has been undertaken. This is clearly the situation of the protagonist at the end of the novel" (169). Given his potential, John may after all be the great son that God promised Gabriel. (Allen is primarily interested in analyzing Baldwin's symbolic uses of biblical allusion and the psychological that establish the novel's universal reference and make it, as critics have said, much more than only a black novel. The novel may be psychological and "universal" as Allen says, but I argue that it has another dimension where it poses black religious belief as a primary mode of knowledge about the world and human existence. From my perspective, biblical allusion and religious belief are not secondary to or symbolic of something else more important, true, or real.)

In spite of his intentions and the destructiveness of his actions, Gabriel may have carried out the Lord's plan by intervening in Elizabeth's life, taking John as his son, and by everything else that he has done as the "Lord's anointed." This is ludicrous from one perspective but not from the standpoint of the novel's intertextual relationship with the Bible, which is an essential and necessary part of the text in spite of its own opposition to it. I have already summarized the part of David's story in which God punishes him by the death of his first son by Bathsheba. God further punishes David through the actions of the "bad" son Absalom, whom David seemingly loves more than anyone, and who is finally slain (2 Samuel 13–19). It is a mysterious story in which God forgives David's sin but decrees the death of the first son and the evil actions of the second "bad" son as punishment for David's sins against Uriah and Bathsheba (2 Samuel 12:7–14). David suffers greatly because of his sons' consequent deaths, but the sin of adultery with Bathsheba eventually leads to the birth of the "good" son Solomon, who brings peace and great prosperity to Israel (1 Kings 2–11). God speaks to both David and Solomon but never explains the logic of the story, leaving only the possibility of David's true heart as the reason for his being "anointed." Gabriel's adultery produces a "bad" son, Royal, who is a punishment to him, and his sin propels him to repent and pray for the fulfillment of God's promise of a royal son (115–16). Gabriel rescues John because he thinks he is the promise fulfilled: "He done give me back something I thought was lost" (188). This could be true; John turns out to be the son who could bring goodness to the world. In spite of Gabriel's sin and his later, more honest rejection of John, his actions lead to there being a "good" son.

There are obviously vast differences between the stories of Gabriel and David, but the similarities are substantive. Gabriel's awareness of the Bible and the novel's broader intertextual perspective connects the stories and in many ways emphasizes and privileges the mystery of both. (Gabriel most certainly would know the entire story of David, although he could interpret it in only a biased, self-serving way. Likewise, David cannot understand the mystery of his own story but only sees it in terms of trying to do the will of God against his enemies.) Within the context of what *Go Tell It on the Mountain* makes possible through its relationship with the Bible, the basic similarity is that Gabriel sins by committing adultery and is forgiven, is punished by the shameful actions and eventual murder of the "bad" son that his adultery produces, and finally gets the "good" son that God promised, although Gabriel cannot see the goodness and accept it.[13] In both stories, morally discordant narrative elements lead to good or the potential of good; these elements constitute important parts of the mystery. It is impossible to analyze the mystery and understand why events occur as they do in David's story, and the same is true of Gabriel's story (and, implicitly, all of human existence). Although Baldwin obviously saw more than either David or Gabriel saw, and was not a faithful believer himself, his novel gives no sense that one can understand reality and deal with it any better than Gabriel and the other characters do through their faith. The novel's complex textuality affirms and simultaneously denies that for unknowable reasons God chooses very flawed men who nevertheless have faith and true hearts to carry out a plan that is ultimately good. The text mocks the comparison with David through its portrayal of Gabriel, and through its vastly different secular setting, but at the same time it makes the comparison powerfully real and true by its own writing of the Bible so thoroughly into the lives of its characters and its own structure.

Florence hates Gabriel and tries to debunk him and his moral pretensions. She is also the character farthest outside the Word of God and in contention with it, which allows her to see the world differently than other women. Florence is seemingly the only woman who has the power to cut through religious doctrine to the reality of male attitudes in a patriarchal society. When they are young, she reminds her friend Deborah, who has been raped and abused by white men, that all men's "thoughts rose no higher [than lust], and they lived only to gratify on the bodies of women their brutal and humiliating needs" (74). She has a natural pride that very early generates a life-long hatred for her brother Gabriel, whom the black patriarchy, as manifested in the attitudes of their mother, privileges. In "Florence's Prayer," she kneels at the altar, terminally ill, thinking about having left Gabriel with her dying mother to pursue the northern life that has only made Florence more bitter. She thinks that if God accepts Gabriel as a holy preacher and as "the Lord's anointed," which Gabriel claims he is, then "she would rather die and endure Hell for all eternity than bow before His altar" (65–66). She "strangle[s] her pride" and keeps on singing, but at the end, Florence continues her important role as the fierce critic who separates Gabriel from his self-righteousness and reminds him of his unchanging pattern of destructiveness in other people's lives: "Who is you met, Gabriel, all your holy life long, you ain't made to drink a cup of sorrow? And you doing it still—you going to be doing it till the Lord puts you in your grave" (212). Her final words to him are that she will expose the "Lord's anointed" for the fake and hypocrite that he is before she dies (214–15).

Florence is right from the novel's viewpoint of human morality, but her interior life makes a substantive judgment of Gabriel more difficult because she accepts his basic view of the Word and of God, although she will never believe that Gabriel is godly. In "Florence's Prayer," what she feels compellingly in her body and spirit is that denial of God has brought his humbling power down upon her. Although she returns to her pride by the end, the novel leaves open the possibility that her total humility may lead to saving grace in the powerful biblical context that she has tried but failed to reject and, even more importantly, in the parameters of *Go Tell It on the Mountain*'s own intertextual relationship with the Bible. "For the message had come to Florence that had come to Hezekiah: "*Set thine house in order, for thou shalt die and not live*" (67; 2 Kings 20:1). The biblical message that death is certain and that "her humility might lead her to grace" (65) is written into her. Florence looks back to her mother, born a slave, and although she definitely sees her mother's highly unsatisfactory life, she also realizes that the "long road, her life, which she had followed for sixty groaning years, had led her at last to her mother's starting-place, the altar of the Lord" (66). It seems inevitable that Florence seek the faith, prayer, and supplication that brought her mother through slavery and life afterwards. The "hands of death caressed her shoulders, the voice whispered and whispered in her ear: 'God's got your number, knows where you live, death's got a warrant out for you'" (91). Feeling utterly lost and damned, she seeks grace in the terms of her mother's tradition; she comes back to the reality of faith in the transcendence of God as the answer.

The thoughts, words, and actions of Florence, Elizabeth, and John explicitly and implicitly criticize Gabriel, but the reality of each one's interior life affirms Gabriel's general faithful vision as much as it implies its shortcomings and limitations. This is also true for Deborah and Elisha, whose interior lives the novel does not portray. Deborah's characterization raises conflicting viewpoints of biblical orthodoxy, sense, and practicality that go unresolved yet at the same time make powerful the biblical reality of the Word. Deborah is a victim of the abuses of white racism and of the desires of the black and white patriarchy imposed brutally on the mind and body of a woman, but she transcends through charitable actions that show her true belief in the Word of God.[14] "Gabriel's Prayer" well expresses the diametric ways that the community looks at Deborah and the indecision of the text itself about her. Deborah went through the "community like a woman mysteriously visited by God, like a terrible example of humility, or like a holy fool . . . [Some mocked her] but their mockery was uneasy; they could never be certain but that they might be holding up to scorn the greatest saint among them, the Lord's peculiar treasure and most holy vessel" (98–99). Although Gabriel's deepest feelings toward her are conflicted during their marriage, she influences him to be his most humane self in his decisions and actions leading to their marriage (107–10). She tries to get him to view Esther and their affair in less self-centered terms and to interrogate honestly his own claims of forgiveness (146–49). Further, she reminds the arrogant Florence that belief in the Word can be used in the best Christian way. In their youth, she responds to Florence's hatred of Gabriel stumbling home drunk: "You know, honey, the Word tell us to hate the sin but not the sinner" (75).

It is possible that Deborah's life represents godliness and integrity just as the life of Deborah the judge and prophet in the book of Judges did (Judges 4–5), and her portrayal most poignantly raises the question of the nature of reality and how the novel judges the world and those around her, especially Gabriel. The novel's multiple perspectives strongly converge in Deborah's characterization because she seems so godly and Christian, and there is no described interior life or selfish, destructive act to provide a basis for criticism. Certainly, it is purely good, if nothing else, always to deal charitably with people as she does, even when one suffers because of it. In the context of Baldwin's oeuvre, subjecting oneself to human engagement, struggle, and, often, suffering is the human goal. Deborah achieves this humanity through belief in the Word and all that it implies epistemologically. This was not Baldwin's belief, but given the novel's intertextual relationship with the Bible that infuses it with the mystery and possibility of God along with its other viewpoints, the portrayal of Deborah and the way she sees the world is powerful.

The novel's overall complex textuality makes Deborah's comments to Gabriel about the Word as substantive and as reliable a basis for reality as anything else implied or stated in the text: "Ain't no shelter against the Word of God . . . You is just got to be in it" (100). Implicitly in the novel, how much do we and can we know about truth and the ultimate cause of human life and interaction? We can know nothing definitively and can only see possibilities that are often opposing. The novel takes part of its stance from a social and human perspective, from which traditional African American religious faith would seem to be a limitation to human growth and visionary, at best. Yet at the same time, the complexity of the novel ties its reality to the African American religious vision, the characters' conviction about the truth of their religious belief, the text's visual representation of the effect of spirituality on the characters, and the characters' internal manifestation of vision and belief.

The text obviously provides no definitive answer as to what goodness means in the secular or biblical setting, but the biblical examples of goodness (David's and Deborah's) are important because they are so thoroughly written into *Go Tell It on the Mountain* and made an aspect of the characters' lives. The novel makes it possible that Gabriel is the "Lord's anointed" whose life is part of a benevolent plan. From a secular perspective, Deborah's characterization is grounds for seeing clearly Gabriel's hypocrisy, but the novel's depiction of his interior life and conflation of his story with David's only deepens the complexity and the mystery. Gabriel's goodness is not perfect like Deborah's, but neither was David's compared to the biblical Deborah's. Gabriel's goodness reveals itself in a strange sequence in which he rebounds from sin and is loving and caring toward Deborah, and then sins again, thus allowing her to play the prophetlike role of trying to bring him to terms with the reality of sin.[15] By the end, Deborah is long dead, but she is important to Gabriel's story that has led to the present, his relationship with John, and John's potential. Gabriel's remark to Florence when she reveals Deborah's letter exposing his adultery and consequent destructive actions is self-righteous yet true in ways that he cannot see: "God's way . . . ain't man's way. I been doing the will of the Lord, and can't nobody sit in judgment on me but the Lord. The Lord called me out, He chose *me*, and I been running with Him ever since I made a start" (212–13). (Deborah continues to hold Gabriel accountable through the letter that she has written Florence. Gabriel believes that it represents "the bitterness she had not spoken" (212), but Florence said that years earlier when she first got the letter Deborah was "mighty worried" about what Gabriel had done. The scene in which Deborah asks Gabriel to come to terms with his actions in the most sincere way for the sake of his own salvation supports the idea that she was genuinely worried and concerned as opposed to bitter and vindictive [148–49]).

Elisha is the other saintly character whose life reflects the biblical ideal, and at the end he and John manifest the potential of faith in the spiritual experience of the Word. In the final analysis, the characters are each other's counterparts. Elisha is John's holy forerunner in the novel's sordid secular world. His holy life is an example for John, and he has a spiritual experience on the threshing floor prior to John's conversion (113, 150, 151). Their shared emphasis on the spiritual and holy dominates the end of the novel. Together, they represent the potential of the prophetic vision captured in their Old and New Testament names. (In Matthew 11:10 and Luke 1:17 and 76, John the Baptist comes before and prepares the way for Jesus Christ. Of course, like any other character in Baldwin's novel, John is only generally associated with Jesus, but his name and characterization obviously suggest John the Baptist and the apostle John in the New Testament.[16] In 1 and 2 Kings in the Old Testament, Elisha is a prophet whose life and vision has resonance in the characterization of *Go Tell It on the Mountain*'s John, as well as the novel's Elisha. The biblical story's underlying epistemology, teleology, and theology applied to the novel's possible underlying essence of reality in the secular world is more important than finding an exact correspondence of the characters' names, specific replication of character, or textual parallel.)

Go Tell It on the Mountain ends by balancing the spiritual life and the possibility of the entire mystery of the Word with the more than subtle suggestions about Elisha and John's suppressed desires of the flesh. Elisha leaves John and exhorts him with a "holy kiss" (221), evoking Paul's instructions to greet with a "holy kiss" (Romans 16:16, 1 Corinthians 16:20, 2 Corinthians 13:12, and 1 Thessalonians 5:26). The time ahead will be hard for both of them because their religious conviction has not allowed them to come fully to terms with their human sides, as perhaps suggested when the pastor catches Elisha "walking disorderly" (16–17; 2 Thessalonians 3: 6) with Ella Mae, and as clearly shown by John's unexplored desire for Elisha. But John's inner struggle, which shows his human weakness, has seemingly brought him to a commitment of holiness as revealed in the life of Elisha, who, like Deborah, is portrayed no less seriously even though the text gives no access to his interior life. The hopeless, destructive battle of Gabriel renews itself in the suppressed human desires of these characters, but the novel also shows the possibility that the negative part of humanity is an aspect of the benevolent plan of God realized through faith, which John and Elisha have already shown.

As John seems to presage in his heart after his conversion, he and Elisha will need strong faith to get through the future after their experience of holy joy among the other "saints" on that night: "Yet, as he moved among them, their hands touching, and tears falling, and the music rising—as though he moved down a great hall, full of a splendid company—something began to knock in that listening, astonished, newborn, and fragile heart of his; something recalling the terrors of the night, which were not finished, his heart seemed to say; which, in this company, were now to begin" (206).

An intertextual relationship to the Bible and a foregrounding of Christian belief are not as central to Randall Kenan's *A Visitation of Spirits;* nevertheless, it is perhaps more similar to *Go Tell It on the Mountain* with regard to these aspects of theme and structure and more generally reminiscent of it than any other novel.[17] Both show characters dealing with crises of faith that are informed by African American religious tradition, and both portray Christianity and the Bible from a complex viewpoint that shows how ineluctable their influences are for African Americans.

The main concern of *A Visitation of Spirits* is the suicide of Horace Cross, a sixteen-year-old who cannot reconcile his homosexuality with the African American Christian tradition that is an indelible part of his being and the foundation of his family, community, and tradition. The novel itself tries to humanely and sympathetically portray and remember Horace's life in the context of African American history and tradition in Tims Creek, North Carolina. In *A Visitation of Spirits,* written texts, oral narratives, and representations of psyche and memory shape and control the characters' perception of reality. *A Visitation of Spirits* uses quotations from the Bible and other literary works as epigraphs, and different texts and narrative and textual modes are referenced and thematized throughout the novel. The Bible, which the narrator and other characters quote, and the Christianity derived from it stabilize and support black individuals and community, and are the strongest influences on past and present African American reality. However, the doctrines of the Bible and Christianity as perceived by black people provide no acceptance of Horace's homosexuality or hope for the spiritual salvation that he seeks. In the final analysis, the text is ambivalent about the traditional Christian belief and faith of African Americans. It acknowledges their power but strongly questions the rigidity of the laws and beliefs that lead to Horace's suicide.[18] In the broader scope of the novel, no written or oral text or representation of reality shaped by psyche or memory, including *A Visitation of Spirits,* is adequate to recreate and preserve Horace's memory and define his relationship to past and present. The truth of Horace's past and the larger context of African American life cannot be known and understood (254). So *A Visitation of Spirits* can only reach a "good" ending with a "once upon a time" romantic narrative about responsibility and humanity holding the community together in the past (254–57). However, the text is still a narrative shaping of reality that aspires to sympathy, knowledge, and understanding, which is all that there can be.

For the two primary characters, Horace and his seminary-trained preacher cousin Jimmy Cross, and the other characters as well, the Bible and the associated religious tradition are either incontrovertible or centrally important (in the case of Jimmy). The text implies and shows the complexity of its viewpoint about Horace's reality and African American history and tradition through its section headings, epigraphs, and parts of its narrative. The novel's major sections are entitled "White Sorcery," "Black Necromancy," "Holy Science," "Old Demonology," and "Old Gods, New Demons." These titles imply beliefs and practices antithetical to the characters' central biblical, religious tradition, and the novel's general epigraphs and those to the last three sections are from nonbiblical sources that symbolize literary and secular constructions of reality and value systems. However, part of the dedication and the epigraphs to the first two sections are biblical, and the novel's third-person viewpoint often draws upon the Bible with neither a clearly ironic nor nonironic intention. On one hand, *A Visitation of Spirits* suggests that literary modes and perceptions of reality such as those referenced in epigraphs quoting Charles Dickens's *A Christmas Carol* (1843) and William Gibson's science fiction novel *Neuromancer* (1984) have the greatest symbolic significance as constructions of reality. Contradicting this, the second dedication is to "the inscrutable grace of the Host of Hosts" for the completion of the manuscript, and the epigraph to "White Sorcery" is "The Lord is in his Holy Temple; let all the earth keep silent before him (Habakkuk 2:20). I was glad when they said unto me, Let us go into the House of the Lord . . ." (Psalm 122:1). Further, the epigraph to "Black Necromancy"—"Whosoever will, let him come"—seems to paraphrase Revelation 22:17: "And the Spirit and the bride say, Come . . . And whosoever will, let him take the water of life freely." The biblical epigraphs invoke the holy and the agency of God, which is what the black characters often do in affirming their tradition. The epigraph to the last section is a dictionary definition of the word *subjunctive,* which points to the narrative's conditionality and uncertainty. Nevertheless, the text itself does not negate the biblically related religious faith that powerfully defines the tradition and people, in spite of the text's inability to tell the story of this definition of African Americans and the apparent fact that the tradition harmfully proscribes and limits human potential in some instances.

Horace cannot deny that he is homosexual nor escape the influence of his African American upbringing that damns him for it. The stress deranges him, and he tries to maintain and manipulate faith to achieve salvation that, according to the religious doctrine that he cannot disavow, is denied because of his sexuality.

He was also a believer in an unseen world full of archangels and prophets and folk rising from the dead, a world preached to him from the cradle on, and a world he was powerless not to believe in as firmly as he believed in gravity and the times tables. The two contradicting worlds were not contradictions in his mind. It was faith, not facts he needed; magic . . . salvation . . . Belief would save him, not only belief, but belief in belief. Like Daniel, like Isaac, like the woman at the well. I am sane, he thought, smoothing over any kinks in his reasoning and clutching fear by the neck. He had no alternative, he kept saying to himself. No other way out. (16)

In "White Sorcery," pushed to the brink of insanity, he attempts to bring together faith and the supernatural to save himself; he wants to retain some kind of biblically related faith, although imperfect, so that he can have a "visitation of spirits." As his references to Daniel, Isaac, and the woman at the well (John 4:1–42) indicate, Horace knows the Bible and understands its concept of faith. To redefine himself and be saved, he tries to combine this knowledge with the power of the supernatural, portrayed in the Bible as ungodly and forbidden. In Exodus 7:11–13 and 8:16–19, and in 1 Kings 21–40, sorcerers, magicians, and ungodly prophets challenge the powers of the prophets of God, and sometimes do miracles that equal theirs. First Samuel 28:7–8 and Isaiah 8:19, 19:13, and 29:4 speak of supernatural "familiar spirits" (occult or netherworld voices "out of the ground" [Isaiah 29:4]), people who possess the power of these spirits, and charmers and wizards. Matthew 8:28, 9:32, 12:22, 15:22, and 17:15, Mark 1:23 and 5:2, Luke 8:2, and Acts 5:16 portray people who have "unclean" or evil spirits, and there are several instances of Jesus casting out these spirits. Later, the novel describes Horace reading these passages and others: "While reading the Bible one day it suddenly came upon him. Sorcery. Had not the prophets battled magicians in the courts of kings and pharaohs? Didn't Saul die in the tent of the witch of Endor? Had not Jesus spoken of such things as demons and conjurers and men who walk in the way of magic? Why would witchcraft not work for him? . . . He had one hope, one faith, one reason, and would warp and distort and realign endlessly to fit his purpose" (240). Using the Bible, Horace creates a new faith in the supernatural, and from such books as *Third World Religions* and *Magicians of the Bible* (18–19), he learns occult practices to transform himself into a hawk (14–15), so as to avoid committing the sins of homosexuality that he will commit if he remains a human being (19–20).

The power of biblical dogma and black tradition prevail over the nontraditional "white sorcery" conceptualized by manipulating the Bible and actualized through occult practices, however. He does not truly believe in the world of books in which powerful demons can do miracles and transform him (26–27), but does believe that the world of the supernatural and its powers depicted in the Bible are bad and cannot be used for good purposes. Horace is unchangeably sinful as long as he is homosexual and can only give himself up to "fiends . . . for this was his salvation, the way to final peace" (28). Eventually, death by suicide becomes salvation and peace.

"White Sorcery" reveals complexities and contradictions that are never resolved; the text's stand on the religious tradition of Tims Creek and its own modes of representing reality is ambiguous. Structurally, the section in many ways foregrounds the text's effort to find a narrative approach. It starts on "December 8, 1985, 8: 45 AM" with an episode from a day in the life of the deceased Horace's family that begins with the words "Lord, Lord, Lord" (3), used generally and customarily to respect and call upon God. It then moves to a romanticized "once, in this very North Carolina town" construction of the past entitled "Advent (or The Beginning of the End)," before portraying Horace's desperate act to transform himself on "April 29, 1984, 11:30 AM." The novel's first words invoking God are those of a ninety-two year old woman, Ruth, ritually invoking God. The text sets this against the short account entitled "Advent (or the Beginning of the End)," "Advent" apparently referring to the second coming of Christ, and the parenthesized title to the romanticized "once" past of hog-killing time, which this narrative depicts. The date and time and the words beginning the novel mark a religious tradition and specific framing of the lives of people, and the date and time at the beginning of the subsection following "Advent" give at least a specific frame of reference to the bizarre portrayal of Horace. The title "Advent" has a very ambiguous connection to its story and is neither clearly a beginning nor an end. Its relationship to the reality of Horace, and even to the truth behind the culture and tradition of which hog killing is a part, is questionable. Perhaps it tries to mock traditional black Christian belief, but it more clearly symbolizes an inadequate narrative mode that lacks the substance to place the complex reality of Horace in the context of tradition. But "Advent" is not totally incongruous with the other two accounts. The stories of "White Sorcery," despite specifying a date and time, are only small fragments with limited perspectives on reality. This is also true of the longer account of Horace in his desperate state of mind, which is at the center of the reality that the novel wants to capture overall.

In "White Sorcery," fragmentary, diverse descriptive modes call into question the text's representation, and the world of Tims Creek and Horace's life are painfully, tragically, and concretely real and abstract and elusive at the same time. In this section and throughout the novel, the signs of the sustaining power of black tradition are there in the physical bodies of the old people who have endured and come to this time on "December 8, 1985, 8:45 AM." The signs also reside in the words of the characters and of the narrative that quote scripture and call on God, even in the words of Horace who tries to use the Bible and God in ways that are not permissible in the tradition. Horace has gone insane because he cannot live up to the same beliefs and tradition that have apparently brought these people through an oppressive past into an impressive, although quarrelsome, old age, and held together a community and a way of life. The tradition, people, and community are real, but the underlying truth about the tradition and its legacy is unclear. It may be implied that the tradition has not been responsive to Horace, but it is not clear how that tradition can be responsible for his tragedy. The tradition has provided survival for many but has perhaps had difficulty encompassing the human needs of sensitive individuals such as Horace, whom it ostracized and defined as abnormal in the process of creating its legacy of survival. Telling this story will be hard.

The novel's quest for a narrative form is most clearly indicated when the first-person "confessions" of Jimmy evolve into a more objective dramatic form to tell Horace's story (40–43).[19] The younger Jimmy is the community's preacher who knows that Horace is homosexual and is highly sympathetic but still ambivalent; his attitude and response to Horace haunt him in "James Malachi Greene: Confessions" in "Black Necromancy" and other sections. The question implied by Jimmy's confessions is how he will understand the feelings that precipitated Horace's suicide and his complicity in the tragedy, and the novel's question is how to understand Horace and tell his story as a part of the tradition strongly based in the religion that Jimmy preaches. The supposedly objectified form of the imaginary dramatic exchange only states Horace's notion that he is possessed by a demon that drives him to evil and his death. Jimmy cannot understand this and can only express disbelief, sadness, depression, and a feeling of inadequacy. Such feelings are also part of the narrative view of Horace as it struggles to understand and place his life in the scope of a powerfully sustaining but also potentially damning tradition. It is easy to feel for Horace but hard to understand and explain the situation.

"Black Necromancy" goes deeper into the tradition and history of the community in which the same beliefs and practices sustain the other characters and condemn Horace; for him, the tradition could be the "black necromancy" that conjures up spirits to punish him because he does not conform. Jimmy is clearly different, but his conflicted relationship to Horace, which is influenced by the religious tradition, makes him complicit. Ezekiel Cross's grounding in tradition alienates him even further from his grandson Horace, and makes him complicit also, if ignorance is complicity. He believes that his extramarital sexual acts that produced children are sinful (60), but he can say "I know heaven is my home, praise God" (57) with genuine conviction because he believes that God has forgiven him. Although he does not specifically describe it, the image of God that Ezekiel has in his mind is the same one that Horace has in his: "The image of God [Horace] carried in his head was a bleak one—the Old Testament God of Abraham and Isaac and David, who took no foolishness and punished true to his word. A vengeful, dusky-skinned Arab with electric eyes and white hair" (101). The difference in Horace and Ezekiel's interpretation of God's willingness to forgive is more than generational; it is based on God's forgiveness of heterosexual transgression in the Bible and biblical intolerance of homosexuality. Because he is steeped in the tradition, the communal and family story of the past, and the consequent present that it engenders, Ezekiel cannot fathom that his own grandson is homosexual and has no clue that Horace's sexuality led to his suicide. However, from hearing sermons in church at age five (72), Horace is acutely aware of the prohibition on homosexuality, as his vivid memory of the preacher's text from Romans 1:28 shows (77), and he never escapes the power of this condemnation.

In part at least, "Holy Science" is the oxymoronic term for Jimmy's and the text's critique and examination of the African American religious tradition from a nontraditional perspective; it is critical of the narrow inhumanity of the tradition and ambivalent about a more "scientific" approach that would replace or improve it. In the scenes that follow, some of the ambiguity is a representation of Jimmy's weak, indecisive character, but part of it is inherent in the text's viewpoint and the complexity of African American reality and Horace's place in it. Talking to people in the community accustomed to harsh, unforgiving judgments, Jimmy thinks "I want to introduce a new way of approaching Christian faith, a way of caring for people. I don't want to be a watchdog for sin, an inquisitor who binds his people with rules and regulations and thou shalts and thou shalt nots. But looking at those eyes so full of past hurt and past rejection and past accusation, I could only smile and let be what was" (110). In another dramatic form of "confession," when Horace presses Jimmy about the possibility that he really is not "normal," Jimmy vaguely alludes to what the Bible says and concedes that he believes homosexuality is wrong (113). He finally tells Horace to pray to God for strength, to search his heart, and to take it to the Lord (113–14). Jimmy's hypothetical religion cannot replace the negatively judgmental practices and beliefs that cause pain but define a place in the community for everyone except Horace. Even the criticized, like those to whom he is talking, accept judgment and find their place as "sinners" whose lives are instructive to "decent folk." Nor can Jimmy reject the prohibition on homosexuality forged from the text of the Bible and cultural belief. The problem with the harsh intolerance of the prohibition is clear, but buttressed by traditional beliefs, the words and text are still powerful. Jimmy, and seemingly the novel too, cannot reject them or offer alternatives, particularly in the unsettling sweep of history and tradition that is both so real and abstract in the present.

Perhaps the most vivid example of criticism of religion and tradition, and of ambivalence, is Jimmy's refusal to forgive and accept his own mother Rose, who has defied and rejected the religious mores of family and community, totally placing herself on the outside. While Jimmy "confesses" and describes the family reaction to his prodigal mother at his grandmother's funeral, the text in parentheses quotes the words of the preacher reading from 1 Corinthians 13:1–4, 9–10, and 12 defining charity (120–21). Jimmy also describes the gesture of his Uncle Lester, the only one to reach out to his mother, as "full of grace." Jimmy seems repelled by the harsh moral law of the Bible (110) and attracted by its Christian grace and charity, and he also seems drawn to the life totally outside community and tradition—including that of the Bible—as represented by his mother. He wonders what she must have learned from her defiance of family, God, and everything else that was important to their community. Like Pharaoh in Exodus, however, he knows his "sin, but was unrepentant"; he hardens his heart and will not go to her (121–22). In spite of feeling negatively about parts of the Bible, he never seems able to deny its possible "truth." He certainly cannot move outside the tradition to follow his attraction or even embrace his mother.

There is a point that Jimmy senses but does not consciously understand and that the novel implies in the structure of its parenthetical quotation from 1 Corinthians. The power of charity is experienced best from within the context of the rituals of the community that is most uncharitable in its attitudes and actions toward those, such as Rose, who are defiant. Jimmy's adherence to the form demanded by the tradition of his community and family is again not just a result of his weakness of character. The force of the tradition itself is too powerful for him to break free. Looking at Rose and thinking about Pharaoh's attitudes and actions, Jimmy "could hear [his] heart ossifying within [his] living breast. It would break before it would soften" (122). Having the sense of observing but not controlling his own heart and body, Jimmy compares himself to the well-known and intricately conflicted character of the king who—under the power of God and facing sure vengeance, the potential of which he can see and which is vividly described to him—still defies God. The family and community ritual centered on the biblical words is what controls Jimmy unconsciously: "Charity suffereth long, and is kind; charity envieth not, charity vaunteth not itself, is not puffed up . . . For we know in part, and we prophesy in part. But when that which is perfect is come, then that which is part shall be done away . . . For now we see through a glass, darkly; but then face to face: now I know in part; but then shall I know even as also I am known" (121). The ritualized words experienced from within the community more than compensate for Jimmy's association of himself with the bewildering, perplexing Pharaoh, a nonbeliever whose story is appropriated and used instructively in African American tradition for the results of his defiance. Jimmy does not go any further in trying to understand his confused rejection of his own mother in the context of this comparison.

The community powerfully projects its love to many and its contradictory scorn to Rose; it does not critique its own Christian failure to extend charity to the defiant outsider. Jimmy's theoretical "holy science," which would lead to a more ideal Christian practice, could analyze the complex implications behind Pharaoh's portrayal, the implications about New and Old Testament contradictions in depicting retribution and tolerance, and the African American appropriation of biblical stories and concepts of defiance, vengeance, and charity. What matters, however, is that the community's traditional interpretations and practices prevail. The promise to those on the inside is the potential that the community will internalize the Bible's words and extend its deepest charity and protection, and the expectation is also Christian salvation in the end. The poetic depth and beauty of the language as spoken by the preacher in this scene is part of the promise and reassurance.

Rose's story and that of Gideon, another young homosexual, also raise questions about whether Horace's plight is the responsibility of the community and its tradition or the tragedy of an individual with great sensitivities. The strength of the tradition can save and protect those on the inside who conform or those on the inside connected by opposition, like the "sinners" whose instructive lives Jimmy describes. The tradition can also condemn and destroy, but women like Rose, who apparently is not overly sensitive about what anyone thinks, can live her life as she wants, although the rejection and ostracism take a great toll. Gideon comes from the family of community "sinners" whose place in Tims Creek is defined by opposition to decency, and not having the concerns of "decent folk" makes it easier for Gideon to be defiant. Like Rose, he also has the tough, insensitive makeup to withstand disapproval: "Gideon Stone was without a doubt the prettiest boy in Horace's class. And everyone used that term for him. Pretty. Gideon had, as the old men say, sugar in his blood. But unlike decent folk, he was not reticent about it; in fact he paraded it about. He cultivated a dainty, feminine air, delicate and girllike. His hands formed flowery gestures in midair, and he had something of a mincing walk. People snickered" (98–99). Being a member of the upstanding Cross family makes it harder for Horace to take Gideon's approach, but compared to Gideon, Horace is a sensitive individual doomed because he cannot withstand the social ostracism resulting from his difference.

The text further implies a connection between Horace's individual sensitivity and his tragedy in its depiction of Jimmy's weakness. Jimmy conforms and finds his place because he is weak and the tradition is strong and persuasive to him in many ways. Perhaps he shares Horace's consciousness in some parts of his "confessions" because he feels similarly vulnerable, and his sympathy could indicate his unconscious feeling that his fate could be Horace's. One has to wonder how he would respond if he were undeniably homosexual like Horace. In all of this, it is impossible to sort out the happenstance of Horace's tragedy from the responsibility of the community and its tradition. There could be innumerable variations of the characters of weak and/or sensitive homosexual men who would not suffer Horace's fate. The communal tradition accepts or includes through opposition many who are both weak and strong, and those who are strong or indifferent and, perhaps, some who are weak or sensitive live on the outside. Jimmy vaguely senses much of this, but does not understand what is true about himself, Horace, or African American history and tradition.

In the last part of "Holy Science," "April 30, 1984, 2:40 AM," Horace wonders if the scenes in his mind and the demon's voice in his ear are real, and the text itself contests its own representation by conflating the concrete world outside him with the uncertainty of Horace's psychic reality. The textual perspective is broader than Horace's or Jimmy's; however, it neither provides answers to the multitude of its implied questions nor shows how one can be sure that its own portrayals are any more substantive than Horace's fantasies. Still, the novel focuses on the suffering of Horace through the factualness of the moment, "April 30, 1984, 2:40 AM." The fact does not reveal the unknowable truth, but at this time Horace was getting ready to kill himself because he felt condemned by his weakness and sin as defined by the tradition. Nothing changes his death or makes it any better from the text's standpoint.

A Visitation of Spirits goes deeper into the implications of narrative interpretations and the incomprehensibility of the novel's story in "Old Demonology"; it shows both the negative and positive power and potential of narratives. The Bible is the African American community's central narrative that has a primary role in Horace's death, but for the theologically educated Jimmy, its relevance is much more complicated. It seems that Jimmy might be utterly lost without the biblically related faith that is part of the religious practice and traditional belief that he perceives so ambivalently. In his "confessions" in "Old Demonology," Jimmy moves from the objectification of faith in his adulterous, now deceased wife Anne, and his consequent despair about Anne's actions and death, to citing Jonah. Jimmy uses Jonah's example of faith in uncertainly asking God for help for him and Horace. He finally incorporates the details of Anne's death into his story after invoking Jonah. Catching Anne having sex with another man makes Jimmy realize that she is the "very personification of my faith" and that he is totally vulnerable: "I was alone and unknown and unknowable, just as she was unknowable, alone" (180–81). Faith in the haughty, light-skinned, upper-class Anne, who betrayed him for reasons that she could or would not explain, is now perhaps, for Jimmy at least, the "old demonology" that haunts him instead of a legitimate faith, which he still needs. Jimmy juxtaposes the scene in which he discovers Anne's infidelity with a dramatic scene in which the Cross family

criticized and chastised Horace for his faith in white people who have oppressed black people historically (181–88). He laments that Horace's world
does not understand him and seemingly does not understand Jimmy, either:
"He, just like me, had been created by this society." "What has happened to
us? Can I cry out like the prophet Jonah and ask God to guide my hand and
direct me toward the proper remedy?" (188). Jimmy defines the faithful example of Jonah as accepting the impossibility of hiding from reality and
"fight[ing] the good fight" in a hard war of life (189). Implicitly, Jonah's imperfect but ultimately faithful example is the model for him and Horace in
the present society.

This is the last of Jimmy's first-person confessions, and he is uncertain
just as the novel is uncertain about how to tell its story. The quest for faith
and the probable need for faith in something beyond Anne are apparent, but
it is not clear how faith affects his life with Anne or how faith in God instead
of white people would change the tragedy of Horace. He cannot answer the
questions he raises, and he does not know what to say about the meaning of
Anne's story. He talks about her death from cancer at thirty-seven and speculates that his grandmother mourned hardest because Anne seemed "so
good, and so young." He accepts Anne and her life by the same faith that he
accepts the death of Horace, which he cannot understand, and he continues
his own life through this uncertain faith.

The main result of these "confessions" is a story in which Jimmy tries to
assert his faith in a mythologized war against an enemy characterized in Old
Testament language; the story is a spontaneous fabrication that encompasses
Horace's tragedy and, most importantly, makes sense of it in terms of faithful prayer to God instead of perception and logic.

> I guess [the black community] didn't reckon the world they were
> sending [Horace] into was different from the world they had con-
> quered, a world peopled with new and hateful monsters that exacted
> a different price.
> . . . Once, oh once, this beautiful, strong, defiant, glorious group
> could wrestle the world down, unshackle themselves, part seas, walk
> on water, rise on the winds. What happened? Why are we now sick and
> dying? All the sons and daughters groomed to lead seem to have
> fled . . . How, Lord? How? The war is not over. The enemy is encamped
> over the hill. With the morning they will come storming over the

wall. They will pillage and plunder, rape our wives and children, destroy our crops, empty our storehouses deface our holy temple. How, Lord? How? How can we defend ourselves and grow strong again? How can we regain the power to lift up our heads and sing? When will the Host of Hosts visit us with favor and strength? (188–89)

The "beautiful, strong, defiant glorious group" is a myth that Jimmy invents, but the invocation of the Lord and Host of Hosts suggests a biblical faith that has greater power to support and affirm than a glorious myth of the past would have by itself. He seems to say that the war of black people is not over, but the world and the battle have changed, and those now waging it, like him and Horace, are no longer equipped to fight it. He fears the dead like Anne and Horace, no matter how many funerals and eulogies he preaches, but he still has faith. In his dreams, "the dead rise, and they wear armor and are armed with bows and arrows and swords and guns and knives. Perhaps the fight goes on. Perhaps the war will be won" (188–89). Still however, Jimmy's sudden invention of a story in which black people fight a great war and the dead rise in his dreams at the end at the very least contests the seemingly greater power of faith generated from the Bible even as he applies it to his fabricated reality.

In "December 8, 1985, 3:00 PM," the text again takes over Jimmy's story and that of his family in the third person and follows in the direction of his last confession's construction of a positively concluded narrative based in romanticism. In the third-person narrative, it is hard to separate the substance of a positive conclusion grounded in the deeply human responses of the Cross family from melodramatic romantic excess of emotion. The text inexplicably resolves a life-long, bitter Cross family feud between Jimmy's uncle Ezekiel and aunt Ruth abruptly, wistfully, and almost magically when Jimmy hears between them indirectly expressed words of reconciliation that are "as pure and as honest as the rain" (207). If the figurative language that describes the reconciliation is not a sign of the text's ironic stance, then the following description of Jimmy is: "On the way to the car a *fat* snowflake pelted him on his face and mingled there with a *fresh and hot* tear" (208, italics mine). The description of the interaction of Cross family members and much of Ezekiel's and Ruth's remembrance of the past contradicts Jimmy's romanticized story in "Old Demonology," and the ending of "December 8, 1985, 3 PM" contradicts its own romanticized conclusion and Jimmy's earlier story.

The last part of "Old Demonology," "April 30, 1984, 4:45 AM," portrays Horace in the hours immediately before his death and makes his whole life an unbelievable phantasm of history and memory/fantasy of his own homosexuality. From this description, Horace cannot be sure of the world around him or even about himself and the rationale of his homosexual being. One of the fantastic aspects of this part of the novel is the account of the Crosstown theater where Horace worked for a summer. The theater is the property of a member of the white Cross family to whom the black Crosses are connected, and the play that is put on, *Ride the Freedom Star,* is a "mishmash of ill-conceived, ill wrought, cliché-ridden drivel . . . doggerel verse and . . . melodramatic romanticizing of Southern American history" (213). The play's construction of white history is like Jimmy's story of black history in its melodrama and romanticism, and its portrayal of slaves in the past, reducing black people to buffoons and caricatures, balances the glorious portrayal of the black past in Jimmy's story. Further, the bad dramatization of white Southern history is similar to the superficial objective "truth" of the drama of Jimmy's "confessions." Ironically, the portrayal of the Crosstown theater relates to the novel's own dilemma, not because the novel does not take black people and history seriously and not because it lacks creative and aesthetic power, but because none of the history relating to the central tragedy of Horace can really be written by any text or captured by any narrative.

The bizarre memory of Horace's summer at the theater calls into question its own reality and the sensual experience of homosexuality. Horace's memory of the Crosstown theater is too strange for the reader to trust as real in the context of the novel's critique of the creation of a substantive narrative, but one particular description of a party is noteworthy in its extremes of "ranting and raving and running up and down the stairs, hanging out windows, throwing water, throwing up" (230). Not knowing if what he sees and feels is real or not, Horace stands in the same cemetery where he went that night after the party, remembering the emptiness of homosexual abandonment.

> Standing here, now, far into the cemetery, over the very spot he had
> originally been with the seven actors, men and women, he was both
> disquieted and fascinated with that night, and dissected it in his mind
> as a true scientist—clinical, clean, objective. The pot. The pills. The
> literal orgy. The strange inevitability of it, for, in a way—like witches

in a coven under a full moon, like wild wolves tearing hungrily at one another's flesh, like hogs wallowing in their own excrement and sin and lonely inarticulateness—they were left to this for expression, this for comfort, this for attention, this for love. But as he did what he did, he did not feel the thrill he expected would accompany such things. It was not the otherworldly event he knew it should be, nor was it satisfying. The moon did not change color or phase, lightning did not flash, the earth did not quake, the sun did not rise. They were left only tired and stoned and dirty and smelly and empty. (230–31)

It is not clear what Horace should or wants to feel sensually, but the physical experience of homosexual sex, in this instance at least, is unfulfilling and tainted with evil and bestiality. Given its description here, the experience perhaps lacks a deeper spirituality that goes beyond the physical, which relates back to the novel's ambivalent treatment of traditional biblical faith and spirituality that Horace believes he does not have.

The novel leaves open the possibility of Horace's need for a biblically related spirituality and faith (although it is important to say that it is only an open-ended possibility) in his graveyard vision of words from the Bible and religious song lyrics structured to evoke nuances of African American ritual; the words represent his calling to serve black people in the context of their history and cultural tradition. The primary words—"Your sons and your daughters shall prophesy, your old men shall dream dreams, your young men shall see visions" (232)—are from Joel 2:28, but Horace cannot answer the call to be a savior in his generation, a call manifested by the horrific vision of black history from African capture to enslavement to oppressive freedom (234). The text echoes 1 Corinthians 13:12: "Horace saw clearly through a glass darkly and understood where he fit. Understood what was asked of him" (234). Apparently he lacks the strength of faith and spirit to answer: "This had been Horace's redemption, and Horace said no."

In his unbelievable world of fiends and demons, Horace maintains, until his suicide, the idea that he must achieve salvation and peace according to biblical and religious standards, but paradoxically by the terms of these standards, he cannot be saved because he is sinful and evil. A belief in words propels him to write his autobiography "to exorcise his confusion" (239), but he burns it. He contradictorily and confusedly grasps for the biblical descriptions of sinful practices of sorcery to avoid sinning (240), which leads him even more fantastically to seek salvation among the demons in his mind and his consequent suicide. Horace cannot escape the tragic situation of growing up in a community with a historically sustaining tradition that alienates and condemns him.

The novel, as it must, finds a way to conclude in "Old Gods, New Demons," but it does not resolve the conflict of tradition and Horace's homosexuality or find a way to portray the truth and substance of this historical and cultural narrative of African Americans that includes Horace's tragedy in the present. In Horace's only "confessions," a self-memoriam that minimizes the social and privileges his humanity as a sentient being ("I remember me" [250]), Horace still "remembers" the threatening mystery of God, "that [God] did not like some people so much," and that he would probably not go to heaven because he lacked the strength to follow the rules (250–51). "April 30, 1984, 7:05 AM" is the specific time that Horace killed himself, but it and other specific times do not make anything clear: "Someone once said that if man is but a figment in God's mind then *the characters in men's imaginations* are no less real than we are. Perhaps. No one can say for certain. But we cannot deny the possibility" (252, italics mine). This conception of God and God's creative role is philosophical instead of traditionally religious; God's creation is like the creations of human imagination, such as the characters in this novel. The chain of creation always produces characters that are real yet uncertain. The last sentences of "April 30, 1984, 7:05 AM" emphasize the uselessness of speculation and even the uncertainty of facts about Horace's tragically real death: "Ifs and maybes and weres and perhapses are of no use in this case. The facts are enough, unless they too are subject to doubt" (254). Then the concluding "REQUIEM FOR TOBACCO" begins, "You remember, though perhaps you don't, that once upon a time men harvested tobacco by hand" (254). And later, "You've heard of these things, I'm sure? Didn't you see it in a play, or read it in a book or . . . " (256). This is a superficial romantic ending honoring the past which foregrounds the self-consciousness of the limitation of its own textuality.

Everything considered, the influence of biblical narrative is central to the theme of this novel, which contests the truth of its own story and narratives generally. From one possible perspective, the Bible's story and consequent African American faith as symbolized in the second dedication and the epigraphs to the first section ("White Sorcery") and the second section ("Black Necromancy") are essential to the ethos of African Americans collectively and individually. This is the case even for Horace in a tragically ironic way. But the titles of all the sections and the section epigraphs after "Black Necromancy" seem symbolically to evolve toward opposing the biblical narrative and religious belief, indicating that in its overall thematic development the novel indicts the biblical and religious tradition. The text cannot adequately tell the historical story, but the community's proscription of homosexuality grounded in biblical doctrine is nevertheless a very important factor in Horace's suicide.

However, no other narrative or literary reality referenced in the main epigraph, a section epigraph, or the text may have the overall power of the Bible, not only for black people but also from the novel's own thematic perspective. The title *A Visitation of Spirits* has strong biblical connotations, but the specific meaning of the words in the title is unclear. The words resonate with the language in biblical stories of salvation as well as of threat and vengeance. For example, in Job 10:12, Job says that the "visitation [of the spirit of the Lord] hath preserved my spirit." But the majority of visitations in the Bible are vengeful and threatening: Jeremiah 11:23 and 23:12, for instance, talk about the Lord bringing evil because of sin in "the year of . . . visitation."

In terms of this approach, *A Visitation of Spirits* does not criticize the Bible; its irresolution attests to the potential negative and positive power of what is *written* in the Bible. On one hand, the title of the last section, "Old Gods, New Demons," can imply an opposition to the biblical doctrine that individuals and nations must serve and follow the rules of one God or suffer an evil onset of demons or "visitation of spirits," which is the story of much of the Old Testament. This may only be "true" in biblical terms, but the Bible's psychological power over the black community and influence on the overall theme and structure of *A Visitation of Spirits* is the point. The bad "visitation" may manifest itself in the communal tragedy that is the underlying reality of Horace's suicide in the present and that jeopardizes the continuation of black leadership in a long historical tradition, but the evil "visitation" most clearly relates to Horace and his thoughts about punishment for sin. The well-intentioned Jimmy can never move beyond his adherence to the biblical proscription of homosexuality, and it is not certain that the text thematically resolves this proscription either, particularly given all of its structural and thematic uses of the Bible. From the viewpoint of Job's story though, the words of the title mean promise and hope, for black people generally, for the spirit of Horace, and even for the text's narrative it-self, which is in part dedicated to the "inscrutable grace of the Host of Hosts." The novel sympathetically portrays Horace's and Jimmy's struggles. Their respective self-indictment and failure to respond adequately to human crisis are destructive but through faith are perceived as part of a gracious di-vine plan. Grace surmounts all evil and potential human shortcomings in light of the inscrutable benevolence.

In spite of the horrible, painful, and tragic fact that Horace killed himself because he was a homosexual whose religious tradition dictated that homo-sexuality was wrong, the reality of what happened is uncertain; no narrative representation of Horace's story and the black tradition connected to it is true and trustworthy. There is a serious, important African American history to record, but it is so very difficult to do, especially with relationship to Hor-ace's tragedy, given the context of the culture's religious tradition.[20] The novel contests the substance and adequacy of its own narrative while at the same time presenting it as a memorial to Horace. There can be no definitive judgments or even clear portrayals of the historical past built primarily on religious tradition and the Bible, but somehow the tradition did bring black people to the present time, although Horace died along the way.

CHAPTER 3

Critiquing Christian Belief

The Text as Prophecy of Different Ways of Seeing Salvation

THE MAIN DIFFERENCE BETWEEN the works analyzed in the last chapter, *Go Tell It on the Mountain* (1953) and *A Visitation of Spirits* (1989), and Toni Morrison's *Beloved* (1987) and John Edgar Wideman's *The Cattle Killing* (1996) is that postmodern approaches subvert the Bible in Morrison's text, and in Wideman's (re)write the Bible's oppression in the attempt to revise the larger oppressive Western narrative tradition. *Beloved* is a boldly different novel that uniquely challenges the biblical and the traditionally sacred at the level of patriarchal privilege and power. It suggests that a different black text can be written that repositions Christian values centrally in the experience of black women, as well as in a cognizance of a wider African and African American folk tradition. *Beloved* does not ignore or trivialize the importance of Christianity for African Americans, but using a subtle, oblique approach, it succeeds in thoroughly challenging and critiquing the *text* of the Bible and the traditionally Christian. *The Cattle Killing* is a great novel for many reasons. It takes a postmodern approach that also challenges the Bible and the tradition of an African American belief in God that is seemingly inseparable from what is written in a pervasive oppressive Western intertext. Unlike *Beloved*, *The Cattle Killing* becomes more immersed in the Western narrative tradition that it opposes and thus is a problematized rewriting of the tradition. Its own narrative opposition to itself is intentionally an important part of the novel's overall impressive critique.

In its own way, each novel reflects African American faithful vision in a postmodern form. Generally speaking, the postmodern mode can be one that restricts the writer to the self-conscious concerns of textuality. But as African American writers, Morrison and Wideman use the flexibility of the postmodern much more creatively to explore the possible impact of received written and oral tradition on black culture and life. Wideman thematizes the pressures and limitations of narrative for the black writer, but even in doing so he manages to demonstrate the power of his writing to interrogate oppression and thus in a sense to challenge it, if not to get beyond it. The postmodern turns out to be a more useful mode for black writers to explore African American history and culture than the modernist was. It is a vehicle of exploration that always challenges faithful vision grounded in the biblical and the religious, but it also shows that vision's central importance in the culture.

As must have been true for millions of black people, the rememories of characters such as Sethe in Morrison's *Beloved* traumatized them to the point of distorting their concept of love and the relationships that define the positive aspects of humanity. Figuratively, the text speaks the "unspeakable thoughts, unspoken" of "the black and angry dead" (198–99), which are also the thoughts of Sethe, Denver, and Beloved inside their house, 124 Bluestone Road, and of all the other living black people who suffered the same kinds of abuses. White hatred has deprived black people of any truly "livable life" (198) and created a rememory of suffering, pain, and consequent anger that can create the need for love that is possessive, greedy, and, in essence, evil. Beloved represents the aggregate black self whose need to be loved is so strong that it pervades everything as a supernatural and possessively evil consciousness. The white oppressors' live their variation of rememory through their internalized "jungle" of black bestiality that they have imagined and imposed on black people out of their need to justify oppression; ironically, what white people have created and carry within themselves is the source of their own fear and hatred of black people (198–99). Implicitly, "whitepeople" need to address their form of rememory that causes black oppression but dominates the oppressor as well; the novel, however, deals much more with the potential of "blackpeople" to change oppressive black consciousness through spiritual and sacred rituals.

The epigraph from Romans 9:25—"I will call them my people, which were not my people; and her beloved, which was not beloved"—calls attention to God and the influence of the Bible at the very beginning. However, although the biblical God as implied by the text is truly inscrutable and may have a benevolent plan, God is an ambivalently conceived agent. The novel has a decidedly political focus on the historical acts of men that produced the deaths and suffering of countless millions of Africans and African Americans. The dedication to the "sixty million and more"—Morrison's estimation of "those who died either as captives in Africa or on slave ships" (Clemons 75)—indicates this. But as the epigraph reveals, the text is also more philosophical in its grand teleological scheme that speculates about divine agency. Romans 9:24 announces the calling and acceptance of the Gentiles and Jews. In this context, the epigraph could affirm a biblical faithful vision of God's salvation and restoration of the lost Africans, the abused and brutalized slaves who suffered the attempt to destroy their human being, and white American humanity corrupted in the process of oppressing black people. Robert L. Broad says that on first sight, the words of Paul from Romans "may suggest hope and comfort. But what happens when we *re*-read that epigraph in the context of, say, the catalog of atrocities spilling from Paul D.'s rusted tin can of memories?" (195). The answer is obviously that the hope initially suggested by the epigraph is no longer there in light of the rereading.[1]

Engaging the centuries-long panorama of horrors inflicted on Africans and African Americans in *Beloved*, one could ask the question that Amy Denver asks when looking at Sethe's mutilated back: "What God have in mind, I wonder" (79). There is no explicit answer to this question, which also challenges faith in God in terms of the epigraph from Romans, but the text focuses on seeking the spiritual and sacred that it reveals in the self and the community more than on the salvation of God as revealed in the Judeo-Christian Bible. The conventional African American church denominations exist in the text's nominally free black community (87), but it is the "unchurched" preacher Baby Suggs who has the right idea as far as finding spiritual resources is concerned: "She told them that the only grace they could have was the grace they could imagine. That if they could not see it, they would not have it" (88). Part of the solution for the characters is to actualize and renew the sacred grace inherent in the self, and thus in the collective community, through community spiritual rituals. In spite of the internalized oppressive legacies that work against the people being the source of their own saving grace, the philosophy of finding wholeness in the self and the community still has greater possibility than conventional religion and traditional concepts of God.

The novel often redefines what is Christlike in the Bible in the characterizations of black women. Generally, it portrays a heterodox cosmology of African and African American folk belief and Judeo-Christian perspective that encompasses multiple possibilities of sacred, spiritual, and supernatural agency. *Beloved* is a secularized prophecy of horrific American history and life that contests received Judeo-Christian biblical traditions of the spiritual and sacred with its own radical vision. Appearing as oblique references and creatively discordant thematic echoes and undertones in the novel, parts of the biblical story are a sporadic but distinct dissonance that clashes with African American life and fails to address it in the way that folk rituals grounded in black historical reality potentially can.

Criticism of the received religious tradition comes from the overall perspective of the novel and not the community, but it is difficult to distinguish the complicated textual voice from the belief system of individuals and the African American community that still adheres to tradition by centering Christianity as the dominant part of a larger system of folk belief. In portraying the black women's preparations for Beloved's exorcism, the text describes their approach, which is a combination of the Christian and the folk. "Some brought what they could and what they believed would work. Stuffed in apron pockets, strung around their necks, lying in the space between their breasts. Others brought Christian faith—as shield and sword. Most brought a little of both" (257). A close look at the text reveals that the community is in fact highly Christian. Baby Suggs, for example, is the advocate for the novel's alternative spirituality; however, she is still a Christian who devises nontraditional practices to deal with black reality. In fact, it must have been at least partly her belief in God throughout her life that allowed her to withstand losing children, including the last child, who bought her freedom, and to survive all the horror of slavery before she finally gave up following the catastrophe in her yard. At the end of her life, it is not so much that she does not believe in God as that she does not understand God's ways and is vexed with him: "God puzzled her and she was too ashamed of Him to say so" (177). Stamp Paid is a Christian, too. Trying to reconcile with Baby Suggs through her kinfolk in 124, he opposes the power of the house's "stepped-up haunting" with that of Jesus Christ: "he would rely on the power of Jesus Christ to deal with things older, but not stronger, than He Himself was" (172). Earlier, he urges Baby Suggs not to give up preaching the Word and not to blame God for what happened (177–79). He affirms his faith: "We have to be steady. 'These things too will pass.' What you looking for? A miracle?" (179). His words sound like a paraphrase of at least two passages: 1 Corinthians 15:58, "be ye steadfast, unmoveable, always abounding in the work of the Lord, forasmuch as ye know that your labor is not in vain in the Lord"; and Matthew 24:34–35, "This generation shall not pass, till all these things be fulfilled. Heaven and earth shall pass away, but my words shall not pass away."

African American Christian belief is ambiguous because the textual voice raises the consciousness of characters and the community to its level while simultaneously and almost imperceptibly portraying African American life realistically in terms of the historical influence of the Bible and Christianity; the significance of the approach is that it allows characters and community to participate in the text's critique. This is entirely appropriate when one realizes that African Americans—who retain racial memory of oppression by whites before coming to America, as well as strands of African ethos— would certainly be capable of critiquing the received tradition of a Western text, predominantly the King James Bible, on this level of collective consciousness at the same time that they privilege it. Collective consciousness is similar to but not the same as rememory; however, I can use Sethe's definition of the latter to define the former. It is shared: "Someday you be walking down the road and you hear something or see something going on. So clear. And you think it's you thinking it up. A thought picture. But no. It's when you bump into a rememory that belongs to somebody else" (36). And it is individual: "You know. Some things you forget. Other things you never do . . . Places, places are still there. If a house burns down, it's gone, but the place—the picture of it—stays, and not just in my rememory, but out there, in the world. What I remember is a picture floating around out there outside my head. I mean, even if I don't think it, even if I die, the picture of what I did, or knew, or saw is still out there. Right in the place where it happened" (36). Collective consciousness is a less violently intrusive, and historically and experientially more encompassing racial memory of the oppressive historical experience with white Westerners than what Sethe defines as rememory of slavery. Collective consciousness is always there even when individuals are unconscious of it or when they die, and its accretion of events exists synchronously in time for the access of different communities. The text often shares with the African American folk community a point of reference, knowledge, and acute intelligence that is collective consciousness, and this equality of viewpoint is its most distinguishing feature. Given collective consciousness, the characters live in, and sometimes speak from the collective knowledge of, the past and present simultaneously.

So the difference between the text and Stamp Paid's and Baby Suggs's vision for much of her life is their belief and the text's contrasting critical approach to the tradition of African American religion and the Bible that largely produced it. Yet at the same time there is often no obvious separation between the text and characters as *Beloved* interrogates the biblical and religious tradition in its own unique and complex way. We forget who could know and who could be speaking to tell us parts of the story. The characters are not set apart from some of the text's most complex structural figurations and thematic ruminations on biblical Christianity and its relationship to African American life. The text's perspective encompasses everything, including the historical perspective of the Middle Passage, spiritual and supernatural consciousness engendered by centuries of oppressive African American experience, and folk retentions of the African past. It is a testimony to the novel's greatness that it seamlessly weaves in individual and community knowledge and awareness without an apparent distinction between them and the text's voice. This is true as *Beloved* develops its main focus on the love between Sethe and her daughter(s).

In its portrayal of this bond between mother and daughter(s), the novel characteristically juxtaposes the Bible to the powerful psychic and spiritual demands of slavery. The novel's most distinct section, structurally and figuratively, depicts the mother/daughter relationship as a supernatural consciousness generated by the exigencies of love (200–217). Song of Solomon may be the most unique book in the Bible because of its amorous language and description of mutual desire between a lover and her "beloved," identified as Jesus Christ through images associated with Christ's birth, life, and crucifixion.[2] There is a broad similarity between the roles of the biblical book and the section in the novel. Each is a radically different portrayal of spiritual and supernatural love that makes it the most atypical part of its respective text. Further, *Beloved* is mainly concerned with Christianity as developed in the New Testament, but the Old Testament book Song of Solomon probably allegorizes the spiritual love of Christ in the most passionate human terms that the Bible provides. It places biblical spiritual love on a level potentially comparable to the deep human commitment in the novel. As is true throughout the text of *Beloved*, however, it relates most strongly in terms of indirect comparison and critique of the Bible instead of general similarity; in its depiction of love between Sethe and her daughter(s), *Beloved* highlights the radical difference between its portrayal of faithful love and the spiritual love in the Bible.

The novel's tense, life-and-death language recalls the language of Song of Solomon and its theme of love: "My beloved is mine, and I am his: he feedeth among the lilies" (Song 2:16); "I am my beloved's, and my beloved is mine: he feedeth among the lilies" (Song 6:3).

> Beloved, she my daughter. She mine. See. She come back to me of her own free will and I don't have to explain a thing. I didn't have time to explain before because [I had to kill her] quick. Quick. She had to be safe and I put her where she would be. But my love was tough and she back now . . . Paul D ran her off so she had no choice but to come back to me in the flesh . . . I won't never let her go. I'll explain to her, even though I don't have to. Why I did it. How if I hadn't killed her she would have died and that is something I could not bear to happen to her. When I explain it she'll understand, because she understands everything already. I'll tend to her as no mother ever tended a child, a daughter. Nobody will ever get my milk no more except my own children . . . I know what it is to be without the milk that belongs to you; to have to fight and holler for it, and to have so little left. I'll tell Beloved about that; she'll understand. She my daughter. (200)

Language and image pull the texts of Song of Solomon and the novel together, refract the biblical, and set the biblical tradition against the incongruous world of slavery. The essence of Sethe's love is spiritual and supernatural because it crosses life's physical boundaries, but it is based in and relates to her oppressive reality. Sethe's intense emotional attachment constitutes the power of love necessary for a black woman to protect her children in the historical setting of slavery. In the language from Song of Solomon implied but not stated in *Beloved,* Jesus is the shepherd who protects his flock and his loved one, and in the more explicit language shared by the texts, he has a complete dedication to his loved one. The biblical language captures the basic theme and is a model for the repeated love motif that defines Sethe's and Beloved's connection. However, Christian love in the Bible symbolized as Jesus Christ's and a female lover's soul-deep love (Song 3:1–4) is still only an idealization that is inadequate and superficial when compared to the emotional and spiritual requirements of Sethe in slavery. In a strong inversion of tradition, Sethe and Beloved become Christ figures because of their suffering, sacrifice, and faithful commitment, thus also making the black female the center of true love, which, by necessity, is very much unlike the biblical ideal.[3] The novel's voice becomes one with Sethe's to create a fascinating angle of vision on the reality of African American mother/daughter love that juxtaposes it to an abstruse book in the Bible and to the patriarchal ideal of Christian love.

There are other disparate, fragmented references that resonate with Song of Solomon but reveal biblical discordance and detachment; the seemingly coincidental is part of a pattern that consists of the common theme of spiritual and supernatural love, and similar words and images provide a basis for comparison that makes contrast clear. Some aspects of the pattern of words and images are more specific and others are general. The section portraying Denver's consciousness begins, "Beloved is my sister. I swallowed her blood right along with my mother's milk" (205). A portion of Song of Solomon 5:1 is, "I am come into my garden, my sister . . . I have drunk my wine with my milk: eat, O friends; drink, yea, drink abundantly, O beloved." The key words are *sister, milk,* and *beloved.* The image of Denver swallowing her *sister* Beloved's *blood* along with Sethe's *milk* contrasts the idealized image of the lover drinking *wine* and *milk* festively and exhorting the *beloved sister* to drink "abundantly." In terms of the more general comparison of Song of Solomon and the three sections projecting the consciousness of mother and daughter(s) (200–17), the novel echoes the biblical passage's description of the chosen beloved daughter through its account of Sethe protecting the sanctity of the daughter(s) and of Beloved being the privileged daughter because Sethe had to kill her. Song of Solomon 6:9 reads: "My dove, my undefiled is but one; she is the only one of her mother, she is the choice one of her that bare her. The daughters saw her, and blessed her." The verse from Song of Solomon obviously does not have the depth of Sethe's love or the intensity of feeling expressed through Denver's consciousness (205–9) or Beloved's (210–13). There are other general comparisons. A good example is a quotation from Song of Solomon 8:6: "for love is strong as death; jealousy is cruel as the grave." Sethe says, "When I put that headstone up I wanted to lay in [the grave] with you, put your head on my shoulder and keep you warm" (204). At this place in the novel, Sethe's words have substance that is incontrovertible. The reality of her fervent love that would make her give up her life and lie in the grave with her child makes the biblical words superficial and inadequate for her. (There are other common references in the two texts that are apparent, given the pattern. For instance, Sethe remembers the "grape arbor" from Sweet Home as she shares the account of the escape with Beloved [202], and the lover in Song of Solomon associates the beloved with "tender grapes" of spring [2:13, 15]. Further, Sethe says she should have recognized Beloved because she asked about the "earrings I used to dangle for you to play with" [203], and Song of Solomon's lover says, "Thy cheeks are comely with rows of jewels" [1:10]).

An overall point of the comparison/contrast centered in Song of Solomon and the consciousness of Sethe and her daughter(s) is that love for women in *Beloved* must manifest itself in forms that are beyond biblical sanction and that redefine the Christian example of sacrificing the body and life. The expression of the depth of Sethe's love goes back to the beginning when Sethe speaks about the "powerful . . . way I loved her," and "there it was again. The welcoming cool of unchiseled headstones; the one she selected to lean against on tiptoe, her knees wide open as the grave. Pink as a fingernail it was, and sprinkled with glittering chips. Ten minutes, he said. You got ten minutes I'll do it for free" (4–5). Sethe's sexual act with the engraver to get the word *Beloved* put on the headstone is an act of sacrificial love as she stands over the grave, which she longs to inhabit with her daughter. She would have been willing to work as a prostitute, to be one of the "Saturday girls" whom she saw selling sex at the slaughterhouse at quitting time to provide for their children (203–4), if that was what getting the engraving done and taking care of her children required. The world of slavery presented black women with alternatives for expressing their love that the "metaphysical comforts" (Guth 93) of the Bible, including its example of Christ's life, did not address.

The section revealing Beloved's consciousness begins by repeating the same theme—"I am Beloved and she is mine" (210)—and completely displaces the biblical ideal with the possessive love that mutates to evil obsession, Beloved's "hot thing." Through repetition and echoes of the word *mine* (172, 181, 199), the text also associates this spiritual and supernatural love/obsession, which is incongruous with the biblical ideal, with the underlying reality of all African Americans as defined by oppression. In part two of the novel, all that Stamp Paid can understand in the "undecipherable language" that he hears outside 124 is the word *mine*. He finally understands who spoke the word *mine* and the others when he finds the ribbon and chunk of scalp from the little murdered girl: "The people of the broken necks, of fire-cooked blood and black girls who had lost their ribbons" (181). This includes Sethe, Beloved, and Denver and implicitly the whole "sixty million and more." The Judeo-Christian ideal is written into *Beloved,* but it is refracted and displaced throughout the narrative as it is in the central section about Sethe and her daughter(s). The subtle critique of the Bible takes place in the overall narrative through the novel's oblique approach.

Baby Suggs does not herself question the Bible or Jesus during the course of her life as a preacher, but the novel critiques the biblical by showing how her words and acts address the reality of historical black oppression better than those of Jesus, which the text subtly references. Baby Suggs "decided that, because slave life had 'busted her legs, back, head, eyes, hands, kidneys, womb and tongue,' she had nothing left to make a living with but her heart—which she put to work at once" (87). Baby Suggs, holy, becomes the preacher who takes the message to the people both inside and outside the church; she "calls" for black people to save themselves by imagining their own grace (88). She develops black folk rituals to deal with the immediacy and specificity of the community's needs within the context of her more conventional religious beliefs but does not reject the work of the traditional African American church. She visited pulpits (87) but "she didn't deliver sermons or preach—insisting she was too ignorant for that—she *called* and the hearing heard" (177). Stamp Paid still considers Baby Suggs's preaching to be the "Word" of God (177–79), and she does indeed use the Word in the Clearing to urge black people to realize the spirituality of their flesh, which is reminiscent of the Word being made flesh in the spiritual body of Jesus Christ (John 1:1–14). Further, the sermons in the Clearing (87–89) are suggestive of Jesus Christ's sermon on the mount (Matthew 5, 6, 7; Luke 6:20–49) but are a commentary on it as well. Jesus goes up a mountain to preach (Matthew 5:1); Baby Suggs "situated herself on a huge flat-sided rock . . . bowed her head and prayed silently" before giving her people a version of the beatitudes (87). She "did not tell them they were the blessed of the earth, its inheriting meek or its glorybound pure" (88; Matthew 5:3–8); she urges poor, mourning, and meek black people to learn to love their flesh. They will be blessed if they love their own free bodies in a white world that loves to enslave and break them. She concludes by dancing out the meaning of loving the freed black body even with her deformed hip, maimed in slavery.

Ironically, the community turns against Baby Suggs when her magical bounty and abundance at a feast of celebration invokes comparisons with the biblical Jesus Christ.

Baby Suggs' three (maybe four) pies grew to ten (maybe twelve). Sethe's two hens became five turkeys. The one block of ice brought all the way from Cincinnati—over which they poured mashed watermelon mixed with sugar and mint to make punch—became a wagonload of ice cakes for a washtub full of strawberry shrug. 124, rocking with laughter, goodwill and food for ninety, made them angry. Too much, they thought. Where does she get it all, Baby Suggs, holy? Why is she and hers always the center of things? How come she always knows exactly what to do and when? Giving advice; passing messages; healing the sick, hiding fugitives, loving, cooking, cooking, loving, preaching, singing, dancing and loving everybody like it was her job and hers alone.

Now to take two buckets of blackberries and make ten, maybe twelve, pies; to have turkey enough for the whole town pretty near, new peas in September, fresh cream but no cow, ice *and* sugar, batter bread, bread pudding, raised bread, shortbread—it made them mad. Loaves and fishes were His powers—they did not belong to an ex-slave who had probably never carried one hundred pounds to the scale, or picked okra with a baby on her back. Who had never been lashed by a ten-year-old whiteboy as God knows they had. (137)

The community is Christian, but the real-world manifestation of a biblical act of Jesus is excessive, arrogant, and incongruous in its life. It is unclear exactly how specifically Baby Suggs models her life after Jesus', but the text indicates that she may consciously use it as an example on which she improvises. The production of the feast that feeds the community is not a supernatural act as was Jesus' feat of blessing a small amount of food and making it multiply (Matthew 14:17–21, 15:34–39; Luke 9:13–17; John 6:5–13). A combination of "her faith, her love, [and] her imagination" (89) are the center of her life. In the context of the novel's overall treatment of the Bible and Christianity, Baby Suggs's faith and love certainly suggest that Jesus is a conscious example for her, but it is as much the folk imagination as Christian ideals that produces the feast. The only explanation for the increase in the amount of food is that Baby Suggs can imagine a positive black community and the rituals to bring it about. Her love and good will, which in this case is making the blackberry pies to commemorate Stamp Paid's labor of love in picking the berries (136), encourages the community to contribute, as Stamp Paid does by also catching fish. The community knows the biblical stories of the miracles of the loaves, but it cannot accept that Baby Suggs makes it reality in their lives: "Her friends and neighbors were angry at her because she had overstepped, given too much, offended them by excess" (138). The community accepts acts of folk imagination such as the sermons and the rituals in the Clearing that lead potentially to their realization of grace, but her creation of the "miracle" from her own imagination and love notwithstanding, the association of her with "His powers" places her outside their experience and their sense of history. Although it is not true, they tell themselves that she has never suffered as they have, which would make her even less than they and definitely not entitled to do Christly things. Their resentment turns to meanness, which makes them abandon her to her own protection since in their minds she pretends to be so "special [and] blessed" (157).

Existing simultaneously in the text's collective consciousness of the past and present, the community in its current Christian reality rejects Baby Suggs, who is legitimately Christly in spite of the community's resentment. From the complexity of its narrative viewpoint, the text ironically uses the resonance of biblical language and images describing the people's abuse of Jesus for his acts to describe the community's un-Christian reaction to Baby Suggs. The people of Jesus' "own country" raise their grievance in the form of questions: "Whence hath this man this wisdom, and these mighty works? Is not this the carpenter's son? is not his mother called Mary? and his brethren, James, and Joses, and Simon, and Judas? And his sisters, are they not all with us? Whence then hath this man all these things?" (Matthew 13:54–58). These questions resonate with the ones asked when the people complain about Baby Suggs: "Where does she get it all . . . Why is she and hers always the center of things? How come she always knows exactly what to do and when?" (137). The community's attitude leads to her further persecution by slavery and eventual death. The community does not openly mock her, as the mob mocks Jesus by putting the gorgeous robes of scarlet and purple on him (Matthew 27:28, Mark 15:20, Luke 23:11, John 19:5), but she does waste away contemplating the colors blue, yellow, green, and pink (201), which is another subtle intertextual resonance that creates irony and narrative critique of the Bible. The implication may be that the Bible portrays an idealized spiritual reality distanced from the African American; according to theory, it has a positive effect on the black community, when in actuality its influence is oftentimes un-Christian.

On the other hand, the text does show the community more positively using the biblical representation of Jesus when it can weave the portrayal into the fabric of its African American folk traditions and beliefs that are strongly informed by an African worldview. Just before the exorcism of Beloved from 124, the text depicts the character Ella's reaction to the knowledge that Beloved has taken over Sethe's life.

> The future was sunset; the past something to leave behind. And if it didn't stay behind, well, you might have to stomp it out. Slave life; freed life—every day was a test and a trial. Nothing could be counted on in a world where even when you were a solution you were a problem. "Sufficient unto the day is the evil thereof," and nobody needed more; nobody needed a grown-up evil sitting at the table with a grudge. As long as the ghost showed out from its ghostly place— shaking stuff, crying, smashing and such—Ella respected it. But if it took flesh and came in her world, well, the shoe was on the other foot. She didn't mind a little communication between the two worlds, but this was an invasion. (256–57)

Ella specifically quotes part of Matthew 6:34 from Jesus' sermon on the mount, but she places the words in a context of the reality of African American oppression and African cosmology. Jesus says, "Sufficient unto the day is the evil thereof" after saying not to worry about tomorrow because God will take care of all things (Matthew 6:25–34). Ella says the same words because there is already in this world a plethora of evil that black people have to take care of without adding otherworldly evil. An underlying reality of African folk tales, instead of Christian ideology, defines what evil is. As Iyunolu Osagie explains, "In an African tale, a demon may sometimes have the same characteristics as a ghost . . . As a concept, the term *demon* is sometimes interchangeable with the term *ghost*. Even Beloved, believed to be a ghost, is sometimes called the 'devil-child' by Ella's troop of praying women" (428).

It is important to reemphasize that collective consciousness is subtle and complex and that it allows the novel to take a range of changing critical perspectives. Ella's response to Sethe's crisis is an example of the text subtly making the characters part of its critique while at the same time portraying them in light of the present where biblical Christianity may have a negative impact or a positive one in conjunction with nonbiblical folk belief. Ella is part of a community of believers who shape Christianity to their needs and devise hybrid sacred and spiritual rituals. Above I say that it is Ella who quotes Jesus from Matthew, but it may be the narrative voice quoting the Bible and raising Ella to the level of textual perception and collective African American consciousness. She would, of course, know the biblical passage, whether she says the words or not, and the aspect of her belief that is African comes from her and the community's collective consciousness of the African past. Throughout the narrative, it is the text as much as it is African American characters and the community that articulates or brings this consciousness to realization.

Further, the text both adheres to and critiques the tradition of Christianity in the black community. In this context, Ella is another black woman who redefines the Christian example by her ability to suffer, forgive, and live a life of service to her people. Ella refuses to love and be loved in the conventional way because "she considered love a serious disability" (256). Her experience with rape and abuse from "the lowest yet" white man, who held her captive, forces her to this conclusion. Her only alternative to combat the evil of this white man is to reject its symbolization by refusing to nurse the "hairy white thing . . . [that he fathered that] lived five days never making a sound" (258–59), which is similar to what Sethe does when she tries to kill her children to keep them from the evil of slavery. In Ella's experience with oppression, conventional love is a "disability" because it prevents her from combating evil. Her service to the community, Sethe in this case, is tantamount to and more practical than showing Christian love because its biblical portrayal does not relate to her situation. In her world she fights evil generated from the complex African American past of oppression that requires her to act appropriately to oppose it, which is what she has done her entire life. After a point, it may sound false and meaningless to say that almost every black woman in the novel rewrites the Christian ideal. However, it does seem to be the text's intention to show the widespread suffering of black women and their ability to overcome and respond with the kind of sacrifice and love that their reality demands. So the general portrayal of women in the novel is part of the subversion of the biblical ideal.

Under the leadership of Ella, an exorcism of prayer and singing by the women of the community that is more than just Christian takes place (257, 261).

The exorcism sounds like traditional call-and-response prayer: "Denver saw lowered heads, but could not hear the lead prayer—only the earnest sylla-bles of agreement that backed it up: Yes, yes, yes, oh yes. Hear me. Hear me. Do it, Maker, do it. Yes" (258). But the later singing is more like the folk rit-ual of the Clearing that draws upon rhythm as well as sound that is "the key, the code . . . that broke the back of words" (261), which is reminiscent of Sethe "picking meaning out of a code" of a language from the African cul-tural past that "she no longer understood" (63). The sound has great power: "It broke over Sethe and she trembled like the baptized in its wash" (261).[4]

This episode plays on and subverts the biblical ideal more directly than the novel usually engages the text of the Bible. *Beloved*'s specific biblical reference in this case is to Matthew 17:1–8. In the presence of his disciples, Jesus "was transfigured . . . and his face did shine as the sun, and his raiment was white as the light" (Matthew 17:2). When the disciples heard a "voice out of the cloud," "they fell on their face, and were sore afraid. And Jesus came and touched them, and said, Arise, and be not afraid. And when they had lifted up their eyes, they saw no man, save Jesus only" (Matthew 17:6–8).[5] In the novel, the "singing women recognized Sethe at once and surprised themselves by their absence of fear when they saw what stood next to her. The devil-child was clever, they thought. And beautiful. It had taken the shape of a pregnant woman, naked and smiling in the heat of the after-noon sun. Thunderblack and glistening, she stood on long straight legs, her belly big and tight. Vines of hair twisted all over her head. Jesus. Her smile was dazzling" (261). Sethe then "lowers her eyes to look again at the loving faces [of the community women] before her" (261–62), sees Edward Bodwin coming, she thinks, to take Beloved from her again, and rushes toward him with the ice pick, precipitating the women to stop her. "The [white] man without skin [Bodwin] . . . is looking at [Beloved]" (262). Later when the people of the community "looked back to the house, [Beloved] was gone" (267).

The text appropriates the Bible's triumphant vision of good to create tex-tual opposition and show its inconsistency with the paradoxical vision of good and evil in its narrative. The women "baptize" Sethe to save her, while the scene in the Bible is all male, but more specific comparisons and con-trasts bring the texts together and undercut the biblical. The words of the "voice out of the cloud" in reference to Jesus, "This is my beloved son, in whom I am well pleased" (Matthew 17:5), recall Sethe's words, "Beloved, she my daughter. She mine" (200), and imply Sethe's love as she stands before the group of women holding her daughter's hand (261), which also reverses the patriarchal paradigm in Matthew. In the biblical verses, the power of the heavenly voice frightens the disciples, but Jesus comforts them and lets them know that they fear needlessly. In contrast, the women are surprised at their lack of fear because of the compelling appearance of the supposed embodiment of evil. The text's intonation of the word *Jesus* registers their shock but also implies the intertextual comparison/contrast between the image of Jesus and the vision in the yard. Jesus' face shines like the sun and his clothes are "white as the light"; Beloved is beautiful, pregnant and fecund in appearance, naked, smiling, and shining black in the sun.

Jesus' image is that of spiritual transfiguration and the biblical ideal of good; Beloved is oppression's transmogrification of loving baby innocence into evil and of vulnerability into threat, which together constitute the intricate web of African American historical reality. Beloved's baby innocence is like Jesus', but at the same time she is evilly obsessive, driven to find the same love that Sethe's loving murder denied her because of its paradox. Sethe sinned but the sin is not really hers: The sin comes from the evil oppression of slavery, especially for black women, which Beloved also embodies in the nakedness and "pregnancy" that are suggestive of sexual vulnerability, which turns to the threat that loving mothers will kill daughters to stop them from being vulnerable, which comes back to Beloved, the conflicted symbol of African American mother/daughter relationships who takes human form to threaten Sethe for denying her life and nurture through the violent act of desperate love caused by slavery. It is a convoluted knot that is hard to extricate. When Sethe looks up and outward, she, unlike Jesus' disciples, does not see a comforting vision but the threat of white oppression again, manifested in the sanguine form of abolitionist Edward Bodwin, who is looking meaningfully at Beloved. (Bodwin and his sister "hated slavery worse than they hated slaves" (137). Implicitly, they feel that slavery reflects badly on white people when they enslave inferior black people. The black caricature figure that Denver sees at the Bodwins' back door has words painted on it that state their true sentiments about the role of black people: "At Yo Service" [255]). Beloved is gone when the people look back at the house, but because her portrayal is ambivalent, the meaning of her disappearance is unclear. The women do in effect save Sethe from her "sin," but the overall outcome is not one represented in the glorious solutions in the Bible.

The novel's characterizations of women redefine the Bible's textual examples of the Christian. Sometimes utilizing this same complex subversive approach, the narrative redefines the male characters in positive human terms through their experiences with women and, in the process, also critiques male exemplars of the Old and New Testaments. Through his relationship with Sethe, Paul D's depiction draws comparisons to the apostle Paul's in the New Testament. But Paul D is a new Paul, sensitive to the needs of women enduring the oppression of slavery, and more practically and realistically compassionate than the idealized and romanticized apostle.[6] The biblical concept of blessedness as articulated by the apostle Paul is central to the comparison/contrast of characters and texts. The apostle uses the word "blessedness" in Romans 4:6 and in Galatians 4:15. He is talking about being justified in the grace of God through faith and not through good works that adhere to the law, which are difficult because of the weakness of the flesh. In Galatians 4:13–15, he refers to his own previous weaknesses of flesh; he asks, "Where is then the blessedness [that the Galatians] spake of?" In Galatians 5:17, he more clearly sums up his point: "For the flesh lusteth against the Spirit, and the Spirit against the flesh: and these are contrary the one to the other: so that ye cannot do the things that ye would." Earlier in Romans 7:24–25, he has stated the solution: "O wretched man that I am! who shall deliver me from the body of this death? I thank God through Jesus Christ our Lord. So then with the mind I myself serve the law of God; but with the flesh the law of sin." On the other hand, Paul D has always had a natural way with women that is "blessed." The text reveals this in his early encounter with Sethe after he sees her for the first time in eighteen years. "Not even trying, he had become the kind of man who could walk into a house and make the women cry. Because with him, in his presence, they could. There was something blessed in his manner" (17). In this same paragraph, Paul D "held [Sethe's] breasts in the palms of his hands. He rubbed his cheek on her back and learned that way her sorrow, the roots of it; its wide trunk and intricate branches." After describing his sexual relationship with Sethe, his rejection of her after he discovers the murder, and then his understanding her better because of ensuing events, the text again refers to his "blessedness." Sethe sees the "peachstone skin, the crease between his ready, waiting eyes and sees it—the thing in him, the blessedness, that has made him walk in a house and make the women cry" (272). At this point, Paul D is not holding breasts: "His holding fingers are holding hers" (273).

What is "blessed" about Paul D subtly but significantly changes to his "blessedness," and his emphasis shifts from sex to greater compassion as he fulfills the biblical concept in realistic ways that contrast with the apostle Paul's abstract terms, which have no meaning in reference to African American life. Paul's treatise on the spiritual life is abstruse; even more importantly, the spirituality that he conceives and actualizes would not address the necessities of slavery. In Romans 7:25, he solves the conundrum of fleshly limitation of the spirit with the invocation of Jesus and the bifurcation of mind and body that apparently separates the spirit and abandons the body to its devices. Paul's transcendentalism is inappropriate for African American life first because his abstract analysis of the flesh is totally separated from an actual relationship with a woman, and slavery was in so many ways about the contestation of African American male/female relationships. Secondly, while black oppression was very much about mind and body, Paul disavows the body to focus on the mind and/or the spirit.

In *Beloved,* the distinction between "blessed" and "blessedness" is important to the overall intertextual comparison. At the beginning when the text's word for Paul D is "blessed," he is already compassionate toward women, but his initial display when he takes "responsibility for [Sethe's] breasts" (18) leads to sex that "was over before they could get their clothes off" (20). "They lay side by side resentful of one other . . . His dreaming of her had been too long and too long ago." After the reality of the torturous experience with Sethe replaces the dream for Paul D, he attains the level of "blessedness" that potentially brings him together with Sethe more compassionately to care about the scars of her body as well as her feelings. Unlike Paul, who calls on Jesus to raise him above the preoccupations of the body and into bifurcated abstraction, Paul D bonds with Sethe as a "friend of [his] mind" (272–73) who supports him in life. The novel has redefined the Christian example through Sethe, and it is after he has come to terms with her reality that the word in the second of two similar descriptions changes from "blessed" to "blessedness" to link Paul D more specifically to the apostle Paul's noun naming the quality. But it is Sethe, and not the biblical Paul, who influences Paul D's blessedness, which is tantamount to a spiritually compassionate concern realized in the face of slavery's monstrosity.

The characterization of Stamp Paid develops to a significant extent from his relationship with a black woman also, but the implied biblical references in his case are grounded in the Old Testament. It is somewhat curious that, with the exception of the reference to Song of Solomon, which is about Jesus, the novel's more overt biblical allusions are primarily to the New Testament. Historically, the Old Testament story of the slavery and freedom of the Jews had a great affect on African American slaves. Perhaps the novel deals so heavily with the New Testament because in essence its thematic scope reaches far beyond the specifics of its nineteenth-century setting to apply to the early twentieth century and the present, where the example of Jesus, along with the New Testament's dispensation to the gentiles, has greater importance for African Americans. Regardless, *Beloved* does critique the Old Testament in its portrayal of Stamp Paid, which leads to a discussion of its uses of the Old Testament that are more subtle and tangential generally.

Initially, the only similarity between his story and the well-known one of Joshua taking the Promised Land in the Old Testament may seem to be Stamp Paid's original name.

> Born Joshua, he renamed himself when he handed over his wife to his master's son. Handed her over in the sense that he did not kill anybody, thereby himself, because his wife demanded he stay alive. Otherwise, she reasoned, where and to whom could she return when the boy was through? With that gift, he decided that he didn't owe anybody anything. Whatever his obligations were, that act paid them off. He thought it would make him rambunctious, renegade—a drunkard even, the debtlessness, and in a way it did. But there was nothing to do with it. Work well; work poorly. Work a little; work not at all . . . It didn't seem much of a way to live and it brought him no satisfaction. So he extended this debtlessness to other people by helping them pay out and off whatever they owed in misery. Beaten runaways? He ferried them and rendered them paid for; gave them their own bill of sale, so to speak. "You paid it; now life owes you." And the receipt, as it were, was a welcome door that he never had to knock on, like John and Ella's in front of which he stood and said, "Who in there?" only once and she was pulling on the hinge. (184–85)

The text later describes in more detail what happened when he gave his wife to the master and changed his name, but there is still no obvious coherence between the stories in which the novel critiques the Bible. Troubling experiences with women—troubling for Stamp Paid, that is—are important in the events that lead to his renaming. First and foremost, the actions of his wife Vashti, along with those of the young master who takes her sexually, bother him, but the reactions of the master's wife, whom Stamp Paid slyly tells about the affair to prevent further liaisons, also disturb him. "I . . . thought she might stop it, but it went right on. Till one morning Vashti came in and sat by the window . . . 'I'm back,' she said. 'I'm back Josh.' She had a real small neck. I decided to break it . . . I been low but that was as low as I ever got" (233). Stamp Paid seems to be as much discomfited and angry because of the women's actions as he is because of the master's, perhaps because he is totally powerless against the master, the real perpetrator. However, the women, and particularly Vashti at his lowest moment, seem to have a great effect on his name change, which is the sign of a profound humanistic development on his part. He stays alive to take care of the victimized Vashti (who later dies although Stamp Paid does not kill her) when she returns from the master, and he remains alive to ferry runaways across the river and to take care of black people later in a redefined existence, which is what earns him entry into their houses.

The connection between the story of Stamp Paid and Joshua in the Old Testament is more oblique and obscure than most of the novel's connections with the New Testament, but small fragments of Stamp Paid's narrative echo the book of Joshua and recast the biblical in light of the exigencies of slavery. Stamp Paid subverts the biblical with the African American vernacular by renaming himself, but this is only the clearest part of a larger subtle pattern. In Joshua 2, Rahab, a "harlot" of the city Jericho, hides the two Jewish spies that Joshua sends, saving them from detection and leading to the success of the mission. Joshua later miraculously parts the waters and crosses over the Jordan River with his people (Joshua 3:14–17), and then he triumphantly "burnt [Jericho] with fire, and all that was therein," except Rahab and her family (Joshua 6:22–25). In *Beloved*, after Vashti saves him by "demand[ing] that he stay alive," Stamp Paid escapes, crosses the Mississippi on a boat (233), and later ferries runaways across the river. Stamp Paid's mundane but great change of identity and crossover are more remarkable than Joshua's miracle because he evolves to a humane self that serves the needs of oppressed black people, and his nonviolent action on behalf of his people highlights Joshua's violence in pursuing the destiny of his. Stamp Paid's characterization also intersects Rahab's in one way, and her characterization conflates with the depictions of the women in his story, who affect and implicitly give critical commentary on Stamp Paid. Like Rahab, he resides among the people whom he helps. Rehab aids the Jews, who are the imperialists from the novel's intertextual perspective, but she is also a powerless victim doing the best she can, as are Vashti and the master's wife. Stamp Paid seems to be angry toward Vashti as if she were a "harlot," and is mystified with the young wife also. But the novel's characterization of them certainly belies Stamp Paid's apparent assessment and perhaps also questions the Bible's characterization of Rehab as a "harlot."

Overall, the stories of Stamp Paid and Joshua in the Old Testament are similar enough to draw attention to their differences. The novel evokes disquieting feelings about the text of the Bible and creates potential ruptures in the story of Joshua conquering the Promised Land. Along these same lines, Stamp Paid's story about his wife disrupts parts of the book of Esther. Vashti shares the name of the rebellious queen (Esther 1–2) whom King Ahasuerus deposes and replaces with Esther because she will not obey his command. From the biblical perspective, Vashti's deposition sets things back in the rightful order of male power. In *Beloved*, Vashti in a sense rebels against the wishes of Stamp Paid. However, he cannot get rid of her, and in turn her actions influence him to be a man who is more compassionate and caring.

Another example of *Beloved*'s subtle critical engagement with the Old Testament is a reference encoded in Sethe's address, Bluestone Road 124. Psalm 124 is a psalm of David to God for being his refuge: "If it had not been the Lord who was on our side, when men rose up against us: Then they had swallowed us up quick, when their wrath was kindled against us: Then the waters had overwhelmed us, the stream had gone over our soul: Then the proud waters had gone over our soul. Blessed be the Lord, who hath not given us as a prey to their teeth. Our soul is escaped as a bird out of the snare of the fowlers: the snare is broken, and we are escaped. Our help is in the name of the Lord, who made heaven and earth." It is only possible to see this relationship between the texts after recognizing the larger structure of other complex but more perceptible ones from the same biblical source; in this context, there is an ironic contrast between the Bible and *Beloved*. Sethe's house number 124 is symbolic of Beloved, the missing third child, as so many critical commentaries have pointed out, but it also refers to the theme of the biblical psalm of David of the same number. David in the Old Testament is linked to Jesus, and Sethe in *Beloved* is a radically redefined Christ figure, who in this instance contrasts with David and again implies redefined Christlike suffering. Sethe has not transgressed as much as David, who commits premeditated murder and adultery, but she suffers as much. House 124 is not her refuge and help; she finds none of the protection and help of the escaped who deserve the protection promised in the Bible. Men do rise against her, and Sethe is almost "swallowed up"; the community through its widely defined folk tradition, along with Paul D, becomes her potential safety and refuge.

Similarly, an aspect of the novel's radical vision is a genesis theory of its own narrative of slavery and oppression. Why does the image of slavery's oppression and suffering exist for Sethe eighteen years after she has escaped? Where does this contemporary novel's narrative come from when the physical and legal institution of slavery has been dismantled for over a century? Early in the novel, as Sethe washes chamomile sap from her legs, the plantation Sweet Home unfolds before her vision as one of the text's figurations of oppression. "She might be hurrying across a field . . . and suddenly there was Sweet Home rolling, rolling, rolling out before her eyes, and although there was not a leaf on that farm that did not make her want to scream, it rolled itself out before her in shameless beauty. It never looked as terrible as it was and it made her wonder if hell was a pretty place too. Fire and brimstone all right, but hidden in lacy groves. Boys hanging from the most beautiful sycamores in the world. It shamed her—remembering the wonderful soughing trees rather than the boys" (6). White people conceived slavery as a "sweet home" beneficial for black people, and generated and actualized the idea with such power that it is indelible and maintains hegemony over the black psyche. The genesis of Sweet Home oppression is the "jungle" that is hatred and fear of black people: The "jungle" that white people conceived as blackness "grew. It spread. In, through and after life, it spread, until it invaded the whites who had made it. Touched them every one. The screaming baboon lived under their own white skin; the red gums were their own" (198–99). Sweet Home intrudes and takes over beyond Sethe's control and likewise produces the slavery of this contemporary narrative. The oppressive "sweet home" and "jungle" of black life are uncontrollable presences in the consciousnesses of black and white people, respectively.

In terms of its own theory, the beginning of the narrative is reminiscent of, and at the same time a parody of, the beginning of the human story in Genesis. "In the beginning God created the heaven and the earth . . . And God said, Let there be [light, the firmament, the world, beasts, and man]: and there was" (Genesis 1). The power, and ultimate goodness, of God spontaneously begins everything. Slavery in *Beloved* just "begins" too: Sethe "might be" anywhere, and with the slightest, most imperceptible thing, Sweet Home involuntarily rolls out before her. But in the novel there is a hellish human design instead of a divine one. The images of trees that resonate with the trees of the Garden of Eden in Genesis also link the texts: "And out of the ground made the Lord God to grow every tree that is pleasant to the sight, and good for food; the tree of life also in the midst of the garden, and the tree of knowledge of good and evil" (Genesis 2:9). The injunction for man and woman is, "of the tree of the knowledge of good and evil, thou shalt not eat of it: for in the day that thou eatest thereof thou shalt surely die" (Genesis 2:17). Breaking this rule is the sin that justifies the beginning of human suffering in Genesis. Unjustified black suffering and death displace the biblical images in *Beloved*. Black people are punished in the Sweet Home creation even unto constant, violent death, and hang from the trees like fruit, without having eaten of the forbidden tree. There is no potential of a meaningful life, as is suggested in Genesis through the tree of life, which is not originally forbidden. Also, unlike the lost paradise of Eden, the Sweet Home reality is one that African Americans would gladly escape but cannot because it is so unforgettably written into the African American and American reality.

From the broadest perspective, *Beloved* is a prophecy of American life that generally parallels the Old Testament's grave vision and simultaneously subverts and displaces it with American reality that gives no recourse to the idealized and abstract. The words of Ezekiel could describe *Beloved*'s narrative: "And when I looked, behold, an hand was sent unto me; and, lo, a roll of a book was therein; And he spread it before me; and it was written within and without: and there was written therein lamentations, and mourning, and woe" (Ezekiel 2:9–10).[7] *Beloved* is "not a story to pass on" (274–75). The book of slavery that is as horrible as the one that Ezekiel sees is hard to "pass on," but it is a story that desperately needs retelling from the standpoint of African American and American history and contemporary reality. Black people must understand and deal with its legacy and influence. Probably even more importantly, the central sins of America and the West are written into the book, and must be acknowledged and expiated. At the same time, the change that acknowledgement would demand is great, and may be too much for an American world set in a different direction and very much assured of its goodness. *Beloved* is a great novel, but there is no assurance that the culture will listen to the story. It likely will not. However, if readers will put themselves into the book and take it seriously, it can surely change many individuals. In this sense, the novel boldly and radically rivals the Bible.

I want to be clear in saying, however, that *Beloved* is a parody of an iconic white, Western *text* that both centers and decenters it, and as such is not a rejection of the basic values that underlie Christianity and other religions.[8] The King James Bible is (re)written in Western terms like other narratives, and it is interpreted from a white viewpoint in this culture. The Bible and Christianity have, nevertheless, had an overwhelming impact on African American life and experience, and a great deal of this has been positive. *Beloved* gives an ironic perspective on the way that the Bible relates to American history and life overall, but it does not negate the importance of the Bible and the religious beliefs associated with it for African Americans. Deborah Guth makes a similar point without specifying textuality: "Morrison's great achievement is her ability to foreground the central position of Christianity in the inner lives of her forbears and simultaneously, through parodic tensions and the discourse of estrangement, to instate an outside perspective through which to dramatize the disjunctions and dire antagonisms that inform this relationship. In her unblinking realignment of the redemptive Christian model with a tortured [African American] past, Morrison thus contributes to the contemporary cultural debate by exposing this central historic relationship without ever denying its beauty or the power it exerted on the lives of those it failed to save" (93). For African Americans, *Beloved* could provide new ways of thinking about what is perhaps their most important historic religious tradition, while at the same time making it part of larger possibilities.

Beloved emphasizes its own postmodern textuality by making explicit its status as a story. From the postmodern perspective, it is a *black* construction of truth that, among its many projects, contests the hegemonic white, Western biblical construction of spiritual and sacred reality with a heterodox cosmology of African and African American belief that redefines what is Christian. Because of collective consciousness, a postmodern concept, black people are narrators of and characters in this story that encompasses the African past and the history of oppression by white people. Just as the black community is both highly Christian in the present and critical of the received Christian tradition from its synchronous positioning with the textual viewpoint, it is also a part of and set apart from the horrible inhumanity in the story. "This is not a story to pass on." Even though African Americans theoretically tell the story through collective consciousness, they may not be capable of dealing with all of its depth, gravity, and complexity in their contemporary lives. Perhaps this is true to a lesser extent than for white people, but the response is similar. Beloved is the full dimension of this story: "They forgot her like a bad dream. After they made up their tales, shaped and decorated them, those that saw her that day on the porch quickly and deliberately forgot her. It took longer for those who had spoken to her, lived with her, fallen in love with her, to forget, until they realized they couldn't remember or repeat a single thing she said, and began to believe that, other than what they themselves were thinking, she hadn't said anything at all. So, in the end, they forgot her too. Remembering seemed unwise" (274). There is obviously a danger here for black people in forgetting the story, just as there is for white people. However, for those who read *Beloved*'s black story and remember, the novel has a potentially more salient role in healing the spirit than does the Bible, which does not address the specificity of the African American historical and cultural past.

John Edgar Wideman's *The Cattle Killing* and *Beloved* are postmodern African American texts of healing that engage and challenge the received text of the Bible with the potential of their own textual messages and that of the textually represented African and African American folk tradition. *The Cattle Killing* deals more directly with the Old Testament and with the Bible generally, and its postmodern textuality is explicitly the self-conscious writing of a metafictional writer who is a character throughout its narrative. The novel has a strong biblical and religious emphasis on the powerful prophetic vision of the Old Testament, but the novel also focuses on the aspects of its textuality that are secular. The epigraphs to parts one and two of *The Cattle Killing* are paraphrases of Ezekiel 12:3 and 13:22, respectively: "Prepare your baggage as though for exile"; "But I will stretch out my hand against the prophets who have false visions and who foretell lies."[9] The novel presents a parallel creation of the history of African and African American oppression and the cultural traditions that deal with it, which are part of a more generalized focus on the highly oppressive human story. The metafictional writer—who also represents a collective voice telling the story that has relationships and connections that reach across three centuries—says that the text contains "*all the books it might have been, could or should have been, buried in its pages. I can't read what's here without mourning what's lost"* (9). *The Cattle Killing* is a palimpsest that presents the religious and secular cultural traditions in terms of its writer's self-conscious theme of the dominance of texts and narratives, and consequently its textual engagement and challenge end differently than *Beloved*'s do.

The novel reveals that suffering and oppression are textual realities that are ineluctable, especially in African American life, and this is not true of Christian salvation. The main character's experience with oppression causes a failure of faith, which leads him to the reality of the enigma of God and forces him away from belief in the New Testament's doctrine of saving grace. The backdrop of the novel is a young preacher's narration of a love story to save the life of a dying woman, who is a composite of many oppressed and abused black women from the eighteenth century to the present, just as the preacher's character is a conflation of the eighteenth-century ex-slave, the metafictional writer of the novel, and other African and African American men in the past and present. Despite his intention to tell a happy, salvific story, he recounts how he lost his faithful Christian belief. Although he is giving an account of losing faith after he has actually lost it, the power of this former belief, which is grounded in the efficacy of the inner light of Jesus Christ that is available to all human beings, and its importance to him and African Americans in general, is a main feature of his narrative.

Although the novel encompasses the influence of the secular folk tradition, its portrayal of black cultural tradition highlights the sacred. Also, the deterministic textual traditions have their deepest grounding in the biblical and religious. The text shows the omnipresent power of oppressive evil, caused by sin, embedded in the inevitable suffering and doom of the Old Testament, other written texts, and mythical narratives. Implicitly in *The Cattle Killing*, Old Testament suffering and doom are transposed historically and culturally into the reality of black oppression, and the dynamics of power subtly but powerfully infuse these traditions throughout secular narratives. The sacred and secular texts become inseparable in effect, and the intertext of African American oppression has greater power because of its base in the sacred. This intertext deeply informs cultural consciousness, which in ultimately produces and maintains physical oppression. Oppression is therefore set in a societal intertext. Generally, according to its own implied theory, *The Cattle Killing* is endless impressions of doomful intertextuality that constructs African American reality. The consequent project of the metafictional writer is to write a countertext of African American salvation, which he entitles *The Cattle Killing,* into this hegemonic intertext of oppression. However, the text is uncertain about the efficacy of its black love story, the true nature of God as portrayed in texts, and the relationship of God, textuality, and oppression. *The Cattle Killing* does not clearly show how to separate African American oppression from this sacred and secular intertextual skein and address it, mostly because *The Cattle Killing* itself is engendered in this common intertextual center of white power and thus deeply complicit. The most definitive aspect of *The Cattle Killing* turns out to be its prophecy of oppressive evil that is a paradoxical manifestation of the potential of God's goodness, which it derives from the Old Testament. *The Cattle Killing* is an ambiguous, problematized black text of salvation that (re)writes the substance of black oppression caused by evil, setting it in a powerful moment of potentially redeeming faith in God and suspending white power in this moment.

The writer at the beginning establishes his intention to unite and save, which is the same objective of the young preacher's storytelling, but his language quickly reveals the oppressive influence of prophecies of captivity and suffering. He says that the Xhosa cattle-killing prophecy *"exiled [them] from the ark of safety that had been home and cattle and heritage"* (7), and his language symbolically links the texts of Ezekiel and *The Cattle Killing* to the Xhosa story as also potentially exiling prophecies.[10] The word *exiled* used by the writer to describe the Xhosa prophecy in his text alludes to the word *exile* in Ezekiel 12:3, which is also the epigraph to part one, thus connecting his novel, the Old Testament, and the Xhosa prophecy. Theoretically, the writer's word is a symbol that embeds the Xhosa prophecy with the same essential codes of oppression and destruction as the narrative of his own novel that portrays it, and as the exiling prophecy of Ezekiel, which is the central story written into all of the narratives in the text. The symbolic becomes "real" because in the writer's story the prophecy sets in motion horrific events that decimate the Xhosas. Again on the theoretical level, the Xhosa prophecy simultaneously inseminates *The Cattle Killing* with its oppression and suffering because the novel tells the Xhosa story, and the same is true of the novel's narration of the story of Ezekiel. The prophecies are intertextual and complementary, and telling one story is tantamount to repeating the underlying reality of the others. All of the prophecies, including *The Cattle Killing,* can warn as well as construct the dangerous, oppressive evil that they prophesy. Consequently, although the writer *"wanted every word of his new book to be a warning"* (7) about the exiling cattle-killing prophecy, implicitly the prophecy of Ezekiel, and possibly other prophecies, there is a chance that his book only repeats these texts and exiles as it warns. This possibility implies broad questions about textuality that the novel specifies through the Xhosa prophecy, the prophecy of the Old Testament, and the prophecy of its own narrative and that it deals with throughout its entirety.

The primary question implied concerns the relationship of African and African American well-being to the oppressive hegemony of white, Western textuality, most strongly symbolized in the perspective of Ezekiel in the Old Testament, which, in the endeavor of the writer and the experience of the young preacher, seems to control the construction of reality to a greater extent than the New Testament's positive vision of renewal. The Xhosa prophecy turns out to be a destructive text of the European oppressor encoded in a story of Xhosa cultural renewal; it *"seduced [them] by false prophesy, false promises, turning [them] away from themselves, [making them try] to become something else, something they could never be"* (7). One mistake of the Xhosas is that they trusted someone else's story; they "looked to the pale people from across the sea to deliver [them] from the destruction they had wrought" (145). And although the Bible as a source of faith is obviously key to black survival in the novel, perhaps African Americans mimic the Xhosas' mistake by accepting parts of this Western text that prophesy oppression and destruction as inseparable aspects of restoration and redemption. The metafictional writer may also be doing this because his book is essentially a repetition of Western stories. Is the prophecy of the Old Testament the deadly warning of doom that in fact dooms the writer and other African Americans in the same way that the cattle-killing myth destroys the Xhosas? Ezekiel is a purported warning, saving prophecy that reveals the inevitable suffering that God promises and manifests. Does this prophecy within prophecy alienate, exile, and oppress black people even as it prophesies that suffering and oppression are inseparable from the will of God? *The Cattle Killing* is prophecy and story within oppressive story that seems almost endless and maddening. Does the seemingly deterministic intertextual relationship of *The Cattle Killing* to other narratives make it another writing of bad prophecy that continues the tradition? Just as it is true that the Xhosa prophecy is in reality a white text, it could be true that *The Cattle Killing* cannot separate itself from white, Western textuality, particularly the Old

Testament, to become a black text. The psychic power of an oppressive textual tradition could be too great.

From the end of the introductory section (15) until near the beginning of the epilogue (209), the metafictional writer largely conflates himself with the young preacher and writes a text that parallels the preacher's oral text and that serves a similar purpose. The preacher unsuccessfully struggles for spiritual belief in the story that he tells as he tries to save the woman with his conception of love that is no longer grounded in the sacred and spiritual. The effect of the love story is ambiguous, but although he is anguished by it, he does seem confident in the pain and suffering that manifests God's existence and will. The writer implicitly tries to construct a secular text of African American salvation as he writes the story of the preacher. However, he cannot elude the heavily biblical, intertextual concept of doom and oppression that opposes the narrative he wants to write and that defeats the preacher's belief in God and potentially negates the influence of his love.

Initially, the preacher's faith is the inner light of Jesus Christ that gives him the benevolent spirit to serve oppressed black people and white people equally. As his faith fails, he hopes the light of artistry will transfigure oppression, but instead it destroys through the horror of its revelation. As his story becomes laden with oppression, he merges into the artistry of Liam, a man that he meets in his story, whose story in turn embodies additional layers of oppressiveness that compel the preacher, at the end of part one, to create the figure of oppression as "circles within circles" of God's body (149). The "circles within circles" are his own inescapable text of oppression grounded in biblical belief, and the "circles" of his text are also the writer's.

At the beginning the novel gives the sense that the light within him creates the preacher and the world around him. His self-conscious awareness of the light originally came from the Bible. The wife of the second, benevolent master persuaded her husband to make his slaves Christians, and she taught the preacher and his brother to read the Bible. He believed its teaching that men are equal in God's sight and salvation is open to all (64–65). The light within the self negates the concrete physical world. The words of another preacher make this point: "This [world] . . . all this, is not real. Yet you steadfastly believe it is. You're taken in. You think you see but you don't. The mountains, the marble-pillared houses of government, have no more substance than taunts and whispering and stares of devil's agents sent to plague you. Phantoms. Ignore them and they have no power over you. Learn to look inside yourselves. Feed the light" (20).

The early account of his experience is reminiscent of a creation myth where he constantly reinvents the world from the power of the saving inner light; he also fears this world each morning as he awakes because of an uncertain sense of its collective past and future that is demonic. At dawn, "he waits, holding his breath while the house that is the world remembers its shape, erects itself again, all the stone and brick and wood piling up without a sound. He goes to sleep alone in an empty place and next morning the cities of his past, the cities of his future, are spread around him. People step over him, around him, through him, always on their way somewhere else. They wear strange shoes, unimaginable shoes, so he understands immediately he is not dreaming, he is awake in a familiar town filled with nameless faces. People wearing shoes cobbled by devils" (18). This early portrayal contains nuances of the angst that the light generates as it reveals more and more earthly oppression. The character feels threat because, as the surrounding narrative context shows, hostile white power threatens his blackness, but he primarily finds comfort in the fact that God has brought him through the night and given him a new day (20–21). The positive power of the inner light is predominant in his belief in spite of uneasiness about the past and future that he cannot ignore.

Prophecy from the book of Jeremiah inspires in the preacher a larger projection of the light that pulls him deeper into the complexity of its paradoxical vision of peaceful transcendence and evil. He is thinking about his text from Jeremiah 5:14: "Behold, I am making my words in your mouth a fire, and this people wood, and the fire shall devour them" (67). A thundering beast and a "storm of lights" (67–68) propel him to a place where "the world was one sight, one luminous presence inventing his eyes" (68–69). He perceives a reality of wholeness and harmony that he cannot recall or put in words (73–74). However, he comes out of his trance speaking Jeremiah's words of warning prophecy, which frightens his black congregation because it sounds like judgment on them; members of the congregation also say that devils possessed his body during the fit he had before he stated his biblical prophecy (72–73).

The world of African community that he sees once his black congregation takes him to their church sanctuary in the woods nearby is a further revelation of his otherworldly experience that is the potential substance of good prophecy and a gift of heavenly grace. The incident begins in St. Matthew's, the white church in Philadelphia that promotes racist doctrines, but later in the woods the strange light from within that generated his fit and the prophecy of Jeremiah shows him a supernatural community of Africans: "Why did the clearing seem so crowded. People everywhere. People in outlandish costumes. Shoes from my dreams. A bazaar of people milling about. More African people than I'd ever seen in one place at one time" (75). The imagery balances and somewhat negates the earlier threatening communal depiction of people "wearing shoes cobbled by devils" created by the light.

However, in the overall textual portrayal of the light, destruction, evil prophecy, and the nature of evil are inseparable from saving prophecy and the character of good; it is unclear what the true source of the light and consequent prophecy is. The beast of death destroying the world in the preacher's apocalyptic vision is evil, but somehow he seems to be infected with evil himself in the fit that the black congregation describes. Although he feels inner peace during the fit, which he believes is nonthreatening and "only a sweet, brief clarity" (73), his first words to his people upon recovery are that those very words will be God's fire to consume them. Further, as the preacher's own thoughts show, he is uncertain about himself and his message; the difference between his prophecy and bad white prophets and prophecies is ambiguous to him. The evil of racist white prophecy for black people as preached by St. Matthew's white minister should be clear (61), but still the preacher cannot distinguish between himself and the white preacher as prophets: "Why couldn't this hair-splitting, chilly priest be a messenger. Was that notion any more preposterous than thinking myself, unschooled, black, poor, a proper vessel to bear truth and prophecy" (67).

Perhaps the young preacher's prophecy is bound in the hegemony of oppressive white oral and written textuality, and he and his congregation cannot escape it and the concrete reality that it manifests. In terms of his education, race, and background—which really are irrelevant—the preacher implies relevant questions not only about his complicated relationship to the white preacher but also about the origins of the text of African American oppression, and about the role of white people and African Americans in creating this text. The evil of white prophecy and oppression and the potential oppressiveness of biblical textuality are indistinguishable from the black preacher, his inner light, and his actions. On one hand, the words from Jeremiah that the black preacher speaks when he regains consciousness are a condemnation of the white racist church people. On the other hand, he says these words to the African Americans after they have left St. Matthew's, thus pronouncing to them the doom and destruction that should apply to white people. The oppressive prophecy of the white preacher for blacks castigates and calls "attention to [them] with a recital of [their] alleged misdeeds" (61), but so could the words from Jeremiah that the young black preacher utters. Where does the evil, oppressive prophecy against African Americans begin, and what is its text? The sources would seem to be white. However, the black preacher apparently has internalized the text of the white preacher, at least to the extent that it has confused him about its possible truth. The white preacher's text specifies a message for black people that has the same general theme of destruction as the prophecy from Jeremiah, which the black preacher articulates under the inspiration of the light. Perhaps the young preacher's prophecy is bound in the hegemony of oppressive white oral and written textuality, and he and his congregation cannot escape it and the concrete reality that it constructs.

It is important to emphasize that the textual brings physical oppression and psychic trauma into the realm of human access and knowledge by giving them linguistic form, thus making the textual, physical, and psychic inseparable "circles" of oppression that are an analytical tautology. Analysis of what the preacher says earlier about the potential of the inner light in one African American man is an example. In the case of a congregant named Rowe, investment in the white religious tradition and the appropriation of the Bible only (re)inscribes an oppressive and destructive hegemony preached by whites and grounded in white, Western textuality. As is true with the cattle-killing prophecy, the potential for self-destruction has roots in a white text and is an internalized form of the oppression that the whites have already imposed physically. The preacher has always wondered what old man Rowe, a devout Christian and the survivor of slavery's almost unbelievable atrocity, sees when he looks into the blue sky as if in a religious trance (63). Rowe's inner light apparently creates a new world like the preacher's does: "Sometime I looks at the sky and close my eyes I see the whole world startin over agin. New day, Reverend. Clean. See a black man and a black woman and a white man and a white woman laid side by side fresh out of the oven and theys the only people God done made" (66). The rest of Rowe's vision and wishful prophecy is the black man's murder of the white man and rape and sexual mutilation of the white woman, which leads to the end of white existence and the perpetuation of black people. Rowe wishes to repay whites for what they did to his own wife and family, but his light illuminates an inner world that the preacher would not have anticipated. The light within Rowe is a longing for retribution that could bestialize and virtually destroy the humanizing qualities of self. Rowe takes a figure of creation from the Bible and reference to God and turns them into an image of oppression that replicates the physical oppression of white people, whose religious text he has appropriated and whose religion he practices. The potential for destruction encompasses Rowe physically and textually, and from within and without, and the analysis of him is hard pressed to escape a tautological knot, as is true for the metafictional writer who is analyzing his own writing and the preacher telling his story.

Through his interrelated stories about a secular artist named Liam and the ministry of Bishop Richard Allen, the preacher's own new secular artistry carries him back to the biblically centered paradox of oppression that is God's only sign of salvation. Secular artistry leads in virtually the same direction as the sacred, which is a problem for the preacher and the metafictional writer. The woman the preacher is talking to wants a happy story, but the best that he can do is the story of Liam and his wife, which only begins happily with them saving the preacher's life (78–79). The story of Liam's life and secular artistry eventually causes the preacher to lose himself "in Liam's eyes" (143) and transports him to "the Africa of Liam's stories," which is the dream state in which the African girl insinuates the destructive European text of the Xhosa cattle killing as her own erotic love story (143–48). The oppression of this story later relates to that in the story about Bishop Allen and his faith in God back in Philadelphia.

The problem with Liam's artistry is that its genesis is European art that reifies butchery and oppression, or at least is complicit in it, like Liam's white mentor's artwork. In his story Liam, an African formerly enslaved in England, models his artistry after that of his former master George Stubbs, an enlightened thinker on race who tried to discover the essence of life and reveal it in his creations (78–149). Liam wants his artistry to liberate the "colors" inside him that are his inner light symbolizing his freedom to be with the white woman he loves and also representing new possibilities in the American world (126). To achieve his goal of liberation, Liam ends up not trying to confine the essence of life in his art like his master; he improvises on Stubbs's example to develop a creative method that frees and gives life through its open-ended, ongoing process. He devises different goals but greatly admired Stubbs's dedication and his work generally. However, there is a larger dimension of Stubbs's life represented by the cattle slaughterhouse owned by his father. The slaughterhouse figuration replicates central nuances of the destruction of the tribe in the Xhosa cattle-killing prophecy that turns out to be a European text: Liam "enters the slaughterhouse, hears the moaning and braying, the panicked squeals of captive animals who smell blood, hear on every side the death wails of their tribes" (110). Symbolically, this is the English pogrom of Africans that is Stubbs's greater reality and that saturates his work, which becomes apparent in one poignant scene. Liam is present when Stubbs and others bid on a pregnant African female cadaver that Stubbs would cut up for his artistic exploration: "She'd been stolen from me and now I was about to lose her again. Knives would slice her open, hack her to bits. They'd find me cowering in the black cave of her womb again, dead and alive, alive and dead" (137). This body could later be Stubbs's black text that is subsumed in his art form, and it strongly signifies the complicity of his work in the oppression that later overtakes Liam, hiding out in America pretending to be his white wife's servant.

Liam's art theoretically and symbolically carries this underlying oppressive imprint, and in its intertextual relationship with the preacher's story and *The Cattle Killing*'s other stories, (re)inscribes it in seemingly endless concentric patterns. Liam's story pulls the preacher into the reality of Liam's Africa that is simultaneously generated by the oppression of the Xhosa prophecy, and both story and prophecy are the same as other oppressive narratives. In the end, the Old Testament prophecy of God and the paradoxical statement of his salvation is a warning like the deadly cattle-killing prophecy, which also purports to be literally a message from God delivered by the African girl Nongqawuse: "Listen with all your ears, child. You must carry my message to the people. Tell them the plague destroying their herds is God's curse upon those who have forsaken His ways. Tell them we must return to the old ways. The sacred path the ancestors walked. But first the people must kill their cattle" (146). However, the prophecy is the voice of the enemy surreptitiously conveying his oppressive "dream" of black destruction (147), which raises questions about the underlying source of the Old Testament text of prophecy. The prophecy's final promise is that the girl "will return in a happier dream in a new land where the cattle are not dying, the children not dying" (148). This false promise parallels the failure of Liam to find freedom in the new world of America: Liam and his "African brethren [had been] ripped . . . from the land of their fathers to preach false prophecies" (148). This is also the false prophecy of Liam's art, which is the story that he tells the preacher that "paints" his life of American freedom, and the actual painting of his wife to represent their love and freedom after the preacher's fellowship regenerates the literal form of his art. In dealing with Liam, the preacher discovers not the voice or the method of his own saving love story but rather the depth of Liam's oppression and his own. The preacher awakens from the dream of the Xhosa cattle killing in Liam's Africa to the reality of Liam and his wife being burned by white people in the physical place of the Pennsylvania country-side, where the preacher has fallen asleep in the white dream of Liam's story.

When the preacher loses faith, Liam's story and all stories conflate in an intertext of God's prophecy that is a profane signification of God's body as *the* figure of African American oppression. The account starts with a happy rescue, but the murder of Liam and his wife propels the preacher "to Phila-delphia to fight the [raging yellow fever] plague, to purge myself of hate, to find you [the sick woman]" (149).

> I found in that city of brotherly love the country of sickness and dy-ing the African woman's dream [of the cattle killing] foretold. And Philadelphia was a prophecy of other cities to come, as my stay in the village of Radnor [outside Philadelphia] had been prophecy and fulfillment of the city.
>
> Circles within circles. Expanding and contracting at once— boundless, tight as a noose. God's throat, belly, penis, cunt, asshole, the same black ditch. The people an unbroken chain of sausages fed in one end and pulled out the other. A circle without and within, the monstrous python swallowing itself, birthing its tail. (149)

The cattle-killing text is prophecy of the real world of oppression in Phil-adelphia, Philadelphia is prophecy of other cities and the world, and God's body, stripped of all connection to salvation in the preacher's utter despair, is the text of everything. This is the repetitious tautology of life, textuality, and analysis, too.

Instead of concluding with the sacrilegious image of God, the preacher in part two concentrates on the biblically associated fearful certainty of God's revelation through his antithesis of evil and suffering, which the preacher sees in the example of Allen; this prophecy of salvation that resides in the constancy of oppression is the only true one. The epigraph to part two is from Ezekiel: "But I will stretch out my hand against the prophets who have false visions and who foretell lies" (151). But who are the false prophets? It seems that all prophets in *The Cattle Killing* are false because they promise liberation and happiness instead of pain and suffering that are a manifestation of God's will and goodness. At the same time, the prophets' supposed texts of liberation are always intertexts of God's oppressive text of suffering; the prophets' voice of liberation invariably speaks an embedded double voice of oppression that is this same hegemonic oppressive text. All the prophets are false ones and true ones that prophesy the oppression that is a dominant aspect of God's text.

Allen and the preacher, before the latter imagines true prophecy through Allen's abject condition, are first false prophets of liberation and later true prophets of God's text. In part two, the young man goes to Philadelphia and meets Bishop Richard Allen. The events of his life, which include taking his congregation from St. Matthew's to the woods in Radnor, parallel the life of Allen, who took his congregation from the white St. George's church to form a new black church (154). These actions are false prophecies because the new beginnings that the men make for their congregations are continued oppression. The preacher's story also returns to Liam in part two. The opposition to the paradox of Allen's oppressive faith is the open-ended textuality of freedom: Liam paints not "what [he] imagined or [the young preacher] imagined or she imagined, but what could come next. After this time. Next and next. Always unknown. Always free" (182). Significantly, the last image of Liam is not of his death but of his artistry, and the preacher and the metafictional writer's secular stories strengthen the opposition of secular artistry. But these texts lack the uncertain power of God's text that the preacher realizes through his imagination of Allen.

It seems clearly implied that although there is one book of suffering that applies to white people and African Americans—God's book—this text at the same time gets rewritten through the hegemony of white power as the central oppressive intertext that serves white intentions and reifies black oppression. In Wideman's story "Fever" (1989), which has many direct connections of character, theme, and plot to *The Cattle Killing,* a character defines God's universal, ineluctable text for Allen: "You do know, don't you, Allen, that God is a bookseller? He publishes one book—the text of suffering—over and over again. He disguises it between new boards, in different shapes and sizes, prints on varying papers, in many fonts, adds prefaces and postscripts to deceive the buyer, but it's always the same book" (154–55).

God's book of suffering in *The Cattle Killing* is similar, but it is more because white people rewrite it as the black oppressive text through power dynamics that evolve historically and in social, political, and cultural processes. As implied in *The Cattle Killing*, the actual rewriting of the Bible takes place in its translation into English and other Western languages, and in its consequent versions, and more explicitly within oral texts such as the text of the racist white preacher of St. Matthew's. Through Allen's example, the preacher seems to accept the reality of this ambiguously constituted book that is everyone's text but still a uniquely black text created by and simultaneously creating white power. He subtly revises the text while accepting it.

Rewritten in the preacher's imagination, God's text is the changeless essence of terrible grace experienced in constantly changing time; the preacher sees this when he visualizes the story of Allen, utterly bereft of everything but ubiquitous evil as the only assurance that God must be always present in a world that would be unbearable without him.

> [Allen] needed God somewhere, somehow keeping track, weaving the ugliness of what was happening into some larger pattern, a tapestry whose myriad scenes he might never grasp but whose overarching design promised that God's hand was active in this, even this.
>
> And what he'd needed had shone forth. A kind of lightness, giddiness when he'd risen to his feet from the boards of the . . . floor [of the white church that is physically forcing black members to the back to worship]. A whispering in his ear. Yes. Yes. Lightness but also iron . . . Now *he* was standing, touching people's shoulders, nudging, hugging, guiding, gathering, moving the others in a body, not to some shameful margin but out the church door, heads held higher than when they'd entered.
>
> Yes. God was there. A rock he'd leaned on. Pushed into a corner by evil, the power of evil rampant, he'd found that the seeming absence of God was God's best proof. The pang of needing Him, the prospect of a world without Him, evil pressing down, no light, no hope, the impossibility of coping in such a world, where evil has the power to consume you, to consume the world—that pang of urgent need and utter desolation, that stab in the heart, reveals Him. (155)

The Cattle Killing foregrounds the faithful moment of "no light, no hope" as the surest and perhaps the most powerful reality in the preacher's life.

Allen looks for the larger design and purpose of his life that manifests liberation as a progressive new start, but in the preacher's ruminations on him, Allen finds only a confining tautology implying the oppressive textuality that is the center of *The Cattle Killing*. Again, the text itself makes the point very well. When he looks at himself closely, Allen does not know if he wants to be white. He begs for "supernatural assurance and signs" from God (158).

> In his heart he does not wish to be white, to be one of them. He's the man he is. Not some other. Yet he is praying for an easier way than the way opening up for him. Why has he been orphaned in this strange land, in this unimaginable city. Divided first from others, then from himself . . . He does not secretly yearn to be one of the whites. No. No. He is praying for a lifting of the burden that crushes them all, black and white, in their tortured, bitter dealings one with the other. He cannot change what he is and they cannot change what they are, and he cannot pray to God to wipe white people off the face of the earth and also keep his heart free for Christ's mercy, Christ's love, so he is not wishing to be white, but if he calls on Heaven to purge whatever it is the whites fear and hate in him, must it also be a prayer for sweet annihilation. (158–59)

Unlike Old Rowe, who potentially loses the humanizing qualities of self in the dehumanizing vision earlier in the novel, Allen understands the conflict between the Christian ideal and the hatred and retribution that would eliminate white people from the earth, and he is not in the same danger as Rowe. But he cannot avoid asking whether his own prayer to be free of the thing that whites fear is for the "sweet annihilation" of his black self. Blackness and whiteness seem to be indelibly written texts that cannot change, and since he cannot pray for white annihilation to solve the problem, he must ask if he wants to annihilate his own self and be white. The inability to see a liberated black self in a world of essentialized racial character, a world that he cannot envision without white people to whom he can only capitulate, could indicate a deep internalization of an oppressive text of whiteness, with the Bible and white oral texts derived from the Bible, such as St. Matthew's white preacher's, being its central aspects.

In the preacher's story, Allen sees an image of himself as a leader and prophet who throws open the way to a new world, but this is a doubtful vision of limited assurance. As he prays, the figure of the receding ocean as a portal that brought him to the American world is like the sea that brought Moses and the Jews out of captivity to freedom (159; Exodus 13). He rises up to go forward in spite of all his doubt and irresolution, but new beginnings are a real question for Allen, particularly in the later context of the novel.

The strength Allen finds in faith through the utter hopelessness of oppression, desolation, and pain is much different than the inner light that the preacher lived by and had faith in. The burning of the black orphans of the Philadelphia plague in the darkness of the cellar where the whites have sequestered them forces the preacher to the despair that gives him his final view of Allen (196–97). The preacher realizes that his erstwhile inner light now potentially reveals only black destruction; this realization is part of his movement to Allen's position of "no light, no hope." The young preacher has stopped praying but considers one last "prayer not to any god anyone has named." But the prayer "might boomerang" him to the beginning of his own birth, and he might "see everything in a blast of white light that also shouts *no no no* because surely as the light reveals it also separates. The seed of him shrivels. His mother moans. Both of them shot and tossed in a ditch beside the road" (199). The "inner light" utterly fails here, and the young preacher is hurled into total desolation and despair, which is paradoxically the presence and proof of God. The preacher rebelled against Allen and only wanted to hurt him by revealing his heresy. Allen, however, responded kindly and moved forward with his sermon: "*From this blackened pit* [of the burned cellar], *from the precious ashes of these little ones called to Jesus' side, the hopes of our people will rise again*" (204). So Allen goes on, and this movement is impressive. But what is much greater than his achievement as measured in progressive change is the strength of his faith as revealed in suffering: "The good bishop's capacity for pain, for bearing pain others cannot bear, is endless." The faith of the endless moment that Allen suffers sounds surer and more powerful than the open-ended text of the secular that *The Cattle Killing* tries to create.

The preacher comes to the point where he must acknowledge the power and significance of God's salvation manifested in the ability of African Americans to suffer and survive the evil of white people with an almost godly power. Through this recognition, the text subtly (re)writes the already rewritten white oppressive text by emphasizing the sheer power of faith in a relationship to an inscrutable God who allows evil, thus placing evil racist white power in the background. The rewriting at least extrapolates somewhat and sets some potential of faith against worldly oppression, whose reality is even more insidious because of its centering in textuality. This is obviously still a problematized conceptualization realized in a context that fails to negate power that serves white oppression. It allows God's suffering and that imposed by whites to remain virtually synonymous, and thus in a sense abdicates African American political and social struggle to faith in the existence of a God who is beyond this world but whom the preacher cannot clearly contemplate through omnipresent grief and pain. This conceptualization is not Christian in its failure to perceive beyond the agony of the moment, but it is Christianlike in its vision of faithful suffering and sacrifice. So while what the preacher imagines implies more than just a hopeless view determined by racism, it is also inadequate and not what the metafictional writer wants.

It is important to reemphasize that *The Cattle Killing* conceives all of this in the realm of Western textuality that, *because it is linguistic*, obfuscates its true role in an oppressive, lethal, and invisible process that is still murky and deadly when made visible by critique. *The Cattle Killing*'s analysis is inconclusive because it is encompassed by the complex history and culture that it portrays and by the oppressive textuality that controls all of it. Everything flows together textually, and it is hard to understand where different realities begin and what the various relationships among them are. Making all of this clear and perceptible, and thus liberating, is the responsibility that the narrative carries. But the narrative reveals a self-awareness that it works against itself because it is part of the intricate intertext that poses its own confusing critical tautology. It is clear, however, that oppression of African Americans does reside in written and oral textuality and so, potentially, does liberation. Still, there are no clear answers. The preacher literally stutters and almost loses the thread of his story but then looks into the future where the story may continue to be told with liberating potential (204–08). The metafictional writer appears as the character Wideman in the epilogue and attempts to give the preacher's life further potential by placing it in another story about the preacher's brother that has "real life" liberating significance (209–12). In spite of these endings, *The Cattle Killing* presents itself as a tentative secular narrative, and according to its own theory it shows uncertainty about liberation.

The power of Allen's moment of faith in God seems equally certain, not because it will bring change and liberation, but because pervasive evil and commensurate African American strength do, in the context of African American faithful belief, make God real. *The Cattle Killing* implies that no other theory works any better, and very few work as well. This is true because it is unimaginable to many African Americans, and apparently to the metafictional writer, too, that black people could have survived oppression without God. Looking at it all, one would find the simple response of Bess to the death of her innocent infant relative in Wideman's *Hiding Place* (1981) an appropriate explanation: "Jesus and Good God Almighty cause what else you gon say" (130). Somewhat strangely, the vision of the metafictional writer, unlike that of the grim, pessimistic Bess, is an Old Testament view that emphasizes the wrath of God and finds less assurance in New Testament grace. This is, however, theoretically the perspective of the individual writer, and while it is different from the broader Christian view held by many African Americans, it does show the reality of the same kind of faith. Bess and the metafictional writer are nonbelievers who reach the inexorable conclusion of the paradox of God derived from the Bible that is more persuasive because of their nonbelief.

The Cattle Killing is a self-conscious postmodern novel, but God and the Bible, implicitly the ultimate postmodern text, are its central, albeit contested, focuses in trying to imagine a liberated African American reality. The text foregrounds the sacred and religious even though the metafictional writer and the young preacher ultimately disavow them. This is consistent, however, with Wideman's fiction from the very beginning. In the early work, which foregrounded a modernist tradition opposed in ideology and practice to black religious tradition, the texts still revealed the importance of the sacred and religious to African American culture traditionally. The same is true in *The Cattle Killing*. The difference is that the novel's postmodern form and theme are more congruent with a critique of the sacred and spiritual from complex perspectives that are revealing. God remains a powerful presence conceived in language and narrative but nevertheless seemingly a final cause, although hidden in enigma and irresolvable paradox, because the story unavoidably creates him, especially for African Americans. For the young preacher, apparently God and religion are necessary because he cannot escape his African American cultural mooring, although he loses his belief. And in spite of never being a believer, the metafictional writer finds God in spite of himself as he challenges God, the Bible, and religion.

CHAPTER 4

Rejecting God and Redefining Faith

Portrayals of Black Women's Spirituality

FROM THE STANDPOINT OF its revision of African American cultural perspective and interrogation of the ethos as it relates to the spiritual and trans-secular, *The Color Purple* (1982) is more complex than it may initially appear to be. On the surface, it seems to be clearly different because it is a bolder and more revolutionary text than *The Cattle Killing* (1996) and *Beloved* (1987), the two rich, innovative postmodern texts covered in the last chapter. It shows none of *The Cattle Killing's* angst about the power of biblical textuality and its creation of a God textually complicit in oppression, but it paradoxically reflects the theological tradition in African American culture as it critiques and rejects it, somewhat like *The Cattle Killing* does. Through a crafty parody, Morrison's novel revises the biblical and Christian and invests spiritual potential in black women. *The Color Purple* does not present the same kind of complex, thoroughgoing parody that uses biblical allusion and structural parallel that produces incongruity. It does parody the Bible and the patriarchy to empower black women as *Beloved* does, but this part of its critique is more straightforward.

In these terms of comparison, Gloria Naylor's *Mama Day* (1988) is not a complex biblical parody like *Beloved* or one embedded with its own paradox like *The Color Purple*. It is an intricate, dense black woman's text that through the process of its complicated narrative decenters the patriarchy and recreates the African American cultural tradition around black women. The novel's complexity is a product of the broad-ranging inclusiveness of its cultural portrayal of the sacred, spiritual, and supernatural, which encompasses the mythical/historical, the biblical/Christian, and the non-Christian/non-Western religious and "pagan," and the good, the evil, and the morally ambiguous. The text is so tightly interwoven thematically and structurally that parts become hidden in the obscurity of the culture's mythical, spiritual, and supernatural reality that is its very source. The text presents a theory of its narrative that implies that structure and theme replicate what is obscure, abstract, and barely perceptible, although deeply felt, in the culture itself. Critics have focused on *Mama Day*'s subversion of male standards, which are grounded in the Judeo-Christian tradition and the text of the Bible, but this is only one part of a vast, intricate exposé that at the same time shows the importance of the biblical/Christian as well as other aspects of the African American tradition that oppose it theologically and ideologically. The subversion of the patriarchy is infused interstitially throughout the novel's structure in a fashion that makes its general effect somewhat indirect. Overall, this aspect of its political critique stands out, but the narrative also highlights diverse thematic features in a depiction of folk syncretism where disparate beliefs and practices often interrelate. This separates *Mama Day* from the more direct challenge of *The Color Purple* and even from the indirect but eviscerating critique of *Beloved*. In the scope of my analysis, the novel is important because of everything that it attempts to reveal about the sacred, spiritual, and supernatural in African American culture and also for the richness that it succeeds in showing.

Celie's story in *The Color Purple* implies a crucial problem for many who do not accept the Bible by faith or who think with a second mind beyond faith. The inferior status of women is inscribed in the essence of life through the myth of the Edenic beginning, particularly in the story of the fall from Eden, and is consistently written throughout the Bible. First, in Genesis 2:23, God creates woman from the body of man, but even more than this, in Genesis 3 woman is responsible for the introduction of sin into human existence and the consequent retribution of banishment from Eden. God's punishment of woman is specific: "Unto the woman he said, I will greatly multiply thy sorrow and thy conception; in sorrow thou shalt bring forth children; and thy desire shall be to thy husband, and he shall rule over thee" (Genesis 3:16). In the Old Testament, this translates into a patriarchal story in which men almost always rule and are foremost and prominent in God's sight. The dispensation of the New Testament changes little, if anything. Perhaps the most important voice in the New Testament after Jesus Christ's is the apostle Paul's; in his epistles to the various churches that he has established, he makes clear the position of women. For example, he says in his first letter to the Corinthians: "For God is not the author of confusion, but of peace, as in all churches of the saints. Let your women keep silence in the churches: for it is not permitted unto them to speak; but they are commanded to be under obedience, as also saith the law. And if they will learn any thing, let them ask their husbands at home: for it is a shame for women to speak in the church" (1 Corinthians 14:33–35). Nothing in the Bible tells man to be abusive and oppressive, but nevertheless it is the belief that woman is subordinate and that man rules her that has produced the concept of male privilege and the consequent misogyny, oppression, and abuse.

As a text, the Bible always leaves open the imagination of a parallel story of the daily lives of women relegated to second-class status by God in the sacred setting; this imagined secular world implies questions of reason and justice verboten by belief in God's sacred omnipotence and by faith in his benevolence. The Bible usually empowers women by expressing their desires when it shows their submissive relationships to God and direct or indirect supplication to him for affliction, or when it reveals their subversiveness that is a part of God's plan. However, their feelings about oppression and terror caused by the men who have power over them is never portrayed. The life of Rebekah as depicted in Genesis 25–27 shows a woman whom the Bible gives some voice and empowerment because she is in touch with God's will. Her husband Isaac successfully entreats the Lord for her barrenness, and she conceives Jacob and Esau (Genesis 25:21–34). Rebekah inquires of the Lord about the turmoil that she feels with the two children in her womb, and the Lord tells her that the younger son Jacob will rule over the elder Esau (Genesis 25:22–23). Through her machinations, she deceives Isaac and Esau to make this true (Genesis 27). In 2 Samuel 11–12, Bathsheba conceives the great King Solomon by her husband King David (2 Samuel 12:24–25). However, before this happens, David saw her, "took her," and then killed her husband before making her his wife. The only reference to Bathsheba's feelings is that when she "heard that Uriah her husband was dead, she mourned for her husband" (2 Samuel 11:4–27). The voice and story of Bathsheba's pain and suffering are stifled in the biblical unfolding of the will of God. She has no recourse for her violation and victimization, which do not exist anyway because they are not written into the narrative.

The Color Purple foregrounds the experience of Celie who suffers the terrors of men because of her belief in the sacred image of God, who is a white man; from one important perspective, the novel is a woman's reimagination of her own story of oppression consequent to male power that the Bible never tells. *The Color Purple* is especially revolutionary in the context of the discourse of African American life and literature, which seldom sets up clear oppositions between the sacred text of the Bible and concomitant sacred beliefs and secular practices, nor makes a negative critique of the sacred explicit. Black society, like American society, is patriarchal, but patriarchal conception does not determine what really happens in interaction between people. African Americans separate daily life and the realm of experience where they deal with the sacredness of God. Many women take Celie's stand toward men and the patriarchy, while few directly interrogate biblical doctrine and redefine God as she does. Not many throw defiance in the face of God by directly challenging the Bible as his divine word and the sacredness of God grounded in the text of the Bible. The idea of God is a defining part of the cultural ethos kept on an abstract level, and his text, the Bible, is used selectively without reference to sections inconsistent with actions in secular life. Therefore, it is not the trenchant analysis of the patriarchy in secular life but the satiric treatment of the Bible and the redefinition of God, along with the novel's implied critique of the Bible's depiction of women, that are so bold because they are contrary to African American literary and traditional practice. However, through the other characterizations, the text portrays an overall conception of God and African American tradition that is somewhat more complex and conflicted than Celie's central point of view. Overall, the novel maintains its subversive approach to the Bible as a text but still juxtaposes a more conventional African American story of struggle and faith with the sacrilegious treatment of God and the Christian. *The Color Purple* radically subverts the sacred spirituality of the biblical God, exposing him as an oppressive textual construction of the patriarchy and thereby subverting the patriarchy, but it parallels its main critique with a less radical one that adheres to the deconstruction of biblical images while retaining faith in God's sacred agency.

Through the influence of Shug Avery, Celie totally redefines her life, but initially she has only a latent consciousness of her own oppression by God and the patriarchy. The voice that imposes itself at the beginning of Celie's first letter to God—"*You better not never tell nobody but God. It'd kill your mammy*" (3)—suggests a subliminal attitude that mocks her belief and a brutal God whom she places beyond the bounds of questions about the suffering that he imposes in life. Throughout significant parts of the text, Celie invokes the God of the Bible who oppresses her in a world in which he has privileged men, white men first and foremost, but black men in Celie's most immediate life. Celie expresses faith by telling God the unspeakable in letters and by enduring hardship and misery as her way to eternal life in heaven. She believes that "long as I can spell G-o-d I got somebody along" (18) and that "life soon be over . . . Heaven last all ways" (39).

She evolves to a conscious revolutionary spirituality that liberates her from God and male domination. Celie first has to see that the Bible is a white text constructed by white people, and then she must divest herself of its influence before she can reject the Judeo-Christian God and live in opposition and defiance of him. Celie initially insists to Shug that God wrote the Bible and white folks had nothing to do with it (166), but Shug has a strong response: "How come he look just like them, then? . . . Only bigger? And a heap more hair. How come the bible just like everything else they make, all about them doing one thing and another, and all the colored folks doing is gitting cursed?" Shug continues: "Ain't no way to read the bible and not think God white . . . When I found out I thought God was white and a man, I lost interest. You mad cause he don't seem to listen to your prayers. Humph! Do the [white] mayor listen to anything colored say?" She says that man puts his image and voice everywhere so that "you think he God. But he ain't. Whenever you trying to pray, and man plop himself on the other end of it, tell him to git lost . . . Conjure up flowers, wind, water, a big rock" (168). Shug basically shows Celie that women empower God by allowing men privilege. Celie had already begun to believe that God was deaf and indifferent (164). She now essentially takes away God's power as an oppressive factor in life when she realizes that He is the symbol that oppresses. Celie then contends with God, who has no more power than she does: "Us fight. I hardly pray at all. Every time I conjure up a rock, I throw it" (168).

Celie recreates a God that manifests *It*-self in the individual and an animistic "Everything" and that enjoys pleasing people and having pleasure, including the pleasure of heterosexual sex and lesbianism. But God is an "It" that is "Everything that is or ever was or ever will be" (167). God is first and foremost within Celie, and when she feels pleasure, she relates to God. As Shug reminds her, God is in the good feeling of their sexual intercourse.

Celie later explains God in terms of smoking reefer and its effects: "I smoke when I want to talk to God. I smoke when I want to make love. Lately I feel like me and God make love just fine anyhow. Whether I smoke reefer or not" (187). Celie writes the last letter to the animistic God who is the opposite of the patriarchal: "Dear God. Dear stars, dear trees, dear sky, dear peoples. Dear Everything. Dear God" (242).

Celie's God gives her the voice that oppressed women in the Bible never have; she breaks the biblical hegemony and exposes the bestiality of men hidden by reverence to the patriarchal God. In the process of her development, she vividly describes the horror of rapes, beatings, and verbal abuse that women under the control of God and men in the Bible must have experienced, but the Bible fails to write this reality into its story. Men are deaf and insensitive to the suffering of women just like the biblical God, and in Celie's view, there is no divine mystery behind God and his plan that makes women secondary to men. Unlike the women in the Bible who are empowered to the extent that they do the will of God and thus fulfill the privilege and destiny of men, Celie comes to her full human realization as she becomes increasingly blasphemous to God and defiant to men.

The novel never undercuts its critique of the Bible as a white patriarchal text or Celie's successful opposition to men who have power because of its textual hegemony, but the same is not true for the subversion of the concept of God as a sacred agent in African American life. The African American community in *The Color Purple* is a recognizable one full of "sinners" in secular life who nevertheless maintain faith in God. In part, through the portrayal of the community around Celie, the novel reconstitutes a more traditional concept of the spirituality of God.

Even Shug, the self-described "sinner" who most contributes to Celie's revolutionary spiritual conversion, speaks in a contradictory voice regarding her belief in God. Shug cites the example of Christ when Celie says that it is hard not to kill the abusive Albert: "Hard to be Christ too, say Shug. But he manage. Remember that. Thou Shalt Not Kill, He said. And probably wanted to add on to that, Starting with me. He knowed the fools he was dealing with" (122). This occurs at a relatively early stage in Celie's spiritual development, and Shug may be relating to her in the most persuasive terms that she can instead of expressing her true belief. Later when Shug is inculcating the most radical ideas about God and spirituality, she still seems to contradict her dominant attitude to God. Celie is blaspheming, and Shug cautions her: "You better hush. God might hear you" (164). This sounds like a sarcastic remark made briefly and in passing, but Shug makes more extensive comments: "She talk and she talk, trying to budge me way from blasphemy. But I blaspheme much as I want to." On one hand, Shug may be forcing Celie to formulate new ideas by advocating their opposition. However, it is also possible that Shug speaks with a contradictory voice because even the most revolutionary thinkers such as she have difficulty canceling the reality of God. Celie seems to affirm this herself at the time that she fully rejects the traditional God: "All my life I never care what people thought bout nothing I did . . . But deep in my heart I care about God. What he going to think. And come to find out, he don't think. Just sit up there glorying in being deaf, I reckon. But it ain't easy, trying to do without God. Even if you know he ain't there, trying to do without him is a strain" (164). Celie is clearly talking about the patriarchal God here, and perhaps what she says partly explains Shug's contradictory stance.

Generally, the novel's African American community pursues a life of "sin" and pleasure without disrupting their sacred belief and ritual, and its women are even capable of violating church ritual while keeping the concept of God sacrosanct. Shug suggests the formal separation between the secular and sacred that allows the two to exist simultaneously. She proudly claims the "devils music," but sets it apart from the church. She says that the woman singing at Harpo's juke joint sounds as if she "can't git her ass *out* the church. Folks don't know whether to dance or creep to the mourner's bench" (98–99). Unlike Shug, Sofia is a revolutionary woman who stays within the general context of the community's traditional belief in God. Throughout the novel, she defies male domination as strongly as Shug, and in the case of her mother's funeral, insists that she and her sisters be pallbearers, thus violating the codes of the church that demand that only men carry out certain ceremonies (185–88). Sofia thinks of life in terms of a conventional Christian journey though: "Mama fight the good fight. If there's a glory anywhere she right in the middle of it" (186). Sofia is not so overly sanctified that she will not smoke reefer with Celie and others, and she and Harpo hear the spiritual humming of Celie's "Everything" under its influence (187–88). But her shock at Celie's reference to making love with God registers her central traditional belief. She and Harpo can experience a lot of what Celie feels, but they separate sacred belief from the secular (as represented by the juke joint). Besides separating them, the members of the community also amalgamate the secular world with the religious and address the former in terms of biblical doctrine. The preacher sometimes takes for his text the lives of "sinners" such as Shug, and the same women who show illicit sexual interest in Albert while they are at church also affirm the preacher's condemnation of Shug for improper sexual behavior. These women would not necessarily act any differently than Shug outside the church, but the church nevertheless gives them a higher forum to criticize her. No matter how much they may stray from it in reality, a concept of the sacred is the standard.

Ironically, however, the main aspect of the text that presents the opposing relevance and power of the Christian God is the characterization of Celie's sister Nettie, with whom she has a strong affinity. The novel establishes the sisters' similarity of belief, separates them, and keeps traditional spiritual belief largely whole through Nettie.

The sisters' undying love conceals the fact that the development of Nettie's theology in her letters retains a focus on God that greatly contrasts Celie's spiritual evolution. The women always have the deepest feeling for each other, as Celie's sacrifices for Nettie and Nettie's sympathy for her sister show while they are together in youth, and Nettie makes this love for Celie primary in her letters. But she emphasizes a reverence for God, too. In the first letter to Celie, Nettie says that she saved herself from Albert's sexual advances with the help of God (107), and later Nettie states that the Olinkas, among whom she is a missionary, most need Christ along with good medical advice. She speaks strongly of the Christian charity and love in her missionary work, and sees the will of God and the working of a miracle in her being sent to take care of Celie's children (111–12). Generally, she implies the belief that God is all-important, which she has shared with Celie from the beginning.

For Nettie, God changes symbolically but not substantively; she effaces images of God while retaining the Judeo-Christian spiritual substance. Her development starts with an analysis of the pictures in the Bible: "All the Ethiopians in the bible were colored. It had never occurred to me, though when you read the bible it is perfectly plain if you pay attention only to the words. It is the pictures in the bible that fool you. The pictures that illustrate the words. All of the people are white and so you just think all the people from the bible were white too. But really *white* white people lived somewhere else during those times. That's why the bible says that Jesus had hair like lamb's wool. Lamb's wool is not straight, Celie. It isn't even curly" (113).

Nettie later goes beyond reimaging Christ to destroying the image of God completely (218). She then believes that God is a spirit who should not have an image and that she and her husband Samuel, a preacher, should "found a new church in our community that has no idols in it whatsoever, in which each person's spirit is encouraged to seek God directly, his belief that it is possible strengthened by us as a people who also believe." This is reminiscent of Celie's attack on the image of God as a white man, but Nettie's words have none of Celie's irreverence. She focuses not so much on the distortion of the text of the Bible as its pictorial symbols, which she implies that white people added, and she seeks a way to reinstitute the traditional God in a Christian church while taking away his power as a white oppressor.

It would also seem that Nettie's more traditional faith has kept her safe and made her good at the same time that the patriarchal God has abused Celie and has been the cause of her revolution. Nettie is sexually inviolate, protected from her stepfather Alphonso by Celie "with God help" (5) and saved from Albert by her own strength through the power of God (107), and she always remains the sexually virtuous woman in the context of biblical theology. She is a virgin until she and Samuel declare their love for each other, and is careful to show that nothing about this love is illicit. She loved him all along, apparently before his wife died, but did not know it because she felt friendship and respect for him and his marital relationship. Her realization of how she feels occurs when Nettie consoles Samuel in his despair about their missionary work: "Celie, it seemed as good a time as any to put my arms around him. Which I did. And words long buried in my heart crept to my lips. I stroked his dear head and face and I called him darling and dear. And I'm afraid, dear, dear Celie, that concern and passion soon ran away with us" (201). She asks her sister not to judge her too harshly for her forward behavior and for the feeling of "total joy" when she is "transported by ecstasy in Samuel's arms." She now feels free to express her "bodily" love for him "*as a man*," but the love is more spiritual than physical: "And I love his dear eyes in which the vulnerability and beauty of his soul can be plainly read." Nettie's life has been a hard journey of faith and steadfastness that leads to spiritual fulfillment in this relationship. The image of God has changed for her, but the concept of God's spirituality that guides her life has not changed. Her desire to establish a new church with Samuel shows this.

Nettie's traditional faith is an integral part of Celie's untraditional transformation. Nettie reinvents their life story (148–50). She tells Celie the "once upon a time" tale about the lynching of their biological father and the consequent insanity and death of their mother, which also erases the fact that incest, "part of the devil's plan" according to Celie earlier (126), produced Celie's two children. However, Celie finds accusation of God in the story: "My daddy lynch. My mama crazy. All my little half-brothers and sisters no kin to me. My children not my sister and brother. Pa not pa" (151). God "must be sleep." On the other hand, tears soak Nettie's blouse when she hears the details of the story from Samuel, to a significant extent because she finds the agency of God in everything that has happened to them. Their stepfather gave away Celie's children to Samuel and his wife Corrine, and Samuel felt that God was answering his and his wife's prayers for children. Nettie's tone in telling the story, as well as what she said earlier about God sending her to Samuel and Corrine to take care of Celie's children, implies that she shares Samuel's belief. Nettie's reinvention manifests her faith while it undercuts Celie's. In a sense, the story reveals God speaking through Nettie in conventional terms at the same time that it leads to Celie's radical ideology. This is ironic, but the point is that the traditional has a bearing on and balances the untraditional.

Further, Nettie's story about the reversal that changes her and Celie's genesis is derived from the biblical gospels in which Jesus often speaks in parables and related paradoxes to show the wonders of God. Jesus almost always talks figuratively to show the unveiling of God's plan, and his general message about faith is often ensconced in paradox that is related to parable. The parables of the barren fig tree in Luke 13 and of the prodigal son in Luke 15 are well known. Two paradoxes built on reversals are Matthew 10:39— "He that findeth his life shall lose it: and he that loseth his life for my sake shall find it"—and Mark 10:33—"But many that are first shall be last; and the last first." Diane Scholl argues that the "'riddling' nature of Jesus' teachings conspires with the unpredictability of the parables to create a 'world of paradox' essentially similar to Celie's world of seeming radical disorder, an improbable world of shifting meanings in which practically no one at the end occupies the same place in which he or she began . . . the world of the novel is figuratively turned upside down in the course of Celie's changing fortunes; and such radical alterations, the stuff and substance of the Gospels' paradoxical stories, inform the story of Celie with an energy that is distinctly biblical" (263–64). Nettie's story is not the entire parabolic source of Celie's, but it is a major influence. Especially in light of her more traditional theology,

Nettie speaks in the biblically inspired voice like Jesus' that "unsettle[s] our complacency . . . prevent[s] our ossification . . . [and] open[s] up new possibilities that usher in the kingdom of God. Walker's methodical destruction of all our social certainties is her means to the revelation, her provocative challenge issued in the spirit and the narrative technique of the Gospels."[1] As a form of biblical parable, Nettie's story takes on an even stronger resonance of traditional faith that juxtaposes Celie's radical theology.

It is important that Celie attacks and rejects the biblical construction of God but does not comment on Nettie's affirmation of spirituality based on a reconstructed biblical theology that includes God. Nettie says that it is not the actual words of the Bible that distort Christianity. There is nothing wrong with the words describing Jesus Christ in the Bible, but the "pictures that illustrate the words" are misleading (113). Neither Jesus nor God is white in the Bible, but the pictures make Jesus, and therefore implicitly God, white. Nettie and Celie see the oppressive power of biblical symbols; the difference is that the symbols are pictorial and linguistic, respectively. Nettie wants to deconstruct all of God's pictorial images to retain his sacred spiritual substance, but the spiritual is essentially the same. Nettie does not, like Shug and Celie, clearly reject the traditional maleness of God. She calls God "he" but says that he does not need a specific form or image: "Most people think *he* has to look like something or someone—a roofleaf [the Olinka god] or Christ—but [Samuel and I] don't. And not being tied to what God looks like, frees us" (218, italics mine). She feels liberated like Celie, but her general perspective is contrary to Celie's. Although she is uneducated, Celie is quite capable of analyzing the difference between her ideas and her sister's—as she demonstrates when she analyzes other problems in the novel—but she does not. The fury of Celie's accusation of God goes into a letter to God initially (151) and then into the letters to Nettie, starting with Celie's assertion that she no longer writes to God but to Nettie (164), and she clearly implies a rejection of much of the religion that Nettie stands for. Although she writes to Nettie, she never speaks to her in an oppositional tone or directly acknowledges or addresses their differences. Nettie writes that they "must have long talks about" her idea that they should destroy images of God and encourage each person to seek God directly in the spirit (218). Celie does not take this opportunity to respond to the similarity or the larger difference between their views.

Nettie educates Celie through her letters, but Celie does not influence Nettie. While the education that Nettie gives her sister is largely about the world, it is still significant that the theology that she develops during her greater experience stands against Celie's without an explicit conflict. The text minimizes the potential differences between the sisters' theology through the fact that Celie's letters return unopened and Nettie never reads them (216).

Like the subtle implications of plot details that undermine the primary narrative theme, the text's formal structure is complicit in mitigating its own radical portrayal of God's spirituality. *The Color Purple* ends as Nettie returns home from Africa, not having heard from or seen Celie in decades. The book concludes before Celie and Nettie can discuss theology, and they never have to come to terms with Celie's belief and lesbianism. It would seem that Celie's religious blasphemy, which definitely shocks Sofia and perhaps even Shug, and probably her sexual lifestyle would be a problem for Nettie. The happy ending obfuscates any potential conflicts that would follow the reunion. The story of the reversal in their lives that Nettie has told has changed them, but like the biblical parables that influence it, the story could not be an aspect of a romantic future as the ending may suggest. The conclusion covers up the results of all the characters' psychological scars and the resulting consequences in their interactions. This final underlying reality of the text is congruent with biblical parable and paradox in which great change that is unexpected and positive does not negate that life is an ongoing struggle that continuously requires faith. Everything that she has said indicates that Nettie would understand this and continue to live accordingly. The good ending therefore hides the biblical implications of faith and faithful living woven subtly beneath the main narrative. Generally, Celie's life and revolutionary character are in the foreground in the novel, but beneath this Nettie's traditional belief stands implicitly and without direct challenge.

In summary, a narrative such as Nettie's might not be necessary if the attack on God and the biblical, which are central to African American cultural tradition, were not so direct and forceful, but given that it is, the novel reinforces the tradition while undercutting it. The "author" inserts herself at the end and therefore more closely associates herself with the text's overall radical portrayal of spirituality. A postscript reads, "I thank everybody in this book for coming. A. W., author and medium" (245), which relates back to the dedication, "*To the Spirit:* / Without whose assistance / Neither this book /

Nor I / Would have been / Written." The "author" being the "medium" who has power and invokes the spirit is clearly in opposition to the tradition of sacred belief in African American culture, but the "author" does write the long and elaborately worked out characterization of Nettie and the portrayal of her theology that respects that tradition. There are many different ways that one can read this, but in the context of my analysis, as Celie says, "It ain't easy, trying to do without God. Even if you know he ain't there, trying to do without him is a strain." I would add that not only is there a strain because God is missing but there is, from the cultural perspective, the possibility that the defiance of God is dangerous. This is especially true because of the "blasphemy" in the text, which shocks even its characters who are "sinners." No matter what the reality of life may be, African American culture adheres to respect for God and the Bible, and refrains from disrespect in word and religious ritual, if not in secular practice. In the novel, the strong rejection of God generates an opposing narrative and other conflicting narrative fragments that restore some of God's traditional spirituality while still critiquing the text of the Bible, including its patriarchal imaging of God, without totally subverting it. This may not be what the "author" is doing consciously, but it is certainly suggested by the counternarrative about Nettie and also by the portrayal of aspects of the community around Celie. It is almost as if certain cultural elements in the story pull it back from its main political direction by virtue of their traditional power.[2]

According to academic criticism of the novel, Nettie's comments often lack political awareness and perceptiveness, but the main body of this criticism misses the point that through Nettie the novel significantly situates traditional cultural belief and practice alongside liberating political ideology. The failure to address the culture outside is related to practice within the academy. In "Alice Walker's *The Color Purple:* Redefining God and (Re)claiming the Spirit Within," Jeannine Thyreen shows that feminist, racial, and other kinds of academic approaches to the novel dominate the criticism about it, while few commentators focus on its portrayal of religion and God. To show how central the theological is in the text, Thyreen quotes Walker's "Preface to the Tenth Anniversary Edition" of *The Color Purple* stating that it was a theological work (49). Critiques that deal with the novel's theology are infrequent because, in terms of the postmodern thinking that is a staple of the academy, God can be dismissed; God is only a constructed truth that can be deconstructed, just like any other supposed transcendental truth.

Thyreen asks: "Does this awareness of the relativity in conceptualizing God lead to an eternal abyss of deconstructing notions of God? Yes. But this need not be seen in a negative light. Hope can be found in such an activity of redefining God, as in *The Color Purple*" (50–51). If God is no different than any other oppressive construct that the academy deconstructs with post-modern analysis, then deconstructing God is a worthwhile academic political project, too.[3] Thyreen shows that because of restrictive academic practices, critics shy away from an aspect of the novel where an important interrogation of oppressive beliefs occurs.[4]

Critics not only ignore an important part of the potential political critique because of the general proclivity within the academy to disregard God, but they fail to consider adequately the specific theological tradition of African American culture outside the academy. The novel and its author have an investment in the culture, although it may be a conflicted one, and the culture holds to the sacred tradition of God and the Bible, even given all of the contradictions of action in secular life. Black people tend to make the sacred a part of individual and community social and political struggle where they can effectively do so, and to separate the sacred and secular to retain both where they cannot, but generally the tradition of belief in God remains essential to the lives of African Americans, including their social and political action.[5] So it is not true that the sacred tradition stops African Americans from fighting socially and politically and from living their lives in revolutionary terms. Therefore, the failure to deal with the theological cannot be justified by saying that it separates the culture, and therefore the academy's critique, from the political and social. The relative lack of analysis of the theological in academic criticism about novels like *The Color Purple* is amazing in light of the cultural centrality of belief in God for African Americans, even for African American students in colleges and universities. The academy's critical commentary has been revolutionary and good, but it has largely neglected the complexity of the culture.[6] A significant part of this complexity resides in apparent contradiction. Sacred and biblical beliefs in effect maintain the status quo inside and outside the culture, and individual and community practices focus toward political and social change. However, the secular and sacred work together historically and in the present for overall survival and enhancement of life.

Gloria Naylor's *Mama Day* is set in Willow Springs, a mythical all-black island off the coasts of Georgia and South Carolina that belongs to neither state. The novel portrays a broad range of African American ritual, practice, and tenet, but Mama Day, her sister Abigail, and others share central values and a belief in God that are, in essence, Christian. Mama and Abigail show their disdain for church people and practices, but live by a strong faith in God, whom they conceive in biblical terms and often invoke. Further, the text generally satirizes the rituals, practices, and conventions of the organized Christian church, but human values common to Christianity and other religions, and supported by belief in the Christian God, are more important than any others in the text's depiction of black communal tradition. The faithful serve a benevolent God (whom the text always refers to as "He") who manifests himself in nature and speaks to them through the Bible in times of trouble, as shown by Abigail's recourse to Bible reading during the hurricane (249–51). God is somehow inscrutably in control of the universe, in spite of abundant oppression and suffering. He is not indicted for complicity in oppression as He is in *The Color Purple*, but it is necessary for people to strive constantly to find the right and good in the world in the midst of so much that is evil and bad.

Although God is "He," African American women, Mama and Abigail especially, are the primary characters who wage spiritual and faithful struggle that is essentially, although not exclusively, Christian. The novel's most immediate focus is the mysterious travail and death of two women of the Day family with the same name, Peace, and two named Grace and Hope. However, it also portrays their female descendants in the present using their greater depth of humanity, which is inherent in women, to resurrect and sustain hope, peace, and love. Mama Day tells her niece Cocoa about the superiority of women: "we got more going for us than them. A good woman is worth two good men any day when she puts her mind to it. So the little bit we gotta give up, we don't miss half as much" (240). By foregrounding the importance of women and satirizing church convention and custom, the novel achieves much of the subversive effect of *The Color Purple* without directly confronting the patriarchal god and African American traditional sacred belief as Walker's text does. Naylor's novel encompasses the African American biblical/Christian tradition and expands it by centering women and suggesting a traditional syncretism of the moral and natural that has African resonance. Through their spirituality and faith grounded in the folk ethos, women achieve hope, peace, and love according to the moral *and* natural order of God in his mysteriously, contradictorily fated world replete with evil, hatred, and suffering.[7]

The narrative starts with a theory of Willow Springs as a primal, mythical African American reality. The story of Willow Springs can be heard if one
listens to the internal voice of the self. At the end of an introductory section
that defines Willow Springs, the narrator says: "Think about it: ain't nobody
really talking to you. We're sitting here in Willow Springs, and you're God-
knows-where. It's August 1999—ain't but a slim chance it's the same season
where you are. Uh, huh, listen. Really listen this time: the only voice is your
own. But you done just heard about the legend of Sapphira Wade, though
nobody here breathes her name. You done heard it the way we know it, sitting on our porches and shelling June peas, quieting the midnight cough of
a baby, taking apart the engine of a car—you done heard it without a single
living soul saying a word" (10). We know the African American reality encompassed in the myth of Willow Springs through the text's narrative, but
we also feel it subconsciously in the rhythms of our lives. It entails a shadowy African past, a history of slavery followed by freedom, and endless personal and family stories of success and failure.[8] In the novel, Sapphira Wade
is the Great Mother figure who embodies the mythical genesis of Willow
Springs. Her family line is Mama Day's. Nobody in Willow Springs, including Mama Day, consciously knows the name of Sapphira Wade, but people
are nevertheless aware of who she is on the level of understanding that is beneath words in subconscious being. On one level, the text of *Mama Day* is a
linguistic construct that symbolizes feeling that is beyond language; the
mythical/folk/natural/supernatural/sacred/secular intertwine to fashion an
eclectic whole and interwoven textual tapestry that formalizes subconscious
myth. Overall, *Mama Day* is an arabesque fictional construction of folk history and trans-secular and secular life that formally replicates its own theory
of itself as a subconscious myth. Thematically, it highlights the agency of
women in a very God-oriented folk tradition that also reaches beyond the
centrally sacred to encompass folk belief and practice vested in a broad range
of the spiritual, natural, and supernatural.

Mama Day includes Christian church worship, non-Christian funeral
liturgy, natural folk healing, divination of nature, destructive hoodoo rites,
and an alternative rite to Christmas that is associated with Africa and
grounded in noncommercial values; its rituals, practices, and beliefs defy description in discrete categories that show clear connections. At the beginning,
the text calls Willow Springs' legendary Mother/Goddess Sapphira Wade a
"true conjure woman" (3). One character in the novel purports to have

hoodoo powers, and another appears to practice it effectively by using nature and the strength of her hate. Mama Day, on the other hand, uses nature to fight the evil of hoodoo and for positive reasons. One episode depicts a card game in which an ersatz hoodoo man applies his abilities to cheating, the scientifically trained city man overcomes him with mathematical calculations, and the scene ends with the group chanting "Take my hand, Precious Lord / And lead me home" as the hoodoo man stands on his hands, "balancing his body so that through the shadows his feet seemed to stretch up to the stars" (213–15).[9] There is a funeral service in the novel that has some trappings of Christian practice, but that strongly belies the Christian idea of earthly finality and implies the continued presence of the deceased in the living community, which seems to be generally suggestive of African belief. Candle Walk, not Christmas, is Willow Spring's main celebration, and it definitely has a connection to the African past. Mama remembers Candle Walk starting as a tribute to the legendary "Great Mother" Sapphira Wade, who left slavery and went back to Africa. In earlier times, people faced east with candles in tribute to her, and they pledged material things to the spirit of the Mother for its journey. According to one legend, Candle Walk began as an agreement between God and "the greatest conjure woman on earth," who is synonymous with the "Great Mother" in various legends, to let her keep the stars that God had flung down so that she could "lead on with light" (110).

Mama Day is decidedly Christian in action and belief, but she embodies the full range of the novel's sacred, spiritual, natural, and supernatural perspectives as well as its historical legacy. She devises herbal medicines to cure people, creates rituals involving natural creatures and objects that positively influence minds, and harnesses the power of nature through an understanding of it that is folk derived but tantamount to scientific. By reading natural signs she forecasts a hurricane more effectively than the hurricane center. She is a healer and diviner who uses nature in retribution in a few instances, but usually for the good and always with an awareness of God's judgment. When the hoodoo woman Ruby makes her niece deathly ill, Mama justifies taking action by calling Ruby out of her house before she repays her in kind by striking it with a cane and throwing a silvery powder around it that will draw lightning: "That'll be her defense at Judgment: Lord, I called out three times [and Ruby did not answer]" (269–70). In talking about the peculiar seasonal change known as "slow fall," the text reveals Mama's thoughts about God's investment in nature and implies her related feelings about the superficiality of the church, which people have corrupted with gossip, meanness, and spite: "They say every blessing hides a curse, and every curse a blessing. And with all of the aggravation belonging to a slow fall, it'll give you a sunset to stop your breath, no matter how long you been on the island [Willow Springs]. It seems like God reached way down into his box of paints, found the purest reds, the deepest purples, and a dab of midnight blue, then just kinda trailed His fingers along the curve of the horizon and let 'em all bleed down . . . you ain't never had to set foot in a church to know you looking at a living prayer" (78). Mama later shows her disrespect for the church as a haven for the sanctimonious and her reverence for nature as the expression of God. She comments on the church through her opinions about Pearl Duvall, who says that her daughter-in-law's failure to conceive is a judgment from God because she and Pearl's son Ambush go out dancing on weekends. Mama thinks that Pearl is "a Bible-thumping idiot," but says, "If Pearl thinks all God got to worry about is two young people hearing some of that silly boogie-woogie music y'all like, then He ain't worth serving" (72).[10] The statement about God is rhetorical: Her words and actions throughout the novel show that God is worth serving, and God is concerned with people's spiritual substance rather than their harmless pleasures.

Natural events are sometimes scientifically explainable but are never completely separable from the supernatural, which can be based in the agency of either good or evil. In *Mama Day*, the supernatural exists independent of the natural, but the opposite is not true. My use of the word *natural* always suggests a connection to supernatural agency. In the family tree just before page one, Sapphira Wade, the "Great Mother" and "true conjure woman," stands next to God as progenitor of Willow Springs. This implies the novel's wide scope that brings together the traditionally biblical/Christian, the portrayal of women that opens and extends the tradition, and other aspects of the historical, natural, and supernatural that are either known or subconsciously imagined. Sapphira had seven sons named after Old Testament prophets, and an asterisk after the seventh son's name, which is Jonah Day, refers to a note: "'God rested on the seventh day and so would she.' Hence, the family's last name." The mythical Mother/Goddess with supernatural powers parallels the acts of God but also reverences him with the biblical naming of her children. Jonah Day carries on the tradition by giving his seven sons the names of major New Testament men. The two generations of Jonah Day's family after this are all females, and the four named in honor of

New Testament Christian virtues, "Grace, Hope, Peace, and Peace again" (10), die tragically. The two named outside the tradition, Miranda (Mama Day) and Abigail, stay alive so that they can bring back grace, hope, and peace for the last Day, Ophelia (Cocoa, also called Baby Girl).

According to the myth of Sapphira, she got her freedom and went back to Africa by using her supernatural powers and her natural womanly powers over her master, and perhaps the father of her children, Bascombe Wade. She was connected to God but also had and used ungodly powers to lay the historical foundation of freedom for Willow Springs. Like Sapphira, Willow Springs has a close relationship to God and Christianity, but its people utilize a range of natural and supernatural rituals and belief systems, as she apparently did. She left Bascombe to return to Africa and, by her act, to establish the Willow Springs legacy of freedom. Willow Springs continues the communal historical legacy of freedom she established. However, because of their own negative emotions, the Day family and the people of Willow Springs generally perpetuate the legacy Sapphira started when she caused Bascombe Wade the pain and suffering of abandonment.

In *Mama Day*'s story, important specifics of a powerful tradition are hidden in myth and mythical history; my overall analysis of the text reflects the intricate, eclectic thematic structure in which this narrative develops. It emphasizes the importance of Christian-type virtues for Mama and the community, but it also follows the intricate textual tapestry of belief and practice of the sacred, spiritual, and supernatural as it weaves and shifts through Willow Springs' shadowy conscious and subconscious family and community history and myth that begins with Sapphira Wade.

"The Days were all rooted to the other place" (285). The life of Mama Day evolves from her subconscious mythical knowledge and history of remembered events of "the other place"; through the text's characterization of Mama, "the other place" is the focal point of Day family and communal myth and history, and of sacred, spiritual, and supernatural tradition. An analysis of the myth and history of "the other place" is central to my overall analysis of the narrative and the African American tradition as the novel presents it.

"The other place" is the physical locality of the Day family house and its surroundings, which include the well and family graveyard, that is part of the family's remembered history, but it is also much more. Mama's experiences at "the other place" have defined her to become the most important person in Willow Spring's recent history; her life at the house made her a mother figure, a healer, protector, and savior of others. She became "Little Mama" after her mother, Ophelia, went insane at the house and jumped in the sound because her own daughter Peace, Mama's youngest sister, drowned in a well. The three-story house and Ophelia are sources of family ambivalence and pain. Abigail says that her mother was "an unhappy woman who never recovered from the loss of her youngest child," while Mama, speaking from her folk perspective, says she was "crazy as a bedbug and she died without peace" (224). In slightly kinder terms, she says later, "She musta been so out of her head that she thought The Sound was the bottom of that well [where Peace drowned]" (278). Mama respects the house but no longer lives there because of her painful associations with it and because she does not understand its past. Abigail will not go to the house where her mother lived her last days because during a storm there in 1920 she miscarried her child Peace, named for Abigail's sister, to bring back what the mother could not find and died for (226–28). But Abigail's dead daughter Grace, who is buried in the graveyard, also foreshadowed her tragic end and tried to perpetuate another tragic cycle by naming her daughter Ophelia after her grandmother. Her reasoning was that her grandmother broke her grandfather's heart when she died, and Grace wants her daughter to break men's hearts because her husband abandoned her (151): "Unyielding, unforgiving Grace. That beautiful baby girl to live for, and she chose to wither away in hate" (278).

"The other place" further stands for the troubling subconscious mythical reality of the Day family that relates to the genesis of Willow Springs. The text portrays Mama and her niece Cocoa's realization of the subconscious as their walk to the graveyard of "the other place" causes a warp in time: "The talk is of avoiding the poison sumac, marveling at lightning-struck edges of tree limbs, the blooms on sweet bays, but they're walking through time . . . The shadows erase the lines on the old brown woman's face and shorten the legs of the young pale one. They near the graveyard within the circle of live oaks and move down into time. A bit of hanging moss to cushion each foot and they're among the beginning of the Days" (150). Back in time, they hear the name of Sapphira that they do not know, and the supernatural voice of John-Paul, her grandson and Mama's father, tells the story of him and his six brothers and his wife Peace, whom his father Jonah warned him about: "Hold back, John-Paul, I can look in that gal's eyes and see she'll never have peace. He passed on before I had the chance to tell him he was right" (151). Jonah's grave does not have a headstone, but they know he is there because they listen and hear him. He remembers "Mama," Sapphira, but says he did not ask her many questions about his daddy and the fathers of his brothers, some of whom did not look like him. The grave of her mother Grace also speaks to Cocoa (Ophelia) about the vindictiveness of her own naming. People in Willow Springs know and, even more deeply, feel the significance of "the other place," but no one outside the Day family will go there because of a foreboding sense of its mystery (254).

For Mama, the house represents the fated paradox that is her life; she finds there both a spiritual revelation of protection and comfort, and the conundrum of the tragic suffering and fracturing of peace in her family history. In a wearying dream of endlessly opening doors that eventually lead to a spiritual place that is "a vast space of glowing light," Mama finds nurturing in her role as "Daughter," which her relationship of "Little Mama" to her own mother and others never gave her (283). Mama's revelation is subconscious; it is a "sense of being" that she "can't really hear . . . 'cause she's got no ears" or articulate "'cause she's got no mouth." However, the dream also forces her to a waking realm of the subconscious in which she looks into the well where her sister Peace drowned. There she sees the baffling reality of Sapphira and her mother Ophelia, both of whom demanded that their men let them go with peace, the former wanting apparently to go with peace back to Africa, and the latter wanting to go with Peace in death. A voice says, "*Look past the pain*," but she has an unvoiced awareness of "circles and circles of screaming. Once, twice, three times peace was lost at that well. How was she ever gonna look past this kind of pain?" (284).

Seeing the painful, complex reality of the house does not afford Mama a clear vision of her past and present, but its realization takes her back to the hope and faith, the essentially Christian, generally sacred/religious values, that guided her throughout her life as the folk Mama, protector, and healer of Willow Springs. Somehow in all this, she feels the assurance of being a nurtured daughter that she never enjoyed and never knew existed, but this is not her earthly calling. Through the tragedy what she most significantly sees is the manifestation of her role as Mama Day. Mama opens her eyes on her own hands, "hands that look like John-Paul's," and the hope and faith embodied in them (285). These virtues engendered in her hands are a family legacy that is paradoxically the result of John-Paul and Bascombe losing someone they desperately loved and needed. John-Paul's loss is "the pain of her childhood," but he also revealed to her the necessity to look beyond the loss, which is to "feel for the man who built this house [Bascombe] and the one who nailed this well shut [John-Paul]. It was to feel the hope in them that the work of their hands could wipe away all that had gone before. Those men *believed*—in the power of themselves, in what they were feeling." Mama cannot understand the tragic past but must translate it into faith and hope—and ultimately love—that will have a positive effect in people's everyday lives in the present and future.

Although she does not have a biblical name and works outside the aegis of the church, Mama magnifies and expands the biblical-like tradition of her father John-Paul, who manifests his double biblical naming through faithful, virtuous striving in response to pain and suffering; their lives resonate with, instead of replicating, the lives of biblical men.[11] The apostles John and Paul, for example, experience persecution commensurate with their blessings and special powers that requires great faith to withstand. John-Paul's characterization is sketchy, but it is clear that he fulfilled his biblical naming by having faith that his good works were meaningful and somehow changed the unchangeable tragic past. In more depth and detail, the text shows how Mama's thoughts and actions similarly raise her to a level where human fallibility and consequent suffering is inseparable from larger-than-life greatness and goodness. As a reaction to the pain, affliction, and suffering bestowed by her family history, she sacrifices for and endeavors to help others, which only causes more distress and makes her complicit in more tragedy. Just as John-Paul must have agonized about his good intentions that led to tragedy, Mama questions herself and supplicates God because of the tragic consequences of her goodness, which is reminiscent of biblical men constantly humbling themselves and praying to be made steadfast as they suffer for doing what is right and good. Mama is the quintessential folk character: Her life is not biblical, but she is a prophetlike and apostlelike figure. Her characterization is an aspect of the text's folk syncretism, which I focus on later and which is central to its portrayal of the sacred, spiritual, and supernatural.

Mama's actions on Bernice Duvall's behalf reveal the anguish and misgiving associated with this biblically related role, and force her to contemplate her entire life in this context. Her attempts to help Bernice bring Mama to grief, just as her family history and so much of everything in her life, which is centered in reverence for God and nature, has come to pain and tragedy. She agonizes: "And only God could change the future. That leaves the rest of us with today, and we mess that up as it is. Leave things be, let 'em go their natural course . . . And would God forgive her for Bernice? But she wasn't changing the natural course of nothing, she couldn't if she tried. Just using what's there. And couldn't be nothing wrong in helping Bernice to believe that there's something more than there is" (138–39). It is important to Mama not to interfere with the natural design of God, but she also thinks it is not wrong to create illusions for Bernice that bring her in line with the natural rhythms with which she has lost touch because of her feverish desire for a child. Mama makes up a strange, "hocus-pocus" (97) ritual involving a setting hen and her fertilized egg to resituate Bernice symbolically in the natural cycle and to inseminate her mind, allowing her to conceive (139). Years after Bernice has a son, Mama is crushed by his death in the hurricane: "You play with people's lives and it backfires on you . . . There'll be no redemption for that. She ain't gotta worry about going on to hell. Hell was right now. Daddy always said that folks misread the Bible. Couldn't be no punishment worse than having to live here on earth, he said" (261). To allay deep doubts and sorrow, she speculates that nothing can be wrong with what she did because she "never tried to get *over* nature" (262). But it is incontrovertible that "it's the people that brings the sorrow. Or the hope. [Her father] told her that she had a little more than others to give. You have a gift, Little Mama. But who asked her for it? Who made her God?" She cannot shake the sense of having the God-given agency to do good that is, paradoxically, part of the fated tragedy of her family and the tragedy that she causes others. Mama resolves this paradox to a significant extent by showing the way to peace and love but not by using methods that are simply and straightforwardly sacred/Christian.

Mama's main project is to bring together the faith that she reaffirms through her vision at the house with the belief of Cocoa's husband George, so that their unified love can save Cocoa from Ruby, the hoodoo woman who makes her deathly sick. The house is thus important in the expanding layers of the narrative; "the other place" is a symbol and a reality connected to the panoply of the African American sacred, spiritual, natural, and supernatural as the text portrays it through the characterizations of George, Cocoa, and Ruby in their interactions with Mama.

Cocoa is a product of folk acculturation and Day family legacy whose life in the world beyond Willow Springs has influenced her but not effaced her sense of connection to family and place. Cocoa is a well-educated, clearly "modern" woman who makes her way in New York City, but she has never truly left behind the reality of Willow Springs: "Home. You can move away from it, but you never leave it. Not as long as it holds something to be missed" (50). In Willow Springs, "it only took a little while for her body to remember how to flow in time with the warm air and the swaying limbs of the oaks." She is "the child of Grace," the "only one left alive in this last generation to keep the Days going" (39). In the graveyard with Mama, she experiences the past life of her mother Grace, her great-grandmother Ophelia, and her great-great-great grandmother Sapphira, which connects her to Day tradition at "the other place" and to the reality of her home town (151). Her deep immersion in family tradition through basically the same subconscious knowledge of the house as Mama's also indicates a folk belief encompassing the sacred, spiritual, and supernatural that may be latent in New York but active in Willow Springs.

Cocoa's relationship to the Day tradition at "the other place" is the key; Ruby incorporates the tradition into the hoodoo to try to kill her. Ruby lives close by the house and uses dust from its graveyard, a plant growing in the graveyard—verbena, "called by some folks . . . herb of grace" (172)—and seemingly the hatred that emanates from Grace's spirit, which is associated with the house's general aura of fractured peace, as the source of power for her hatred that manifests itself in a potentially deadly natural concoction. (It seems to defy common sense that someone steeped in local tradition like Cocoa would come, at Ruby's deceptively kind-sounding behest, to have her hair braided and thus have the concoction massaged into her body (244–46). Since Mama and Abigail knew, Cocoa must have known that jealous Ruby suspected an affair between her husband Junior Lee and Cocoa, and that Ruby would get revenge (152–57). However, Cocoa going to Ruby's makes sense in the context of the narrative because after Cocoa has an altercation with George, Ruby appeals to her as a woman disrespected in the same way that Junior Lee has disrespected Ruby [244].)

From the perspective of Ruby's characterization, "the other place" means the power and the enigma of hoodoo, which allow her to turn negative human emotions into destructive natural creations. However, *Mama Day* reveals that, although Ruby is clearly evil, it is hard to judge the part of the house's tradition most closely connected to hoodoo, which Ruby turns to evil purposes, just as it is difficult to understand why so many painful, tragic things happened there. There is a kind of "hoodoo" in Grace's naming of Cocoa (Ophelia) to get revenge on Cocoa's father, which Ruby takes from the graveyard in the physical form of graveyard dust and in the symbol of the verbena plant, the "herb of grace." When Cocoa subconsciously moves back in time in the graveyard, she envisions Grace associating her retributive naming to her grandmother Ophelia "softly" breaking her grandfather's heart (151). The grandmother's act was not conscious and intentional like Grace's, but it is a link to the feat of the great-great grandmother Sapphira, "the greatest conjure woman on earth." To gain her freedom and return to Africa, she apparently conjured Bascombe and "tore [his heart] wide open" when she left him. The text does not clearly distinguish among the "hoodoo" women, Sapphira, Ophelia, and Grace. Sapphira used her powers to do what was necessary against slavery, and the other women were compelled to follow her legacy. Ophelia was not in possession of herself. Grace perhaps had alternatives but seemed powerless against hate and her sense of the past of Ophelia, whom she knew about, and Sapphira, whom she did not know. Mama herself uses hoodoo for positive purposes, and Abigail and Cocoa also carry on Sapphira's legacy positively at the same time that demented Ophelia, hate-crazed Grace, and Ruby negatively perpetuate it. Submerged in the mythical subconscious that has dim associations with Africa and cloaked in the practice of the supernatural in real life, the general legacy of hoodoo from "the other place" is too complex to analyze in concrete terms of good and evil. Ultimately, hoodoo is a tradition inseparable from the demands imposed by oppression in the shadowy past of "the other place."[12]

Mama disavows the existence of the non-Christian supernatural that includes hoodoo, but the text and her thoughts and actions contradict the disavowal. She agrees with Abigail: "This hoodoo mess is just that—mess" (155). Mama attributes much of hoodoo's power to the hatred of the one practicing it (157) and says further that what people believe—"the mind is everything"—is responsible for much that happens to them (90). This idea would apply to her effect on Bernice, whose mind she claims to influence with the appearance of "hocus-pocus." She gets her remedies from nature: "There's something in [the woods] for everything . . . if a body knows what they're doing" (207). However, while realizing that it starts with the emotion of hatred, Mama has to acknowledge Ruby's power and implicitly the power of evil to oppose good (156). Although she is confident that her more than ninety years have given her the remedies to deal with Ruby, she wonders, "Or had they?"

(173). She also reveals that there is much more than the natural: "She talks what she knows, not what she's afraid to remember. So the ginger vines on that tombstone whisper in vain under all her chatter. And she don't say nothing about them, and least of all, Candle Walk" (207). Mama has knowledge about nature, but Bascombe Wade's tombstone mysteriously speaks to her, which relates to the mystery of the beginning of Candle Walk. Mama learned as a child when her sister Peace died that "*there is more to be known behind what the eyes can see*" (36). This applies to the general relationship between the natural and supernatural as well as to that between natural, herbal medicine and hoodoo, and between hoodoo and the "natural" mind. There is only so much that is explainable in natural, scientific terms, and a lot that is supernatural in *Mama Day*. Mama's powers are probably more supernatural than natural, a strong element of the supernatural being hoodoo.

She would definitely not call herself a hoodoo woman, but her overall portrayal reveals that she is one. Her power over nature, the mind, and the spirit is significantly attributable to the supernatural agency of what people in Willow Springs call "hoodoo," an often evil force residing outside the realm of God that the characters access through ritual concoction based in nature and that human senses and natural laws and theories cannot fully explain. Although her practice with Bernice, which she would say is natural, may be ambiguously both hoodoo and natural, Mama actively and more clearly assumes the role as a hoodoo woman when she takes on Ruby. Ruby, who some say has powers equal to Mama's (112), is a hoodoo woman for many of the same reasons. In the final analysis, hoodoo in the novel is like the traditional practice of hoodoo in large segments of African American culture; it is recondite but fearful and powerful. African Americans profess disbelief but have an underlying respect and use it when its extra-godly agency requires a response in its own terms. Mama's attitude toward hoodoo and contradictory practice of it embodies what is traditionally true for African Americans inside and outside the novel.[13]

I digress briefly to develop a general context for thinking about hoodoo that encompasses the novel and also goes beyond it. Mama, Abigail, and the people of Willow Springs seem to associate the word *hoodoo* with the practice of evil, contrary to what Mama herself actually does and contrary to the overall implications of the text. The characters' attitudes are like those of African Americans generally. While they may unknowingly engage in practices congruent with hoodoo practice and belief in the diaspora (or even perhaps suppress the knowledge of their action), African Americans beyond the strong influence of the culture of New Orleans relate the word *hoodoo* to a dangerous world of the occult. (In New Orleans, according to Zora Neale Hurston's *Mules and Men* (1935), black people adhered to practices of the voodoo religion like those in Haiti [193]). Hoodoo can be good when it counters evil constituted in its own realm; however, if not definitively evil because its practices can save and help as well as destroy, hoodoo is still fearful because it is outside the domain of God and the Christian. The next chapter analyzes Erna Brodber's *Louisiana* (1994), in which the main character calls herself a hoodoo woman and references God as the ultimate power. It confirms that hoodoo / voodoo for adherents of the larger tradition of the diaspora, which begins in West Africa and reaches to Haiti and beyond to the New Orleans area in a highly concentrated form, is not an evil-tainted practice of the occult. It is a sacred/religious way of life that easily tolerates and embraces other religions. Voodoo "is the ancient African vision of man's relationship to the mystery. The origins of Voodoo lie in the African past, in the quasi-universal belief in *ophiolatry* (serpent worship), which held that the founder of the race originally sprang from a serpent. For this, the serpent is revered as a symbol of fecundity and wisdom, and as a life giver. Others honored include the god of war, the great spirit of the waters, and the goddess of fertility . . . Voodoo has no argument with any other theology. It has a place in its system for any way of perceiving man's relations with the unknown. It is flamboyantly undogmatic" (Hogue 243; see also Laguerre 21).[14] *Mama Day,* then, would seem ambivalently to incorporate the larger view of the diaspora—in the myth of Sapphira as "the greatest conjure woman on earth" who has a supernatural connection to the present, for example—as well as the predominantly African American one.[15]

The difference is significant between voodoo syncretism and African American folk syncretism that makes a conscious distinction in the mind, if not always in actual practice, between hoodoo and the Judeo-Christian and privileges the latter. Although the same difference is not always clear in the text, the culture of the novel reflects more strongly the African American folk syncretism of the characters that places the all-important Judeo-Christian God at the top of its belief system than it reflects a diasporic voodoo syncretism that positions in the vanguard of its religious hierarchy a God who still has only relative importance in spite of his power and ascendancy. In the conclusion to *Voodoo Heritage* (1980), Michel S. Laguerre discusses religious songs that present the voodoo "perception of the universe" in Haiti. The songs "speak of existing relationships among God, spirits, and the Upper Belair [an area in Port-au-Prince] congregation. In the songs . . . the name of God is rarely mentioned, except in a few cases where one praises His goodness or invokes His protection. However, God is believed to be the creator of the universe and therefore has the power to reward or punish both spirits and humans. Based on a careful reading of the songs, it is correct to say . . . that a search for the true nature of God does not seem to be the primary preoccupation of Voodooists" (181). This view that focuses relatively minor attention on God in the overall scheme of things is the diasporic voodoo perspective and not the one of the people in Willow Springs, which is slanted toward God and Christianity, or that of African Americans, largely speaking. Laguerre's description of voodoo as a Haitian religion that does not glorify God reveals why African Americans, who are more heavily influenced by the Bible and the Judeo-Christian tradition and highly vested in a belief in the centrality of God, would disavow hoodoo while still including it in their syncretized system of belief and practice separate from the sphere of God in the church. W. Lawrence Hogue may be right when he says that the reason for the African American turn toward the Judeo-Christian and God in New Orleans at the end of the nineteenth century was the "rise of a powerful, middle-class, Christian African America whose goal it was to enter the American mainstream" (55). Whatever occurred in New Orleans, however, African Americans set hoodoo apart from the sacred/religious in America and in New Orleans as well in the twentieth century.[16]

In the novel, the practice of hoodoo moves in convolutions, contradictions, and ambiguities—from Sapphira to Ophelia (who is linked to Sapphira by marriage to her grandson and later by the actions and intentions of Grace, Ophelia's granddaughter) to Grace to the second Ophelia to Ruby, who appropriates the power of Day family hate to hate and kill a Day. The difference between production by pure will and intention linked to ritual creation becomes blurred in the line of women who produce the negative human effects that are part of a "hoodoo" tradition, and so does the distinction between good and evil. Mama and Ruby's opposition consequent to Ruby's act against Cocoa is more straightforward. It focuses on a clearer confrontation between good and evil centered in different practitioners of hoodoo, who rely on their minds and on ritual production and the natural concoctions that are the result of it.

Making the house her central location physically and symbolically, Mama practices hoodoo for the relative good to save Cocoa and take revenge on Ruby, thus balancing Ruby's evil and hatred, and shifting the novel's emphasis to her folk / Christian value system. Ruby has already hoodooed and made crazy the ex-wife of her husband (112), and killed a woman named May Ellen with hoodoo for a supposed romantic entanglement with the husband. As Ruby prepares to hoodoo Cocoa because of jealousy, Mama thinks, "A jealous woman. Creeping through the woods, picking up nightshade and gathering castor beans. Coming to the edge of the other place, the full moon shining on twisted handfuls of snakeroot. May Ellen's twisted body. Ain't no hoodoo anywhere as powerful as hate. Don't make me tangle with you, Ruby . . . I brought you into this world [as a midwife]" (156). While emphasizing the power of hate, Mama is alluding to using hoodoo to fight Ruby's evil hoodoo. Mama's primary motivation is love for Cocoa; she wants to empower George to help her save Cocoa with his own love. Although Ruby's hoodoo has the power to destroy life, religious and sacred ideals such as sacrificial love are stronger and stand above hoodoo in the hierarchy of Mama's belief. Mama and Abigail have faith that George can save Cocoa because his love, which is so great that he will give his life for her, is "a power greater than hate" (267). It is clear that God's judgment is paramount to Mama in the fight, as shown when she calls on the witness of God before she draws lightning down on Ruby's house (269–70). The bonding of the godly and the extragodly that underlies essentially folk Christian values is implicit and unspoken, and resides in ambiguity and contradiction.

It is important to emphasize that this African American folk belief and practice coincides with the Judeo-Christian and creates a syncretism between it and the natural and supernatural. Throughout the Bible, there is a strong injunction against anyone who "useth divination, or an observer of times, or an enchanter, or a witch, Or a charmer, or a consulter with familiar spirits, or a wizard, or a necromancer" (Deuteronomy 18:10–11). Mama brings together the natural and supernatural in ways that the Bible definitely implies are the province of magicians and sorcerers. After she thinks about her defense before God on Judgment Day, Mama "brings that cane shoulder level and slams it into the left side of [Ruby's] house. The wood on wood sounds like thunder. The silvery powder is thrown into the bushes. She strikes the house in the back. Powder. She strikes it on the left. Powder. She brings the cane over her head and strikes it so hard against the front door, the window panes rattle" (270). George later provides a scientific hypothesis of how someone with significant scientific knowledge could make lightning strike Ruby's house more than once in the same storm, as it does later, a virtual impossibility (274). George's account leaves it open for speculation that Mama has the knowledge to precipitate such a natural occurrence as well as the supernatural power that she demonstrated earlier, when she called down lightning on a troublesome white policeman (79–80). For Ruby and Mama, the natural is never separable from the supernatural and includes hoodoo, and the folk syncretism of Mama and of Willow Springs is the basis of their practice and belief system that privileges the Christian/sacred.

The description of Mama, Abigail, and Willow Springs during the peril of the hurricane suggests the text's syncretism. As the storm rages, Abigail reads from Psalm 77:1, 4, 6, 12, and 17–19 before Mama closes the Bible and places their hands together for comfort and reassurance. The episode ends: "them winds will come, rest, and leave screaming—*Thy way is in the sea, and thy path in the great waters, and thy steps are not known* [Psalm 77:19]—while prayers go up in Willow Springs to be spared from what could only be the workings of Woman. And She has no name" (249–51). The prayers of Mama, Abigail, and all of Willow Springs are apparently consciously to the God of Psalms, but also to the great supernatural agency of Woman that the text reveals is a subconscious mythical reality.

To a significant extent, Mama has to meet Ruby on her terms, which at times means moving into a realm of belief and practice where folk syncretism distances Mama from the sacred/Christian in her more conscious thinking, or at least makes her belief in the sacred/Christian ambiguous. This is perhaps clearest in the scene when she tries to use Bascombe Wade's ledger and John-Paul's walking cane in a ritual to access George's faith in self and combine it with hers to save Cocoa's life (295–96). Worms generated by Ruby's hoodoo are putrefying Cocoa's body from inside: "they were spreading so rapidly because they were actually feeding on me, the putrid odor of decaying matter that I could taste on my tongue and smell with every breath I took" (287). Mama tells George to take the book and ledger to her chicken coop where a hen is setting, search in the back of the nest, and bring whatever he finds to her at "the other place." George is outraged at this advice to use "mumbo-jumbo" but does what Mama asks when he penetrates Cocoa's body sexually and finds a worm (297–98). George will locate nothing behind the hen's nest but his own hands, but Mama wants him to bring her those hands in which he has faith. Achieving faith remains the goal of this strange hoodoo, but the focus and source of faith seems to slip into vagueness and uncertainty as George leaves Mama to go to the chicken coop: "She don't even watch as he slowly takes that bend away from the other place. She done already turned her face to the sky that's well beyond the tip of the pines. Hot. Vacant. It ain't a prayer. And it ain't a plea. Whatever Your name is, help him" (299). Without pleading or praying, Mama yearns for the intervention of some unknown deity of nature. The power of hoodoo evil and the necessities of her own measures to deal with it draw her away from the sacred / Christian center.

This drawing away does not question or diminish the inscrutable power of God, who is still there. Maybe Mama's speculation regarding God sending the hurricane explains her thought and action that imply a contradiction in belief. What God allows to happen "ain't got nothing to do with us, we just bystanders on this earth. Sometimes I think we was only a second thought— and a poor second thought at that" (228). Whether her words are an adequate explanation of what Mama thinks and does, and for whatever reason God leaves her to her own devices, this is an instance when hoodoo's extragodly agency requires a similar response.

Mama brings George to "the other place" to put his nontraditional belief together with her belief to fight the power of Ruby's hoodoo. Through a method that defies natural, scientific explanation, Ruby has woven the Day family legacy into a death curse that has turned Graces's hatred for a man back on her daughter to consume her. It will take the combined power of Day family love and the love of George to save her because love is always stronger than hate. In a not-so-strange logic that also apparently underlies the mystical, supernatural legacy of the Day family and the supernatural power of Ruby's curse, a man's love is a primary antidote to the hatred that Grace had for a man. George must supply this part of the cure because Cocoa is committed to him. Mama "needs his hand in hers—his very hand—so she can connect it up with all the believing that had gone before. A single moment was all she asked, even a fingertip to touch hers here at the other place" (285). The problem is that George's faith in the self developed in a setting that is the antithesis of "the other place." Raised in an orphanage and trained to focus on the present, George earned a degree in engineering, and believes that he must rely on his education and scientific observation and analysis for everything. Ruby has made it difficult by making it necessary that George at least briefly share

Mama and Abigail's belief in the sacred, spiritual, and supernatural represented in the house and the community (267). Although this is the ideal solution, George has the power to save Cocoa by himself, too, but Mama "won't even think on that" (285).

The "atmosphere" that George sensed in Willow Springs—"More than pure, it was primal" (185)—represents African American traditions that refute his narrow belief. Even before he gets there, the town's traditions affect George in ways that belie his belief that science and objectivity account for all that happens to him. For example, Mama tells Cocoa to write to George and let her mail it: "Use some of Abigail's yellow writing paper, the one with the little flowers at the bottom" (50). Mama puts powder in the letter, or at least the text implies that through some abstruse process she is responsible for it being there. When George feels the powder in the letter, it feels like touching a goldenrod flower (54). The figure of speech suggests the flowers on the paper and also an earlier description of Cocoa growing up in Willow Springs as a sunflower and as "kind of blooming from pale to gold" (47). Along the same lines, while at lunch with his business partner, George subsequently opens a fortune cookie whose message reads, "All chickens come home to roost" (56). George is in complete denial of its "total nonsense" but recommends Cocoa for a job after the paper crumbles into powdery, yellowish dust. (The fortune-cookie message also foreshadows his later visit to the chicken coop in Willow Springs.)

In Willow Springs, George must come to terms with the reality of God as well as the extragodly. Prior to the hurricane, George had not thought much about God: "I might take a deep breath and say, God help me, really meaning, Let the best in me help me. There wasn't a moment when I actually believed those appeals were going beyond me to a force that would first hear, secondly care, and thirdly bend down to insert influence on the matter. No, I saw the Bible as a literary masterpiece, but literature all the same; and Christianity owed its rules and regulations to politics more than anything else . . . But the winds coming around the corner of that tiny house on that tiny island was God" (252).

He undergoes no conversion, as shown by his later reliance on himself, but he briefly achieves a spiritual awareness that extinguishes his self-centeredness and generates the desire for peaceful oneness with God and loving connection with people. He felt "even smaller than them [the house and the island]. Trivial. Every thought, ambition, or worry diminished as it became my being against the being on the other side of two inches of wood. Fear never entered the picture: at first an exhilaration of the possibility of having the barrier broken and, for one brief moment, to be taken over by raw power. What a magnificent ending to an insignificant existence . . . the growing and pervasive realization of my insignificance caused a lump in my throat. You yearn for company then, any company, to have some minor evidence of your worth reflected back at you." This is only a moment, still colored by scientific analysis and rationalism, however, especially in light of George's comparison of the power to the running of a "nuclear steam turbine generator" that could light up New York City (251).

Overall, George reveals his shaping beyond the sacred, spiritual, and supernatural beliefs and practices of Willow Springs by indicating that he cannot take "the other place" seriously in spite of the palpable spiritual and supernatural reality that he senses there. George hears the story of the house from Mama (206–7) and Cocoa (218), and he witnesses the presence of the troubled spirits of Sapphira and Ophelia that are alive in its mythology and history. "That house had known a lot of pain. And more than what you [Cocoa] talked about: your great-grandmother, Ophelia, losing her baby daughter at the bottom of a well; closing herself off from her husband and her children . . . No, there was something more, and something deeper than the old historical line about slave women and their white masters. A slave hadn't lived in this house. And without a slave, there could be no master. What had Miss Miranda said—he had claim to her body, but not her mind. Yes, that house resonated *loss*. A lack of peace" (225). In spite of what George seems to perceive is true, his juxtaposed vision of the house and his proposal of action to change its tradition, as well as what he does later, show that he refuses or fails to understand and accept its reality. "But, God, it was a lovely place. Why not move out here for the last week of our vacation—a sort of second honeymoon. We could wake up and see what those morning glories entwined around the pillars would look like in full bloom. There was an ancient bed on the second floor, a mahogany headboard ten feet high, and we could call the girl [conceived there] Mahogany . . . Let's bring ourselves into the house and erase a little of the sadness" (225–26). Although George insists that he is not joking (Mama would utterly reject the idea because the house is no joke to her [226]), his romanticized allusions imply a superficial conception of the house's grandeur isolated from human oppression and tragedy. He thus trivializes its pain and suffering and the serious difficulty of changing its legacy, calling into question his belief in the truth of the spiritual and supernatural that he perceives but cannot see. What George truly believes is limited in comparison to the reality of "the other place" and Willow Springs' folk syncretism.

In an ongoing process of syncretism, Mama forcefully and purposefully manipulates George to access his narrow, nevertheless strong belief in self to save Cocoa and, concomitantly, to shift the Day family tradition toward positive spirituality. He does not believe in Mama's way but is "beaten down to believe" (299) that he must try it by her persuasion and the gravity of Cocoa's condition. George goes through the ritual in the chicken house and reaffirms the importance of "*my* hands" (301) instead of discovering the need to put his hands together with Mama's in communal folk belief that ultimately asserts positive values over the negative. George consequently dies; Mama realizes he "went and did it his way, so he ain't coming back" (302). But he finds peace: "The worst thing about the blinding pain that finally hit me was the sudden fear that it might mean the end. That's why I gripped your [Cocoa's] shoulder so tightly. But I want to tell you something about my real death that day. I didn't feel anything after my heart burst. As my bleeding hand slid gently down your arm, there was total peace" (301–2). Mama in effect adds a new kind of faith in the self based in the rational and in the objectivity of the senses to her belief and that of Willow Springs as she guides George, unintentionally, to peace in death and, intentionally, to save Cocoa and give her peace in life. Mama triumphs over Ruby and evil, but since she is unable to keep George alive, her life retains the paradox of her great spiritual power and seemingly fated link to human tragedy, which is also part of her characterization as an apostlelike and prophetlike figure. George ascends to a spiritual place that he would never have believed in while he was alive.

Through its folk syncretism, the text subsumes an essentially religious and Christian spirituality into an ethos that encompasses good, evil, and the nondescript but privileges faith in the goodness of the inscrutable course of human events. Near the end, Willow Springs' collective folk voice summarizes this faithful affirmation: "Another Candle Walk. This one's gonna be a bit sparse, there being more than [Willow Spring's] share of troubles this year, what with the hurricane and losing crops, some even losing their jobs beyond the bridge [to the mainland]. And it ain't easy watching the young pass on, the life that [Bernice's son] Little Caesar never started or Cocoa's husband finished. Still, it ain't about chalking up 1985, just jotting it down in a ledger to be tallied with the times before and the times after. We figure it'll all even out in the end" (305). The folk voice speaks in a secular idiom that reveals its human values and underlying faith in spiritual revelation.

Cocoa must figure out what it means in the context of a folk worldview in which human beings can only know so much and for the rest must trust in the revelation of a benevolent spirituality. Mama realizes that George has made possible a positive future in which "the other place holds no more secrets that's left for [Cocoa] to find" (307). However, Cocoa must move beyond the immediacy of grief to a higher spirituality for this to happen. "He's gone, but he ain't left her. Naw, another one who broke his heart 'cause he couldn't let her go. So she's gotta get past the grieving for what she lost, to go on to the grieving for what was lost" (307–8). He has broken his own heart, literally and figuratively, loving her and trying to keep her alive with him, but leaving her in death as he did is a sacrifice with the opposite effect of Cocoa's father's desertion of her mother Grace. Also, his sacrificial love is superior to Bascombe Wade's obsessive, possessive love. George's spiritual attainment has opened the way for a new relationship and new knowledge.

> My daddy said that his daddy said when he was young, Candle Walk was different still. It weren't about no candles, was about a light that burned in a man's heart. And folks would go out and look up at the stars—they figured his spirit had to be there, it was the highest place they knew. And what took him that high was his belief in right, while what buried him in the ground was the lingering taste of ginger from the lips of a woman. [Bascombe] had freed 'em all but her, 'cause, see, she'd never been a slave. And what she gave of her own will, she took away. I can't tell you her name, 'cause it was never opened to me. That's a door for the child of Grace to walk through. And how many, if any, of them seven sons were his? Well, that's all left for her to find. And you'll help her, won't you? she says to George . . . And there'll be another time . . . when she'll learn about the beginning of the Days. But she's gotta go away to come back to that kind of knowledge. And I came to tell you not to worry: whatever roads take her from here, they'll always lead her back to you. (308)

The "child of Grace [can live] up to her name"; Cocoa can change the Day tradition, make the unknowable known, and manifest the ultimate in spiritual connection—up in "the stars" above the emotion that "buried [a man] in the ground"—that is always inherent, if unrealized, by bonding spiritually with George. She goes away and returns to do this as Mama suggests (308–11).

George becomes part of the spiritual connection to Cocoa that is beyond words, beyond this world, and beyond death. This spiritual connection is a nexus incorporating the text's formality, which replicates its own theory of itself as subconscious myth, and further incorporating the sacred and a positive valuation of the supernatural. From the beginning, *Mama Day* theorizes itself as an open-ended story that changes "depending upon which of us takes a mind" to tell it (3). A subconscious myth, spoken within the self and not by the novel's voice, generates the story: "Think about it: ain't nobody really talking to you . . . the only voice is your own" (10). Subconscious knowledge of the story here is not clearly nonlinguistic, but the novel does later define the nonlinguistic as an unspoken and unheard "sense of being" when it describes Mama's spiritual awareness (283). Narrative subjectivity, indeterminacy, and even nonlinguistic "sense of being" (283) do not truly represent an unfulfilling lack of knowledge, though. The text encompasses them in its ultimate spiritual knowing, which is through a state of peace and love that transcends the material and human figuration that constructs knowledge. As Mama predicted, Cocoa does "get past the grieving for what she lost, to go on to the grieving for what was lost." The utmost loss was more than herself and more than George: It was love (309–10). Cocoa echoes the novel's concepts of its indeterminacy and subjectivity in her spiritual communion with him: "Because what really happened to us, George? You see, that's what I mean— there are just too many sides to the whole story" (311). However, the indeterminacy and subjectivity of their story are within the domain of spiritual apprehension where linguistic signification is unnecessary. She now communes with him through a spiritual "sense of being" in which "there ain't no need for words as they lock eyes over the distance. Under a sky so blue it's stopped being sky, one is closer to the circle of oaks [around the graveyard at "the other place"] than the other. But both can hear clearly that on the east side of the island and on the west side, the waters were still" (312). This is how the novel ends in love and peace that surpass all, which represent spirituality that is inseparable from the sacred and the positively supernatural.[17]

Mama Day is a radical narrative invention that creates its own textual theory and folk belief system.[18] The text is a labyrinthine formal construction of subconscious/unknown knowledge and the related tradition. One might say that the narrative is a complicated literary portrayal of African American atavism, particularly as it pertains to the Day family connection to its history and the African past, and the African past and mythic knowledge generally. In the context of its theory and system, the logical and the provable must quickly give way to acceptance of the ambiguous and contradictorily true; the unexplainable, nondefinitive, and nondescript; and to the acceptance of the paradox of subconscious knowledge that we perceive spiritually. Analysis, like the text itself, inevitably progresses into contradiction and ambiguity that necessitate recourse to the text's self-conceptualization and folk syncretism. This is part of the overall point implied thematically and formally, though: One must accept the narrative's theory and belief system in order for it to be real. This is obviously true for many novels that violate the expectation of linguistic replication of supposedly linear, concrete, and easily accessible reality, whereas reality is nonlinear, dense, abstract, and inaccessible through language. The narrative, then, devises a theory and folk belief system that are the basis of a *representation* of African American reality. It is a way of understanding and positively coming to terms with what we know without being fully conscious of knowing it, which is what the characters in the novel accomplish through the belief and practice of their tradition and ethos.[19]

The portrayal of the tradition has a resonance of truth at its most radical margins and much stronger believability as one gets closer to the center of belief, practice, and ritual that is still extant and recognizable. The sacred and spiritual as they relate to the Bible, belief in God, and religious worship are real and true to many people in the present day. The reality of hoodoo and the supernatural is more recondite, but it still is part of the African American consciousness because it lingers in memory, situated there by stories, somewhat like the effect of the subconscious in *Mama Day*. In the final analysis, the novel tries to do something very difficult, which is to capture the full essence and truth of an entire tradition by situating it in the place of Willow Springs and the specificity of the Day family and its women. In the process, *Mama Day* presents perhaps *the* most comprehensive novelistic portrayal of African American sacred, spiritual, and supernatural tradition as it relates to myth, history, and secular life.

Finally, I want to make a point about an aspect of the novel that is integral to its radical narrative invention and overall portrayal of the tradition. *Mama Day* is among the important revolutionary black women's novels of its time. It brings to fruition the political critique of misogyny and sexism in Naylor's first two novels *The Women of Brewster Place* (1982) and *Linden Hills* (1985) by centering the entire African American tradition around the agency of Mama Day and the lives of the Day family women and making men secondary.[20] However, this critique is less direct because it is indigenous to a complicated narrative that theorizes its invention of a system of syncretized folk belief and practice. Published in 1988, *Mama Day* carries on and adds new dimensions to the movement of revolutionary black women's fiction that includes Toni Morrison's *The Bluest Eye* (1970) and *Sula* (1974), and Alice Walker's *The Color Purple* (1982).

CHAPTER 5

Reshaping and Radicalizing Faith

The Diasporic Vision and Practice of Hoodoo

JAMAICAN-BORN NOVELIST ERNA Brodber brings together the larger sacred, spiritual, and supernatural tradition of the African diaspora and shows its relationship to the African American in her novel *Louisiana* (1994). In its portrayal of hoodoo, *Louisiana* reveals an important part of the religious tradition indigenous to the African and diasporic past that Western culture and many African Americans have rejected. Brodber's novel is similar to Gloria Naylor's *Mama Day* (1988) in its portrayal of a black cultural milieu in which hoodoo is a significant factor. The novel makes black women the spiritual center in a hoodoo cultural tradition reminiscent of the spiritual centering of women in the syncretic cultural tradition of *Mama Day,* and thus similarly decenters Western patriarchy. (Alice Walker's *The Color Purple* [1982] does so in a somewhat different context.) *Louisiana,* however, goes further in portraying hoodoo as a religion of the African diaspora that can, in some cases, forge a link to the Bible but revise the Judeo-Christian tradition and create an alternative vision of the sacred, spiritual, and supernatural. The analysis of hoodoo as a religion of the black diaspora in *Louisiana* opens the way for a critique of Ishmael Reed's *Mumbo Jumbo* (1972), in which hoodoo is a religion that is even more oppositional to the Western tradition that proscribes it.[1]

Reed's novel secularizes the voodoo religion, investing the sacred, spiritual, and supernatural in the human desires and actions of daily life, and the text vilifies God and Christianity instead of portraying *Louisiana*'s syncretism. Heaven, portrayed in *Louisiana* as a separate spiritual place that nevertheless has a strong connection and clear relationship to the earth, does not exist in *Mumbo Jumbo*. In Reed's novel, voodoo manifests itself almost totally in a mythicized, highly spiritualized temporal world. The novel's reality is greatly defamiliarized by a voodoo mythic history and story of the past, and by hoodoo's supernatural influence in present-day life, in which its spirits possess people constructively and destructively, use them to create art that expresses its essence, and generally inseminate the world with their greater than human power.[2] However, the novel mainly focuses on the secular that is mythicized and spiritualized. Two kinds of spirituality exist, the kind that is good because it allows life to prosper and the kind that is evil because it oppresses and destroys. According to voodoo philosophy, everything always inscrutably evolves to the triumph of life; the only evil is the attempt to limit and obstruct the ways of infinite spirits that influence the expression and celebration of life in all of its diversity, this restriction being tantamount to death. The biblical and Judeo-Christian traditions are considered evil and deadly, just as voodoo is bad from the perspective of Christianity. In this context, *Mumbo Jumbo* does not engage the Bible directly to revise it to the same extent as *Louisiana,* but its narrative fully opposes the biblical story and the Judeo-Christian with its counterstructure and theme. In theoretical terms the narratives of both novels are structurally and thematically human artistic productions inspired by voodoo spirituality, meaning that we must judge them according to a hoodoo aesthetic that is encompassed in the general scope of postmodern textual theory.

In *Louisiana* voodoo/hoodoo redefines Christianity to create an alternative religious cosmology; it is not just a powerful and feared aspect of the culture that is peripheral to Christianity and highly proscribed. Main character Ella Townsend is a hoodoo woman in late-1930s New Orleans whose belief and practice has evolved from the diasporic tradition.[3] She is the priestess who is the primary oracle of the spirit of Vodun. (See the discussion of Vodun in chapter 4, note 14, and of voodoo in the analysis of *Mama Day* in chapter 4.) Characteristic of voodoo/hoodoo derivation and evolution in the diaspora, she syncretizes hoodoo and Christianity. Ella's hoodoo worldview secularizes the heavenly and spiritual and spiritualizes the secular, and decenters God, foregrounds women, and focuses on the human. The emphasis on the human perspective is partly responsible for the proscription of hoodoo among Westernized black people acculturated to revere the sacred Judeo-

Christian God. However, reverence and positive human action constitute Ella's whole life. Besides accepting herself as a hoodoo woman, she calls herself a soothsayer and a prophet, clearly implying that she is a holy person of the voodoo/hoodoo religion. Although God is not her primary focus, she is devoted to helping people on earth and oriented toward a concept of heaven as home where the renewed spirit can manifest itself in the image of youthful rejuvenation. Perhaps African Americans and others know hoodoo most popularly through the story of Marie Laveau, the nineteenth and twentieth-century New Orleans oracle/priestess of hoodoo who had supernatural vision and power and who combined hoodoo with Catholicism. Unlike the legendary Laveau, Ella's practice is totally nonadversarial and salvific. By portraying Ella in this way, *Louisiana* minimizes her association with carnality, destructive human conflict, and the evil occult attributed to Laveau.[4] The hoodoo religion takes the secularized form that Ella gives it but emphasizes morality, virtue, and spirituality.

What the text projects through Ella's portrayal is a faithful vision of black spirituality linking life and death and effacing the barrier between earth and heaven. It is tantamount to African American faithful belief in a centralized Judeo-Christian God and his sacred, spiritual realm beyond the human and secular. Ella becomes a hoodoo woman mainly because of the supernatural intercession of the secularized dead—the dead in heaven who spiritually maintain contact with their earthly past and the present—and the spiritualized living—the living on earth who are constantly in conversation spiritually with heaven and who are in transit there. They imbue her with the powers to see the heavenly world and the personal histories of the living, which she uses to help people confront their pasts in positive, uplifting ways. She begins as a Westernized, Christianized black American of Jamaican birth. Her parents were snobbish Episcopalians who held themselves apart from other West Indians and Americans. Ella stops going to church early in life, but she retains the strong desire to succeed in conventional terms, first by attending medical school for a year and then by going to Columbia to become an anthropologist. Being a hoodoo woman is the last thing that she wants to do; however, this is what she turns out to be, initially with great misgiving and fear, and then with growing self-approval and joy. The change begins for Ella when she undertakes a project to retrieve the oral history of African Americans in St. Mary, Louisiana. She interviews and records Sue Ann Grant-King, called Mammy, and soon discovers that the tape recorder miraculously records her own thoughts. It also captures a voice saying a phrase that Ella is not conscious of knowing, and a conversation among her, Mammy, and Louise Grant, called Lowly.[5] Lowly (dead in heaven and constantly in communication with Mammy) and Mammy (in transition between life and death) initiate Ella into a different reality that amalgamates the earthly and heavenly and leads to spiritual transcendence in a humanized heaven. She accepts the cosmology of Mammy and Lowly, themselves hoodoo believers and practitioners, moves from St. Mary to New Orleans to learn the hoodoo practice from Madam Marie—whom Mammy and Lowly select—and succeeds her when she dies. By the end, Ella dies, making the transition to the heavenly home and thus continuing the connection between a secularized heaven and a spiritualized earth. Her husband sees her smiling as she goes over the rainbow, and hears her singing among jazz-inflected voices of a heavenly communal chorus.

In *Louisiana,* God is no longer the enigmatic but all-controlling God of the Judeo-Christian Bible. He has the ultimate power but resides ambiguously in the background, as in the classic Haitian practice of voodoo (Laguerre 181). As she develops and changes, Ella gives human beings more earthly importance and human power in heaven, sans the direct intervention of God, thus implying a spiritual mystery even greater than that portrayed in the Judeo-Christian tradition, in which an all-knowing, inscrutable God controls. Ella is influenced by the spiritualized living and the secularized dead, who inspire the supernatural revelation of the secularized life histories of individual West Indians and African Americans, and revelation of a radically redefined heavenly world where they exist with spiritual hegemony and communicate with each other and the human community. Besides this influence, Ella converts because she revises the Bible, in the process changing the role of women and the perspective on them, and critiques her earlier life as a Christian. Another aspect of Ella's conversion to hoodoo is her realization that a mysterious spiritual power works through her to write the narrative that is *Louisiana.* In line with hoodoo's integration of the spiritual and secular, her immersion in the hoodoo-inspired aesthetics of everyday folk life, especially the improvisatory creation of folk songs and jazz that bonds black people culturally, impacts her creation of the improvisatory text. Apart from Ella's perspective, the narrative also theorizes its creation by the investment of supernatural power, defined according to non-Western hoodoo belief, in Ella and in the African American community, and it practices the theory. Overall, this theory and formal practice and the portrayal of voodoo/hoodoo as a religion, presented primarily through Ella's characterization, are central in my analysis. In *Louisiana*'s theory and related formal practice, hoodoo power, invested in the centered black woman writer and repeated throughout the extended black community, produces the narrative. Challenging Western ideas of the sacred, spiritual, and supernatural by revising the text of the Bible, redefining women's religious role, and deepening existential mystery, while still typically retaining a syncretic relationship to the biblical and the Judeo-Christian, voodoo/hoodoo is a religion of faithful vision of the agency of black people existing in its reality of the secularized spiritual and of the closely associated spiritualized secular.

The prologue in the form of an editor's note establishes *Louisiana* as a black woman's novel that presents its own theory of reality and narrative construction; the theoretical publisher positions itself with Ella and the community as a participant in the hoodoo practice that creates the text. The manuscript mysteriously just "appeared on our desk" at a "small black woman's press . . . looking for works on and of black women . . . The text argues persuasively that Ella came under the influence of psychic powers. Today the intellectual world understands that there are more ways of knowing than are accessible to the five senses; in 1936 when Ella Townsend received her assignment it was not so. The world is ready. We are. The manuscript's arrival is opportune. And in more than one way" (3–4).[6] Ella's "psychic powers" that the theoretical editor refers to are much more than the ersatz ones of the psychic as viewed in the Western world; they represent the true reality of hoodoo as a fully realized religion with a supernatural vision that is different than the West's. These powers connect Ella spiritually to an earthly and heavenly community and inspire her production of the narrative in conjunction with the community. The press has become a communal participant in the process of supernatural creation: "We have subjected [the manuscript] to little editing. What looks like part of a letter, accompanied this manuscript . . . We have appended this note as an epilogue, using its last sentence as a heading, in line with the style of the rest of the work. This is our major intervention, mandated we think by the distinctly communal nature of this offering, an approach which is most obvious towards the end of the manuscript. Here a voice, which we presume to belong to Ella's husband, appears" (4–5).

The press's addition of the "Prologue" and "Epilogue" and minor editing do not make the novel less cryptic or easier to decipher; the manuscript that evolves before the reader has the abstruse form marking the mystery of its supernatural production. The first section of the text is a recording of conversation between earth and heaven that Ella initially transcribes. After this, she continues transcribing, learning more of the supernatural revelation of the story and, along the way, reshaping herself, which entails becoming a part of the community and being influenced by its creativity. After a point in her development, Ella stops using the tape recorder, and communication takes place through a pendant that her husband gives her. Subsequently, the voice of the husband, who also immerses himself in the community and essentially becomes a hoodoo man, appears strangely and abruptly in the text. Ella does some editing as she transcribes, but largely her story has a spontaneous form. The press's prologue is formally similar to the rest of the text, which includes the epilogue produced by the hoodoo-influenced husband. Overall, the narrative has a spontaneous, ungrammatical form that represents its theory, as stated by the press, that supernatural power, working through Ella and the community with which she interacts, writes it.

The prologue's next-to-last paragraph is particularly important because it practices the theory and replicates the overall thematic revision using the narrative's unique form.

> The text came to us divided into six parts—1) I heard the voice from heaven say 2) First the goat must be killed 3) Out of Eden 4) I got over 5) Louisiana and 6) Ah who sey Sammy dead. Is there a message in these titles, we asked—I heard the voice from heaven say, "first the goat must be killed (and you get) out of Eden and get over (to be) Louisiana." Den a who sey Sammy dead, (if this can happen). A hypothesis. We called the epilogue, our appended note from Ella's husband (?), 'Coon can', to complete this thought/hope, entering by this act into the community of the production. (5)

From implicit and explicit perspectives, the paragraph supportively rereads the revision of the Judeo-Christian in a form symbolic of the larger hoodoo manuscript. Underlying its reality is the repetition of hoodoo in everything, making all one—Ella, her heavenly and earthly community, the press, and this very text of *Louisiana,* produced by Ella and the others, that critically engages the Bible and Christianity. The form is ungrammatical to symbolize implicitly the volition of its spontaneous supernatural production.

It generally duplicates the structure and theme produced by the working of the spirit in Ella acting in concert with the community, with the press entering the communal production by adding the prologue, written in the form of the rest of the manuscript, and appending and editing the epilogue. On the explicit level, the press says that it gets the manuscript in six parts. It is not the manuscript's sole or primary agent but cryptically reinterprets the revision of the Judeo-Christian in the already revised form inscribed by hoodoo, which is simultaneously Ella's writing of the text and rewriting of the biblical and Judeo-Christian in the context of the hoodoo community. I emphasize that thematic and structural repetition in the analysis fits the levels of thematic and structural repetition implied in the paragraph.

Ambiguity is an additional sign of hoodoo spiritual mystery working in everything and everyone against and in syncretism with the Judeo-Christian. In the press's reading of *Louisiana*'s revision, the voice from heaven is not the traditional voice of God. It says "first the goat must be killed (and you get) out of Eden and get over (to be) Louisiana." What may be clearly implied is the rejection of the biblical figure of Eden and movement toward the folk reality of the people embodied in Ella's renaming and characterization as Louisiana. However, the more ambiguous reference to the killing of the goat is an allusion to revision of biblical symbolism. In Leviticus 16:5–10, Aaron the priest is instructed to offer a goat on the altar and also to send a "scapegoat" into the wilderness symbolically carrying the burden of the people's sin: "And [Aaron] shall take . . . two kids of the goats for a sin offering . . . And he shall take the two goats, and present them before the Lord . . . And Aaron shall cast lots upon the two goats; one lot for the Lord, and the other lot for the scapegoat. And Aaron shall bring the goat upon which the Lord's lot fell, and offer him for a sin offering. But the goat, on which the lot fell to be the scapegoat, shall be presented alive before the Lord, to make an atonement with him, and to let him go for a scapegoat into the wilderness." Isaiah 53:6 alludes to Jesus as the sacrificial bearer of human iniquity: "All we like sheep have gone astray; we have turned every one to his own way; and the Lord hath laid on him the iniquity of us all."

My reading is that in terms of biblical intrarelationships, the latter verse implies that Jesus is the savior sacrificed for sin like the "goat" and that he is similar to the symbolic "scapegoat" for sin whom the priest sends into the wilderness. *Louisiana* revises the biblical through Lowly and Mammy's displacement of Jesus as the traditional biblical (scape) goat for human sin.

When they die, in the context of death in the hoodoo religion, they open the way for Ella to break free of the biblical paradigm of sin. Ella changes her name to Louisiana, symbolizing her conversion to the hoodoo religion and her consequent cultural and spiritual oneness with black people. She leaves behind the inhibiting concept of sin inscribed in the human experience of Eden and Jesus' redeeming sacrifice, and goes on to a different life and a different salvation. Lowly and Mammy allow Ella to get "out of Eden." They "kill" Jesus Christ the (scape) "goat" for sin who leads to salvation as constructed in the Bible; their authority replaces that of Jesus Christ, who is *biblically constructed* through the authority of white middle class values and power, which stand behind Ella's Episcopalianism.

The analysis is specific, but keep in mind that ambiguity is central.[7] This is a reading of the press's reading of textual form that destabilizes the Judeo-Christian with ambiguity representing the mystery of a contending hoodoo vision. The manuscript overall provides biblical references and references to Ella's biblical critique that are a context to make the reading of the prologue possible and appropriate. However, the meaning of the working of the spirit is only revealed in nondefinitive signs. The main point is that hoodoo changes the world by pulling everything into its powerful but mysterious reality.

"Den a who sey Sammy dead" and "Coon can" are the main symbols of formal structure and concomitant mysterious spiritual message generated through the agency of Ella/Louisiana and the black community, which includes the press. "Den a who sey Sammy dead" is a West Indian dialect song lyric that Ella has forgotten. She remembers where she heard it when the West Indian men in New Orleans sing the words in a communal setting. She swoons under the spirit's influence, which takes her back to her infancy in Jamaica where the community sang the same song at her grandmother's funeral (88–89). The words become formally coherent and readable for her only in terms of the hoodoo communal experience and supernatural reality, which she understands in the course of understanding her own life as a hoodoo woman. When in the swoon, she learns that the response to "Den a who sey Sammy dead" is *"Sammy no dead yah. Sammy gone a"* (91–92).[8] Although the words have more of a literal meaning to Ella now, it is never explicit to her, or at least she never tries fully to signify the meaning. The language seems primarily symbolic of faith in the spirit that is greater than death of the physical body, but it leaves the reality of existence open-ended and mysterious. For the reader, the linguistic figure (and the text generally) is less decipherable as a sign of the concrete, and is even more clearly representative of faith in what is ultimately a mystery. *Louisiana* unites the spiritual with the communal in a formal structure that requires faithful acceptance of a perspective that generally defies the senses and Western theology. Hebrews 11:1 perhaps helps to make the point here: "Now faith is the substance of things hoped for, the evidence of things not seen." The difference is that this is hoodoo religious faith that is as significant as the biblical but based on different beliefs.

"Coon can" *is* hoodoo religious faith in the context of the prologue. The press's "hypothesis" is that "'Coon can'—the black community *can*—be the mystery that is "Den a who sey Sammy dead" because of its hoodoo belief and ritual practice. Coon can is a card game played by black people, but it has greater importance as the figuration of the black secular/communal that cannot be separated from the hoodoo empowerment that unites human life and spiritual mystery. Coon can only has true meaning when one understands that the spirit works in all the secular activities of the black community, and bonds and almost equalizes those in heaven and on earth. It implies faith in the salvific power of the hoodoo spiritual mystery encompassing earth and heaven.

Louisiana's first section, "I heard a voice from heaven say," introduces the reader into the form of the mystery of hoodoo that is its narrative, and starts the process of Ella's initiation into the spiritual reality that totally defies her Western upbringing. The section comprises Ella's unedited recording done at the earliest stage of her development. It is, of course, a version of the story that ultimately evolves toward a linear plot sufficiently to be allusive of the point about hoodoo spirituality. As it is written, however, it is the most difficult part to read because it provides few clear markers of a definable experience embedded in narrative structure and characterization. At the beginning, Lowly reminisces about hearing a song at her own funeral—"Is it the voice I hear / the gentle voice I hear / that calls me home?" The most repetitive linguistic element of the section for Ella is her own taped voice, which she does not recognize, saying the unknown words "Ah who say Sammy dead." The phrase is interjected for the last time in the section just before this passage: "There is no question about it; it is as clear as a bell. Somebody spoke. A voice very familiar and it isn't her Mammy's. The ears are hearing other frequencies. The child has come through. Anna, she'll make it" (28). Mammy and Lowly speak Ella's repeated words as they prepare her for spiritual conversion. The three already speak in a common voice that signifies their shared being. This voice, speaking through Lowly to Mammy (Anna) at the section's end, is talking about the beginning of the conversion. Ella will soon be able to see the unfolding transition to the hoodoo mystery, which the reader also sees as the story develops, but the text is totally perplexing here.

At the beginning of the second section, "First the goat must be killed," Ella talks about the voice and her name change under the influence of Mammy and Lowly: "The above is as true and exact a transcription as I Louisiana, the former Ella Townsend, now Kohl could with guidance over the years manage to make of my first encounter with my teachers. '*Ah who sey Sammy dead.*' They had placed that message in my head. It was my voice that kept saying it, though nowhere was that phrase in my consciousness at the time. I now know that it is the refrain of a folk-song from home but I didn't know the song, having left there at an early age . . . Nevertheless the voice that uttered these words was inescapably mine, less recognisable at first but finally leaving me . . . with no doubt of my involvement with the exchange" (31). The voice speaks ambiguously throughout the first section about what happened to Mammy and Lowly in the past on earth and about their current interaction with Ella. They use the unknown phrase spoken in Ella's voice to bring her into the mystery of the secularized spiritual and the spiritualized secular that is her changed reality. This relates back to the prologue's penultimate paragraph. In theoretical terms, the press's revision of the theme—already revised in the first section and throughout the manuscript it has received—similarly brings the reader into the hoodoo mystery that changes the world. The revisionist spirit replicates itself everywhere.

"First the goat must be killed" depicts Ella's movement into the community that impacts her conversion to the hoodoo religion and life that transforms her. Ella's communal experience starts in St. Mary during the interview when Mammy and Lowly are initiating her into the reality of hoodoo and when Ella goes to Mammy's funeral. Ella shouts out "*Ah who sey Sammy dead*" at the funeral and also physically expresses great emotion as in a vision she watches a young Mammy ascend a ladder over the rainbow, but she does not remember shouting or her physical acts at the church (34–35). The interpretation that her husband Rueben picks up walking through the village is that "Mammy had passed, leaving her soul with me" (37–38). The people say that Ella "was being taken on a journey into knowing and was resisting as first timers sometimes do." Ella is embarrassed at her behavior and does not share with Reuben her vision of the heavenly world and the fact that she hears voices (38). However, as she inevitably changes, she is increasingly exposed to a black community about which she was completely ignorant. This hoodoo community is immersed in the same cosmology as Lowly and Mammy, and supports Ella's conversion to hoodoo by providing a context of sympathetic belief. The community's sense of Ella's taking a "journey into knowing" does not suggest she will obtain final knowledge with God in heaven but that her new way of "knowing" is an ongoing revelation that leaves the role of God ambiguous and the ultimate design behind a secularized heaven and a spiritualized earth mysterious. The constantly unfolding vision empowers black people, particularly women, because in it they take positive roles in the entirety of their existence.

In this section, the hoodoo reality on the tape recorder forces Ella to deal with her earlier church life and to begin the revision of the Bible concomitant to her religious transformation. There are several quotations from Ella's Episcopal past supernaturally produced on the tape by the spirit; she remembers these words from her own former life when she hears them. The words "control large spaces" and "sit over large holes," which is to say that they buttress Ella's middle-class religious values and respectability inherited from her parents. After hearing what is on the tape, she and Reuben "[fall] off the end of that reel right through those word holes" (43). The words do not hold them up or support them against the alternative spirituality expressed on the tape. A quotation from Psalm 2:4 confronts Ella: "He that sitteth in the heavens shall laugh: the Lord shall have them in derision" (45). She specifically recalls the second half of this verse from her mother's psalter but does not understand clearly her great discomfort about it. Implicitly, Ella feels distress because the supernatural revelation on the tape and her vision, which includes Mammy's ascension, of a more humanly autonomous heaven mocks the biblical image of an all-powerful, wrathful God in heaven.

Actual and envisioned diasporan communities that conflate are the initial context for biblical revision and Ella's renewal. Words from 1 Corinthians 15:55, which she did not realize had impacted her so greatly, come to mind: "Death where is they [sic] sting / Grave where is thy victory?" (51–52). Revelation of these words comes after Ella compares the singing on the tape and Lowly's description of her funeral to the singing, ceremony, and regalia at Mammy's funeral. Lowly and Mammy are one being that Ella/Louisiana also becomes, and similarly Ella realizes that in her mental picture the two funerals in Jamaica and Louisiana are essentially one (50–51). This indicates that the hoodoo communities where the funerals take place (both named St. Mary) are basically one. In accordance with the passages from Leviticus 16:5–10 and Isaiah 53:6 mentioned earlier, Jesus is the sacrificial figure who resurrects in 1 Corinthians: "But thanks be to God, which giveth us the victory through our Lord Jesus Christ" (1 Corinthians 15:57). As I have said, the hoodoo perspective to which Mammy and Lowly give her access from the realm of the dead is the background for Ella's vision of life and resurrection that is not so much grounded in the biblical / Judeo-Christian idea of sin and death. Concomitantly, the beliefs and rituals of their community, such as those practiced at the funeral(s), challenge the whole meaning of the biblical, and Ella starts to become uncomfortable with the biblical when she juxtaposes it with images of the response to death at the funeral(s). She will later more consciously define herself as a hoodoo woman through biblical revision.

The end of "First the goat must be killed" portrays Reuben and Ella's acceptance of their communal remaking that in turn immerses them in the community. It depicts the hoodoo spirit of creativity working in the community and the repetition of its creativity in Ella as she becomes the creator of the manuscript in the communal context, and in Reuben as he participates in communal musical creative processes and rituals. Instead of being a standoffish Episcopalian like her mother and an elitist academic doing research on the community as she was formerly, Ella is now "a woman among women," which refers specifically to her connection to Mammy and Lowly, and her inclusion in the community because of it. Through the act of revising the tape and writing it as a manuscript, Ella "had entered. I had listened, been with them and hadn't collapsed . . . I had . . . grown to their size, stabilised myself and was hobnobbing on equal terms. I had arrived. Passed through my rite of passage with flying colours. I . . . was in, ready and willing to be and see something else. Transform, change, focus. Transform, change" (52). The ungrammatical form symbolizes the creativity of hoodoo that is open-ended repetition in Ella, in the community, and in the manuscript; the words convey the theme of transformative creativity repeated everywhere. The repetition of creative hoodoo spirituality throughout everything is also clear in the characterization of Reuben. He has finally found the black experience for which he has searched. He already knew jazz and blues from New

York, but here was "feeling them in the making . . . The man was being made anew" (52–53). He is much more a part of the spiritualized secular that creates jazz than he is of the secularized spiritual that inspires Ella's heavenly perspective, but the two are never separate in the text, especially because Ella makes him privy to her vision and he takes her into his musical world. Experiencing and participating in the making, he is also being remade in the process. This applies to him, Ella, the community, the text—everything.

At the beginning of "Out of Eden," Ella presents an ironic analysis of an image of Jesus on the stained glass window at her mother's church that is congruent with Mammy's and Lowly's earlier displacement of Jesus, consistent with Ella's changing values as she develops, and associated with the specific and direct biblical revision that follows and that is integral to the process of hoodoo in everything. The image from her mother's church is "a thorn-headed picture of Jesus the Christ, his head slightly leaned to one side, his arms open and his fingers delicately crooked reminding me somehow of the proper way of drinking tea. You could see his heart—it was heart shaped and had, I think, a dart going through it. At his feet in halos were women, the Marys I presumed" (57). The picture projects the superficial middle-class values that produce it and that contrast Ella's view of the world as she changes. Overall, Ella's language sounds sarcastic to reflect her attitude. The most unmistakable indication of the negative is Ella's feeling that the picture reminds her "somehow of the proper way of drinking tea." Further, the subservience of women in the picture also stands in opposition to the role of women in her developing hoodoo perspective.

Assaying the underlying reality of God is also an aspect of the development; although Ella does not negate God in the description of the image and church ritual that she talks about as she continues, she makes his role ambiguous to fit hoodoo cosmology.

> The picture was a mosaic, like a jigsaw puzzle. Someone must have painted it on glass, broken it into pieces of uneven sizes then stuck the parts together in that large window sited over the altar. How did they do this and why? The picture responded to light, so that bits of it or the whole were only visible as it was directed towards them. There was no street lamp or beacon close by, revelation had to depend on God's natural light. In winter therefore, there was hardly more of this picture to be seen than the raised lines in the mosaic

where the parts were joined. With the coming of the sun and the summer, the whole picture was there and for a considerable time.

The services my mother attended began at six AM . . . It was more often than not dark then and no picture to be seen for the whole hour and a half at that church but as the days grew longer I could watch the parts individually revealing themselves and I'd leave the church with the whole picture in my head.

The stained glass window vied with the over-shirts of the processing men for my attention . . . I did have a good view not only of the stained glass window but also of the men walking slowly and reverently behind each other and behind the man who carried the cross. Those over-shirts bothered me. Who did that delicate embroidery? It had to be a woman . . . I dropped out of church-going before I entered high school. (57–58)

Does the sunlight reveal the individual parts of a production of human desire and power, or is the picture a representation of the divine whose wholeness she can only see in "God's natural light"? Ella implies that humans make the picture, and the hand of men is more explicit in her account of the subjugation of women integral to creating its associated dramatization at this middle-class church of West Indians whose conception of God is so different from hoodoo religious belief.[9]

Most importantly, in "Out of Eden" Ella starts directly to oppose the biblical; she contrasts its conception of God with her own counterimages of the hoodoo community in which the spiritual is grounded in the secular and the secular in the spiritual. She remembers words from Exodus 20:5 and other Old Testament passages associated with the church: "For I thy God am a jealous god" (59). Ella responds: "Cane is a jealous god. It needs every ounce of energy of every man, woman and child. This is especially so in November going on to December . . . This is reaping season and every stalk must be in before the winter sets in. I was in my cottage with the venerable sisters . . . All concerned were now, I imagined, happy with me. I certainly was happy" (74). She consciously moves from a preoccupation with the fearsome God constructed in the Bible to a focus on the work of the community that includes her and the heavenly sisters.

Ella figuratively leaves the life conceived in terms of the biblical (scape) "goat" and Eden violated by human sin at the end of "Out of Eden"; an alternative black community that is inseparably earthly and heavenly, and propelled by a plan significantly grounded in mystery, precipitates her action. Ella describes her departure: "before morning broke, I had left Eden, guided out by Mrs. Forbes and Reuben's enthusiasm for her plan. It was months after, that I could fully appreciate the intervention of the venerable sisters" (74). Reuben, then Ella's boyfriend, arrived just as Mammy was dying. He is Congolese and likes the plan to go to Congo Square in New Orleans because he has already involved himself in the diasporan community in St. Mary and because he will, in a sense, return to his home. Mrs. Forbes is the one who carries out Mammy's plan for Ella to live with Madam Marie in New Orleans to become a hoodoo woman. A man is supposed to go with her, but Mammy's only "clue" about his identity is that he is "coming from far" (73). Mammy's uncertain knowledge of Reuben is an element of the constantly developing mystery that works out right. Ella suggests trusting and letting the mystery develop when she says that she does not see the connection of the "venerable sisters" to what she does until later. She lets events direct her and has faith that the sisters will take care of her. As she perceives later, "they would hold me up on their knees: they had done so. They had sent me to Madam Marie and allowed me to continue my work. They had placed Reuben in his home and settled the visa problem. Let me take this leap in the dark knowing that I would not dash my foot against a stone" (80). In their existence as the secularized dead, Mammy and Lowly have power over human events, but their communication to Ella shows that they do not fully know or determine the mystery. Along the same lines, Ella only learns some of their history and that of the other characters and even less of the future as she develops her hoodoo powers and makes her own transition to the secularized dead.

In "I got over," Ella continues the ongoing revision of the Bible and reconceptualization of God as she becomes a hoodoo woman under the tutelage of Madam Marie. The salient part of the development is that she learns what it means to be a hoodoo rather than a biblical prophet. Believing in and acting on the revelation that evolves from the mystery of life instead of waiting for the word of God like biblical prophets appears to be the key.

Right after Ella takes the faithful "leap in the dark" based on her belief that Mammy and Lowly will guide her, she receives Mammy's strange communication that reveals aspects of the story of Mammy's grandfather with respect to prophetic inspiration. The cryptic story becomes somewhat clearer near the end of *Louisiana* when Ella learns more about what happened to Mammy. The grandfather was a slave whose deep thinking led him to run away and to be captured and killed (80–83). The grandfather "just get up cool like and go. You know how when the prophets of God get the word" (82). Later, Lowly gives Ella details about Mammy's life as an activist that are comparable to the description of the grandfather, who was the first in the family to take action against oppression.

> She had been thick into the longshoreman's strike [in New Orleans]. Like happened to the prophets in the Bible, a voice came to her, a hand touched her on the shoulder and guided her away to the train. Somebody out of the blue paid her fare. News came after of the shooting and jailing of the strikers. She could never explain to herself how she had left something that was vital to her and in such a flash. [She later saw] herself as selected by a higher authority to have a set of experiences different from that of her relatives and selected for another task. Whoever controlled the world she now felt, had said that enough of her line had been wasted in battle, that she should take a new approach to fighting. (154–55)

On the surface, the acts of the grandfather and Mammy may seem to be similar, but in substance they are quite different.

Mammy lets instincts and feelings guide her, but she does not think before she acts. The master and the male slaves think about the condition of slavery, and the grandfather cogitates deeply before he takes bold, decisive action. The emphasis on male reliance on analysis, which leads to the deaths of the grandfather and master (who commits suicide after he kills the grandfather), implies its shortcoming when set against Mammy's nonanalytical approach that leads to her survival. One cannot take this aspect of the analysis too far because, although the text does foreground women, it only juxtaposes the negative characterizations of men to those of women to a limited extent, most notably in this depiction of Mammy's grandfather and Ella's analysis of the mosaic and account of Episcopalian church ritual.

What is clearer is that the text compares the grandfather and Mammy to prophets in different linguistic figurations that redefine the concept of the prophet and the prophet's relationship to God in an ongoing revision of the Bible. The specific language describing the grandfather and Mammy is important. The revelation came to Mammy "like happened to the *prophets* in

the *Bible*" (154, italics mine). It is the ambiguous "higher authority—" who-
ever controlled the world"—and not God that speaks to her.[10] Mammy acts
with the inspiration of prophets in biblical stories. However, she trusts an
unknown power and lets the mystery guide her. She is thus a biblical-like
prophet who changes the concept of prophet, the prophet's relationship
to the known God, and consequently the overall characterization of God,
and the text revises the Judeo-Christian Bible in the process. The grandfather got the word like "the *prophets* of *God* get the word" (82, italics mine).
Although the text does not use the word *Bible* in the case of the grandfather,
it describes him taking action like God-inspired prophets in the Bible. In the
comparison with Mammy, the problem with the grandfather is that he follows the sure word of God, which turns out to be unsure, and not the voice
of hoodoo mystery. However, the grandfather himself is also a part of this
mystery that will evolve positively.

By trusting in life and implicitly believing in the mystery working in the
secular and spiritual realms, Ella gets the gift of prophesy that makes her a
biblical-like prophet much like Mammy. As is true throughout the text, im-
mersing herself in the hoodoo community and its faith is the key. Ella learns
to relax among the people: "I felt in step with my group and liked the feeling. That was how Madam and Reuben behaved: they didn't worry that there
was little work and little money. For Madam, another boat would turn up;
for Reuben, just being was learning and learning was living" (84). This communal setting is where the singing of the compelling but unknown lyrics by
the West Indian men inspires the supernatural revelation of men's histories
that she will utilize in giving them helping, healing prophecy. When Ella
heard the words, "Sammy dead, Sammy dead, Sammy dead oh," she fell and
"just sat there. Madam indicated to them that they should let things be, so I
sat there unable to move without help and with no help forthcoming. Then
it was prophesying. I went on with the weak no-go body into prophesying. I
looked at the faces of the men sitting around me and I saw stories" (88–89).
Ella is helpless in the grip of the spirit as she sees the unknown in her past as
well as the pasts of others, but this is how the spirit works in revealing aspects
of the mystery of individual lives that are part of the larger, ongoing mystery.
At the beginning of "Louisiana," Ella has become a prophet and essentially
"gotten over" to be Louisiana at this point. She experiences "hegemony of
the spirit" (98), and just stops working and thinking and lets things happen
(97–98).

The spirit continues to prepare Ella to be a hoodoo prophet, and early in "Louisiana" this entails recontextualizing biblical stories in the secular setting of her development in which she trusts and waits on the spirit. When Ella/Louisiana asks Madam to help her understand the change that she is undergoing, Madam allows the spirit to guide her and spontaneously "just got up and read" from the Bible: "It was the creation story. Genesis one. I didn't have to think long about her message either . . . 'And God saw that it was good.' This refrain occurs at the completion of nearly every stage of creation. Madam was pointing me to the action of being totally satisfied with step one before taking the other steps. Remarkable! My self was on a kind of sabbath, evaluating stage one and resting/strengthening and absorbing the lesson there before tackling stage two. Not to worry, she seemed to be saying. I wasn't worrying" (98). Madam helps Ella to shift the idea of Sabbath to apply to her life as the spirit inspires her to wait in the process of development that will lead to action. Like Madam, Ella "take[s the Bible] up and let[s] it open itself as it will" (99). The Bible opens to the Elijah/Elisha story in 2 Kings 2: "it jumped right from the page and just hit me right between the eyes. It was meant for me" (100). Ella appropriates the story of the passing of the spirit from Elijah to Elisha to explain the passing of the mantle from Mammy and Lowly to her. In recontextualizing the story, Ella changes the gender of the prophets and the setting from Judeo-Christian to hoodoo. She also sees her relationship with Mammy and Lowly in the context of the transfiguration of Jesus (Matthew 17:2–8, Mark 9:2–10, Luke 9:28–36)— "Two dead people talking to a live one, just like Mammy and Lowly and me"—that her setting similarly redefines.

The story of Elisha and the one about the witch of Endor in 1 Samuel 28:7–20 are the main focuses of Ella's critique of the biblical concept of prophet. King Saul has banished the woman because she is a "familiar spirit," a supernatural power proscribed in the Bible: "A man also or woman that hath a familiar spirit, or that is a wizard, shall surely be put to death: they shall stone them with stones: their blood shall be upon them" (Leviticus 20:27). Only when God forsakes him does Saul resort to her to conjure up the prophet Samuel. The woman successfully brings back the spirit of Samuel from the dead, but he foretells Saul's doom. She follows the orders of Saul, the man of God, when he expels her and orders her not to use her powers and when he tells her to use them, but her portrayal is still highly negative in the biblical context because she has powers that do not come from God. On the other hand, the Bible authenticates Elisha as a prophet although he uses God-given power to curse little children and cause beasts to kill them right after Elijah passes the prophet's mantle to him: "And he went up from thence unto Bethel: and as he was going up by the way, there came forth little children out of the city, and mocked him, and said unto him, Go up, thou bald head; go up, thou bald head. And he turned back, and looked on them, and cursed them in the name of the Lord. And there came forth two she bears out of the wood, and tare forty and two children of them" (2 Samuel 28:23–24). Ella wonders: "Now why is he a prophet and not a witch? . . . Why should that unfortunate lady be ashamed of herself and Elisha not?" (101). She realizes why: Elisha is a "Man of God" who "took his orders from God," and "the little lady was running a private enterprise, her own corner store, stoking her own fire." This is the woman's problem, but Ella will not let it be her own.

Ella's biblical revision frees her to use supernatural powers that are like those of the woman of Endor and to be a prophet in the hoodoo context. In spite of Elisha's power, Ella wants to be a different kind of prophet. The biblical prophets believe in God, who is definitive and arbitrary, and the hoodoo prophet relies on the divine mystery. She contrasts Elisha in the story from 2 Samuel and Peter in the transfiguration from the New Testament with herself and Madam.

> Prophets wait for God. Elisha must have been grey-bearded with waiting for Elijah to be promoted and he to be appointed in his place! Nobody turns on prophets nor do they turn on themselves. They wait for God's orders. That makes the difference and I saw Peter, poor "winjie" human—mother's word—making an effort to be useful, practical and controlling—"Let us make three tabernacles," when the higher authority had already made those tabernacles and put people in them, so much so that the occupants had long since passed on or were about to pass on. I laughed and had to share with Madam. "That's why we are so fat," she said. "We eat while we wait." I was waiting for a higher command. That's it. I vowed then and there to be a vegetarian seer. (101–2)

She will not wait on the orders of God, who controls and determines everything, like biblical prophets do, but will trust and wait on the "higher authority" or "higher command" through which the mystery works ambiguously in secular and physical as well as heavenly ways. Ella will then utilize her powers with no "sign of fear or dissonance" like Mammy and Madam and unlike the woman of Endor (101).

At times, Ella seems to contradict this theology with Judeo-Christian nomenclature. In talking about Mammy's communication of some stories and not others that Ella also wants to hear, Ella says: "Who can control Mammy? Only God" (109). Although she uses the word *God,* this is not the God who controls Mammy like God controls biblical prophets. She relates this God to acts of Mammy's supernatural intervention that seem autonomous in the overall hoodoo mystery, and thus "God" here is implicitly like the "higher authority" who is ambiguous and not the biblical God who asserts control and proscribes "familiar spirits."

In generally characterizing herself as Louisiana the hoodoo prophet, Ella similarly expresses her devotion to a divinity named "God" that she defines according to hoodoo theology.

> I join the world of the living and the world of the spirits. I join the past with the present. In me Louise and Sue Ann are joined. Say Suzie Anna as Louise calls Mammy. Do you hear Louisiana there? Now say Lowly as Mammy calls Louise and follow that with Anna as Louise sometimes calls Mammy. Lowly-Anna. There's Louisiana again . . . I was called in Louisiana, a state in the USA. Sue Ann lived in St Mary, Louisiana, and Louise in St Mary, Louisiana, Jamaica . . . I am Louisiana. I wear a solid pendant with a hole through its centre. I look through this hole and I can see things. Still I am Mrs Ella Kohl, married to a half-caste Congolese . . . I am Louisiana. I give people their history. I serve God and the venerable sisters. (124–25)

Ella prophesies and as Louisiana represents a collective hoodoo spiritual and secular reality. In the character of Ella, she reverences God along with Mammy and Lowly. God is worthy but is not the assertive, definitive Judeo-Christian divinity. As individuals in the secular world with supernatural powers of vision like the woman of Endor, Ella, Mammy, and Lowly would all be "familiar spirits" condemned by this God.

Generally, "Den ah who seh Sammy dead" stands for Ella's faith in the spirit that transcends death and manifests itself in the evolving mystery of existence. As the title of the last section before the epilogue, the phrase symbolizes the fruition of belief through her realization as a hoodoo prophet and concomitantly the text's narrative realization, both of which only temporalize the still ongoing mystery. Many West Indian and American men successfully "make use of the history [Ella] hand[s] them" (129), and her parlor is a "matrix" for the folk songs of the diasporan community (130). Through a pendant that Reuben gives her, which replaces the tape recorder as the oracular medium, Ella sees heaven where the sisters are and where she now wants to be (136–37). She also achieves a new phase where she speaks but Reuben hears the voices of Mammy and Lowly: "I record on paper what comes out of my wife's mouth" (142–43). Reuben becomes even more integral to the process by assuming Ella's role on earth as she makes her passage to heaven. As the creator of the text, the spirit gives her supernatural access to defining facts and details in the stories of Mammy and Lowly which are essential to the creation of *Louisiana*. With regard to communication from the spiritual realm, Ella has wanted "a narrative plain and straight of [Mammy's] life and doings in South West Louisiana" (109). She never gets the full story because the spirit maintains the mystery of existence, but in this section Mammy and Lowly do tell her about significant aspects of their lives that allow her to put their stories together in a more linear fashion. Together, Ella and Reuben achieve a transcription of the narrative that is the text: "This really did happen and we have just made what I believe to be the only existing record of it" (158).

The tale of *Louisiana* is the creative repetition of the spirit in the community and everywhere; it is a not fully revealed but positively evolving mystery of the earthly and heavenly that is a harmonized black song. When Ella dies, Reuben hears "angel voices" (161). "My wife's voice was there too. Different chords, different tunes, different octaves. Sheer jazz. One sound. From one body. A community song: *It is the voice I hear, I hear them say, come unto me* . . . Louisiana, my wife . . . was smiling and singing. She was going over the rainbow's mist with her knowing smile. I know now what she knows: Mammy would not tell the president nor his men her tale for it was not hers; she was no hero. It was a tale of cooperative action; it was a community tale. We made it happen." The spirit works through everything and everyone in the community of the spiritualized living and the secularized dead to create the tale, which is also the text that Ella writes and the story of her recreation in life and death.

The press adds the epilogue and entitles it "Coon Can," signifying the black communal, to continue the text's ongoing creation by the community, and the epilogue in turn includes Reuben, extending the possibility of communal creation to Africa. After Ella's death, Reuben contemplates the pre-civil rights era at the end of *Louisiana*: "I am here, which might not be very long. There is marching . . . Protest is all about and our people are making their discontent known. Is this my community? Have I any business in this? I am hearing of Kasavubu and Lumumba. I am beginning to think that I must put down my spade in the Congo where I was born . . . The prospect is exciting. That would be an extension of the community. Isn't that exciting! The coon can" (166). The extension of the community in the epilogue is the open-ended evolution of the text that is the spiritual mystery repeating itself. This repetition is the thematic and formal substance of the narrative in important ways. As was true in the earlier analysis of the prologue's paragraph symbolizing the narrative's overall theme and structure, repetition in the structure of my analysis of the epilogue and the rest of the novel is a critical praxis that engages the narrative's theme and form.

The message of "Coon can" coincides with the text's overall project of making African and diasporic culture and community coterminous with ascendant black spirituality and making secondary the "white" Judeo-Christian, thus adding another dimension to the body of novelistic portrayals of religious belief relating to African American and diasporic life and the racism and sexism that are always a part of it. Hoodoo is an African American and diasporic religion engendered in Africa. *Louisiana*'s hoodoo-derived reality of the spiritualized secular and the secularized dead constitutes black life. Its hoodoo cosmology implies that the positive sources of black spirituality reside deeply in the African past instead of in the Judeo-Christian tradition, and it positively focuses on a black religion and a black view of the sacred, spiritual, and supernatural proscribed in white, Western culture.[11] This is what makes its view different from that presented in most African American novels.

Generally, the hoodoo worldview and religion change the identity of the divine, the human perspective on oppression, and the cultural context in which black people express faithful vision. In *Louisiana*, black people in diasporic cultures confront oppression with faithful vision just as much as they do in novels that deal solely with African American culture. However, the oppression is less apparent because hoodoo spirituality reveals it in the course of closely connected events that are all moving in concert toward positive fulfillment in both the otherworldly and terrestrial realms.[12] Instead of placing faith in the Judeo-Christian God to get through the travail of white oppression, which is the focal point in life, black people rely on a different spirituality. It is more mysterious because its source and identity are ambiguous, and it manifests itself equally in the secular and the heavenly, thereby always keeping human beings in touch with a spirit that is moving them beyond oppression. The characters have faith that events in heaven and on earth are constantly evolving toward positive human expression and renewal under the aegis of the spirit. Women who have the oracular power of the hoodoo priestess are primary in changing the cultural setting, which they do by showing faith from the hoodoo viewpoint.[13] They embody faithful vision as they critique the male-centered Judeo-Christian and tell the spiritually inspired story that gives a new perception of heaven and earth, in part by portraying new roles for themselves. Further, the theoretical foregrounding of the role of a hoodoo woman in the creation of the text, which reveals the spirit and the centering of women in the positively developing events of black life and political struggle, are aspects of the novel that are integral to the hoodoo system of faithful belief.

Finally, *Louisiana* is written by, and is an ever-changing form of, the spirit that guides by faith, centers the text's religious belief, and has an interrelatedness in everything. Along these same lines, it is the focal point of the novel's aesthetic. Belief in the spirit that open-endedly moves toward the revelation of the virtuous and positive in human existence constitutes a hoodoo narrative aesthetic. This is not a story with a definitive ending written by a definitive author. It is the communal text of the people's faithful vision of their lives written by the spirit using Ella and others as oracles. The text continues to change shape and express itself as the voice of the spirit as it constantly brings generations of the people to spiritual fruition. It is an unerringly developing narrative of the spiritual and not a human one. Theoretically, this is the only aesthetic judgment that one can make, which again goes back to *Louisiana*'s hoodoo faith in the spiritual work taking place in all things.

Louisiana's depiction of hoodoo is a step toward *Mumbo Jumbo*'s radical religious vision. Reed's novel breaks away from voodoo syncretism with Christianity, takes the voodoo religion and its spirituality out of the realm of the otherworldly, foregrounds the secular world where human beings respond to life through their desires and artistic creations, opposes the concepts of Christian morality and virtue, and centers the good in the triumph of a voodoo-influenced limitless expression of human desire and intention in life. Readers and critics have said that the text is a critique of the novelistic tradition and a satire of Western beliefs and values, including those that are Christian, but few have focused in depth on the work's portrayal of the anti-Western religious beliefs of African Americans and black people of the diaspora. Along with its other thematic features, however, it is indeed a novel that purposefully espouses a different black religious view of the world and faith related to it that deserve treatment from this perspective.

In *Mumbo Jumbo,* life in all of its mystery and diverse expressions and outcomes, which are inherent in the practice and belief of the voodoo religion, *is* good. The novel reverses the dominant Judeo-Christian mythology by making Christianity evil because it opposes this conception of life and its inherent religion. At times, the text makes it seem as if one of the two basic rites of life that it creates, the "Petro," is evil, but the main character PaPa LaBas concludes that neither the Petro nor the "Rada" is "inherently good or evil; it depends upon how they are used" (213).[14] Evil is native to "Atonism." "Atonist" uses of the rites to constrict life are the inception of evil. In belief and practice, evil is Atonist life-constraining intolerance of cultural forms, artifacts, and ways of thinking and acting that do not adhere to European standards and intolerance of voodoo because it is a non-Christian religion. Atonism is more than Christianity, but Christianity is integral to and inseparable from it and consequently from evil.[15]

Christian/Atonist suppression and oppression are tantamount to the death of other cultures, and literally kill when they take the form of holy wars and other brutal physical acts of the past and present. Atonism is not exclusively white. According to the text's cryptic myth, a few early Atonists such as Moses derived Christianity from VooDoo because of the Atonist proclivity to focus on one standard and thereby to control life (186).[16] Whites have shown this same inclination most strongly. They are in the forefront of those who try to use Christianity and political power to prescribe one way to think and be that limits life and controls others. Many blacks also share their Christian / Atonist beliefs, although even blacks with highly Atonist attitudes are likely to show the influence of voodoo in some way and may not act toward other black people as white people do.

A way to describe voodoo's inherence in and synonymy with life is to say that the belief and practice of voodoo is the emanation of the mystery and diversity of life, which *is* good, and consequently voodoo *is* good also. But the deduction that life / voodoo *is* good does not mean that it is a construct connoting only pleasure and gratification. Voodooists act under the impetus of numberless spirits who sometimes possess them, but possession can be painful and harmful because it is generated from a world that human beings can not fully understand and sometimes do not properly access and approach. However, neither the influence of voodoo spirits, the human action that leads to the adverse effects, nor the possession represents evil because, again, life in all of its mystery and diversity *is* good emanated in voodoo. From this perspective, making mistakes that lead to painful possession is one diverse consequence of life, and even the negative consequence of death as one of life's possibilities, as opposed to death caused by Atonism's control, is part of the good. Of course, the unstated implication is that since life/voodoo *is* good, the gods and spirits responsible for it must somehow be ultimately good in all their mystery and contradiction that make them appear so humanlike in desire and action, and that can produce human conditions and situations that seem so bad, and should be trusted as such. (This is similar to the way that Christians trust God to be always good even when they suffer adversity, but God is always suprahuman and righteous in action and desire.) In this context, hoodoo practitioners like PaPa and his friend Black Herman can often cure harmful possession resulting from ignorance because they believe in the gods and spirits, and accept that life is their creation and humans must work through them when they encounter problems entailed in the mystery. The hoodoo men get in line with the mysterious intentions of the gods and spirits and appease them, their conjuring of the possessed always including the emotion and sensuality that are expressions of life. The contemporary form of voodoo possessing Harlem, where PaPa and Black Herman practice, is "Jes Grew," a manifestation of the mystery that speaks through a variety of art forms, including the text of *Mumbo Jumbo*. It inhabits people and makes them demonstrate the vitality of life in a broad range of ways.

Near the end, PaPa tells a story within the story of the war between good and evil, VooDoo and Atonism, that goes back to ancient Egypt and is ongoing in the present. The origin of voodoo is black; according to PaPa's story, the Egyptian Osiris, a prince and apparently also partly the god of classic Egyptian myth, learned its rites "from the long-bearded Black men in the university at Nysa" and practiced it in Egypt (162). Historically, as a predominant cultural belief and practice, voodoo has evolved from black Africa to Haiti to black New Orleans and the rest of African America, but all people in all times, and not just black people, reveal the influence of voodoo/hoodoo mystery. The gods and spirits inspire PaPa's story about the continuing struggle between the opposing forces of good and evil, but still do not give him definitive answers about why things happen and what will happen. However, the story strongly indicates that life in its multitudinous expressions will always successfully resist Atonist cultural deracination and physical oppression. In the still-evolving mystery, PaPa practices hoodoo in his Mumbo Jumbo Kathedral in Harlem, and the story he tells is an assertion of faith that he has a role in his own scenario in which good overcomes evil as represented by Atonism. Overall, PaPa's narrative is strongly informed by the mythical and the spiritual that are conflated in the secular; its setting is an incongruous mythicized, spiritualized temporal world, the term *spiritualized temporal* meaning that human beings act from the impulses of physical desires and the contradictorily and similarly human effects of supernatural voodoo possession in everyday life.[17] Prominent in PaPa's account is a sacred text of voodoo that opposes God, Jesus Christ, and the whole Judeo-Christian tradition, and is antithetical to the Bible in all ways. Overall, PaPa's story highlights the theme and structure of the rest of the novel: a contemporary hoodoo version of PaPa's sacred voodoo text, *Mumbo Jumbo* is thereby also a counternarrative to the Bible that symbolizes its oppositional story in its "mumbo jumbo" portrayal of mystery. It renounces God, belief in his biblical and spiritual revelation of existence and truth, and the Judeo-Christian, instead maintaining faith in the outcome of the mystery defined in terms of the text's myth projecting the triumph of life/voodoo in all its possibilities of human creativity and feeling in the spiritualized temporal of everyday life.

Artistic creation, especially improvisatory art, is a large part of hoodoo religious expression in *Mumbo Jumbo,* where the unholy secular, according to the Christian perspective that the text rejects, is the locus of the spiritual. Haitian Benoit Battraville says the following to African American poet Nathan Brown, who wants to be inhabited by the contemporary hoodoo Jes Grew.

[African Americans] have synthesized the HooDoo of VooDoo. Its blee blop essence; they've isolated the unknown factor which gives the loas their rise. Ragtime. Jazz. Blues. The new thang. That talk you drum from your lips. Your style. What you have here is an experimental art form that all of us believe bears watching. So don't ask me how to catch Jes Grew. Ask Louis Armstrong, Bessie Smith, your poets, your painters, your musicians, ask them how to catch it. Ask those people who be shaking their tambourines impervious of the ridicule they receive from Black and White Atonists . . . Open-Up-To-Right-Here and then you will have something coming from your experience that the world will admire and need. But your musicians are dying your novelists are exiled for telling the truth your poets are pawning their coats for 10 dollars. He continues: "You [African Americans] are walking fetishes. You are indeed beautiful." (152–53)

African American do not understand the mystery of loas or spirits, but embody its essence when they let the loas play out the mystery in their lives, especially through improvisatory black creativity. Black artistic and cultural forms are the vehicles of hoodoo, and black people only have to accept art and the range of cultural expression to experience and propagate life / hoodoo. The important point is that the hoodoo spiritual and supernatural becomes fully humanized, secularized, and manifested in the artistic creations of black people, as well as in everything else that they do that shows human desire and emotion.

PaPa and Battraville are mediator/artist types; their narratives further elucidate *Mumbo Jumbo* as a mysterious improvisatory text inspired by the gods and spirits. Battraville describes the source of a narrative of the history of voodoo's struggle with Atonism that is also implicitly the source of PaPa's later history: "Agwe, God of the Sea in his many manifestations, took over when I found it difficult to explain things" (138). Battraville and PaPa's stories come from supernatural possession by a god or spirit whose strange and different shapes represent themselves in mythic narratives that ambiguously illustrate the mystery but at the same time celebrate the rites of life/voodoo and project its victory. These are improvised creations like *Mumbo Jumbo*. The spirits speak through Battraville and PaPa to create parts of the story within the story in the same way that they speak through the theoretical artist of the novel.

Black Herman is another mediator/artist whose work is a different model for the writing of *Mumbo Jumbo*'s theoretical artist, as shown in a scene in which he uses improvisation to cure harmful hoodoo possession. PaPa's assistant Earline does not understand that she has to feed or supplicate the loas with which she interacts in Mumbo Jumbo Kathedral (28). As a result, she suffers a powerful possession that is potentially harmful to her and others. PaPa says that Earline "picked up [a loa] . . . the one with the red dress on. The one known in Brazil as Yemanjá; you know what W. C. Handy called her: St. Louis Woman" (125–26). Like most things in the novel, Earline's case remains significantly a mystery, but it seems that her failure to deal properly with the loas causes her habitation by the spirit Erzulie (130), a spiritual double for Osiris's sister/love mate Isis (162). This spirit also turns out to be a voracious sexual side of Earline's self that shifts her life toward predation and self-destruction. Black Herman and the hoodoo women assisting him access Erzulie in her powerful supernatural state through a mysterious traditional conjuring ritual, but Black Herman also plays the blues, "a loa that Jes Grew here in America among our people" (128), and has sex with Earline before Erzulie leaves her (125–30). Although he is capable of dealing with hoodoo spirits and their mystery, PaPa fails with Earline. Black Herman reminds him that he cannot cure Earline because he is not ready to improvise sufficiently: "You ought to relax. That's our genius here in America. We were dumped here on our own without the Book to tell us who the loas are, what we call spirits were. We made up our own . . . Doing The Work is not like taking inventory. Improvise some. Open up, Papa. Stretch on out with It" (130). Black Herman improvises by adding music and sex to his hoodoo spiritual ritual that succeeds in restoring sexual balance to Earline. His whole process defies concepts of Western reality and the standards of Christianity relating to spirituality.

Mumbo Jumbo's artist similarly redefines reality and spirituality by improvising a formal structure of unconventional novelistic forms that thematically portrays the importance of accepting and celebrating the diversity of life that comes from a mysterious world of gods and spirits. Hoodoo is a mystery, but the positive and negative of its life experience represent good that opposes Atonist evil. Battraville says that "no 1 knows how a new loa is formed. But we know that when 1 comes about it must be fed, similar to the way you feed your [African American] Ragtime and Jazz by supporting the artists and making it easier for those who are possessed by those forms. Buying records and patronizing those places which are not in the hands of Atonists. You know that if you don't do this, Ragtime and Jazz will turn upon you or unfed they will perish" (151). Dealing with the mystery of supernatural hoodoo possession in its many forms may produce positive or negative

effects, but everything associated with hoodoo *is* good, just as Atonism's repression of life stands for evil. The reconceptualization of good and evil is a
major redefinition of the text. In the narrative that the artist writes and in
Black Herman's improvised conjure, dangerous supernatural possession that
produces voracious sexuality and sex that has its source in human desire, as
well as a range of musical and cultural expressions such as jazz, are diverse
aspects of the mysterious hoodoo spiritual life that are not evil or profane.
Death is also an acceptable possibility of negotiating the mystery of the spiritual life. The case of PaPa's other assistant Charlotte is a textual mystery related to the general spiritual mystery. She makes mistakes in dealing with the
mysterious gods and spirits and practices "dilute dances of The Work" (104),
which apparently leads to her murder (123–24).

The theoretical artist is also like the artist of the original Book of Thoth
who illustrates the mysteries to reveal the work of the gods and spirits, and
to allow others to improvise on his text to deal with the always-cryptic mysteries. The original text, the Book of Thoth, is a book of the mysteries created in response to outbreaks of the life-supporting dances of Osiris that
were "something strange" because they disrupted the people's work (164). A
"certain artist . . . called on Osiris 1 day and argued his theory that the outbreaks occurred because the mysteries had no text to turn to. No litany to
feed the spirits that were seizing the people, and that if Osiris would execute
these dance steps for Thoth he would illustrate them and then Osirian priests
could determine what god or spirit possessed them as well as learn how to
make these gods and spirits depart." The artist created a "Book of Litanies to
which people in places like Abydos in Upper Egypt could add their own variations." The book is one for people to improvise on to develop their own
textual variations, in whatever creative or expressive forms that they take, to
negotiate the spiritual realm that is the source of life. *Mumbo Jumbo* is a further variation of the highly improvised secular "litanies" to hoodoo that me-
diate between the spirits and the people.

However, artistic mediation is not exclusive to privileged individual
artists like *Mumbo Jumbo*'s; the book of hoodoo is an indestructible text of
various musical, cultural, and physical media, including the human body,
and endless written, oral, aural, and visual forms constantly being improvised by artists of all kinds among the people who jointly contribute to a
tradition. Significantly, PaPa never finds the ancient sacred text that he
searches for during the Harlem Renaissance of the 1920s when Jes Grew is

also looking for its source, which is the text. Likewise, Jes Grew does not find it and consequently withers and dies in the 1920s. However, as PaPa says, this is not the end of hoodoo because black people can make their text: "We will make our own future Text. A future generation of artists will accomplish this" (204). African Americans can textually embody the mystery in themselves and their creations if they let hoodoo spirituality express itself in their lives. In the final analysis, there is no set way to create the text, and any person can be an artist/mediator who takes part in its creation.

The comments of Henry Louis Gates Jr. in his seminal book *The Signifying Monkey* (1988) are useful in my analysis of hoodoo mediators who are creators. He describes a central figure of black mediation and interpretation as the "divine trickster figure of Yoruba mythology, Esu-Elegbara" (5).

> This curious figure is called Esu-Elegbara in Nigeria and Legba among the Fon in Benin. His New World figurations include Exú in Brazil, Echu-Elegua in Cuba, Papa Legba . . . in the pantheon of the loa of Vaudou of Haiti, and Papa La Bas in the loa of Hoodoo in the United States. Because I see these individual tricksters as related parts of a larger, unified figure, I shall refer to them collectively as Esu, or as Esu-Elegbara. These variations on Esu-Elegbara speak eloquently of an unbroken arc of metaphysical presupposition and a pattern of figuration shared through time and space among certain black cultures in West Africa, South America, the Caribbean, and the United States. These trickster figures, all aspects or topoi of Esu, are fundamental, divine terms of mediation: as tricksters they are mediators, and their mediations are tricks. (5–6)

Gates delineates a dissemination of African cultural and religious tradition that is generally similar to Reed's. In *Mumbo Jumbo,* the emphasis is not the artist/mediator as a trickster, but the trickster is comparable to Reed's creative figures because his mediation and interpretation, which Gates later encompasses in his concept of textual indeterminacy, creates and leaves open the mystery, the illustration of which still gives access to the spirit world and the basis of life. (Gates's analysis also reveals that Reed portrays PaPa LaBas as an artist/mediator by naming him in conformity with a tradition of black diasporic interpreter figures.)

I am making a similar but somewhat different point than Gates; I am centering the novel's explicit theme of voodoo spirituality and its influence on narrative creation through mediation, which is at most secondary in Gates's critique.[18] He shows why *Mumbo Jumbo* is one of the great texts of black indeterminacy (227–38). In his analysis, indeterminacy is the rich and profound play of textuality that always leaves interpretation and meaning ambiguous, and mystery is a thematic and formal aspect of textual indeterminacy. Gates points out the mysteries of the novel that are unsolved, partially solved, and solved, but all contribute to an overall mystery that is the text's indeterminacy (229–30). The mystery of "Voodoo/Hoodoo exposition" that deals with the Haitian Benoit Battraville and ends in the capture of Atonist Hinckle Von Vampton is the last of seventeen that Gates lists (230). My point is that voodoo/hoodoo is *the* source of mystery that is also the text's indeterminacy according to the novel's own theoretical statement about the origin of its story. It comes from the gods and spirits who make it mysterious in theme and form, and at the same time an expression of life grounded in human desire and daily endeavor. The gods and spirits make themselves known through human mediators who construct a strange myth of their existence and through their manifestation in the actions and other productions of mediators. (The construction of myth is similar to Christians gaining understanding of God by creating his myth in various kinds of religious stories, although *myth* is not a word that most Christians would use.) The emphasis on voodoo/hoodoo spirituality and narrative mediation is in the background of Gates's analysis and others' criticism, and I place it in the foreground as it is in the text thematically and formally.

Hoodoo spirituality produces a narrative that debunks Christianity and the Bible; an important part of this is the novel's unequivocal rejection of the idea of the one, almighty Christian God. It seems that Atonists constructed God by reducing multiple voodoo gods to one: PaPa says that "all of the gods who were rivals of the 1 they called Jehovah . . . were driven underground and the many were reduced to 1; even Muhammad, 1 of Jehovah's allies in the priesthood, is depicted in a church carving as the devil" (170). Earlier when chastising Abdul about Islam's intolerance of the belief in other gods that is just like Christian practice, Papa asks "where does that leave the ancient Vodun aesthetic: pantheistic, becoming, 1 which bountifully permits 1000s of spirits, as many as the imagination can hold. Infinite Spirits and Gods. So many that it would take a book larger than the Koran and the Bible, the Tibetan Book of the Dead and all of the holy books in the world to list, and still room would have to be made for more" (35). The novel builds mystery upon mystery in the context of its overall theme that everything is a mystery produced by hoodoo spirituality, and the origin and nature of innumerable gods and spirits is an aspect of the mystery. However, the text clearly suggests that the construction of God's divinity and supremacy by Atonists is an evil human device that has the purpose of empowering Atonists and negating voodoo spirituality that is indigenous to human life. Atonist evil is very real and apparently the necessary binary opposition in the struggle between Atonism and Voodoo, which is destined to end in the latter's triumph, but it is unclear whether God was originally one among the infinite gods somehow transformed to evil by Atonist appropriation or more purely an evil Atonist fabrication. Again, almost everything is mystery, and this includes the construction of God in this instance. What is clear is that God lacks the spiritual substance of voodoo gods. The text effectively reverses the biblical paradigm that God is authentic and that other gods are bogus and powerless.

Like God, Jesus Christ is an Atonist construction, and his power in the novel is sorcery, which is ironic and purposeful because in the Bible a sorcerer is a fake and the evil opposition of Jesus. PaPa describes Jesus in terms of his voodoo belief: "Mary was the mother of the Atonist compromise Jesus Christ. They made him do everything that Osiris does, sow like a farmer, be a fisherman among men but he is still a *bokor*, a sorcerer . . . Lazarus [whom Jesus raised from the dead] was a zombie!" (170). Two examples from the New Testament show that sorcerers are simulators of godly powers and anti-Christs. Acts 8:9–11 describes an insidiously evil man: "But there was a certain man, called Simon, which beforetime in the same city used sorcery, and bewitched the people of Samaria, giving out that he himself was some great one: To whom they all gave heed, from the least to the greatest, saying, This man is the great power of God. And to him they had regard, because that of long time he had bewitched them with sorceries." In Acts 13:4–12, Paul and Barnabas in their ministry to the Gentiles encounter "a certain sorcerer, a false prophet . . . whose name was Bar-jesus" (Acts 13:6). He tries to prevent Paul from converting an official of the gentiles to Christianity, and Paul cites his evil and opposition to God: "O full of all subtlety and all mischief, thou child of the devil, thou enemy of all righteousness, wilt thou not cease to pervert the right ways of the Lord?" (Acts 13:10).

Mumbo Jumbo's specific reference to Jesus Christ as a "sorcerer" juxtaposes biblical textuality and the novel's voodoo textuality; it turns the Bible's negative signification of sorcery as evil back upon the text and Jesus Christ, its archetype of good. Belief in the spiritual significance of the biblical story in which Jesus Christ is sacred is an icon of Western and African American tradition. It reduces religions other than Christianity, voodoo in particular (in America and among African Americans), to superstition at best and at worst to sorcery, evil practice and belief that may have unexplainable but somehow unreal and ungodly power. *Mumbo Jumbo* reverses the Bible's powerful indictment of voodoo and consequently of the voodoo text. In the novel, just as Jesus Christ is in reality a sorcerer, an evil impostor, the Bible is an evil text of sorcery and the voodoo text is truly spiritual. Further, the Bible is the main text of Atonist reduction of irreducible multiplicity; as such, it is the antithesis of truth instead of the spiritual revelation of divine and human reality from God. PaPa's remark about the incapacity of religious books to encompass numberless voodoo gods and spirits helps to make the point. The Tibetan Book of the Dead is not a part of the novel's negative critique, but implicitly, all voodoo/hoodoo texts, *Mumbo Jumbo* among them, are more truly "holy books" than the Bible and Koran because they are imaginary, highly improvised responses to the true mystery of thousands of gods and spirits. *Mumbo Jumbo* sums up its perspective on the Bible with the statement that PaPa would not "dare touch the accursed thing [the Bible]" (47–48).

Improvisational voodoo textuality creates large ruptures in the form and structure of the biblical text; an example is the novel's account of Moses, which deconstructs a central biblical theme and human characterization. PaPa says the "VooDoo tradition instructs that Moses learned the secrets of VooDoo from [his father-in-law] Jethro and taught them to his followers. H. P. Blavatsky [who is quoted in the text and cited in *Mumbo Jumbo*'s 'Partial Bibliography'] concurs: 'The fraternity of Free Masons was founded in Egypt and Moses communicated the secret teaching to Israelites, Jesus to the Apostles and thence it found its way to the Knights Templar.' But this doesn't explain why he received the [evil] Petro Asson instead of the Rada [or good]. My theory is that it was due to the fact that he had approached Isis at Koptos [where she kept the Book of Voodoo] during the wrong time of the Moon and stirred her malevolent aspects thus learning this side of the Book. Others say that shortly afterward Moses and his Atonist followers went into exile" (186–87). Theoretically and practically, the novel's improvisation produces a text of religious mystery that defamiliarizes the Bible's narrative by giving an account of Moses that relates him to Atonist evil. The improvisation in *Mumbo Jumbo* is an esoteric plot of incongruous incidents, characterizations, events, and references cloaked in the text's overall mystery. The novel has an entirely different narrative semblance than the exhaustive linear narrative of Moses in the Old Testament, which covers four books and which conventionality has made seamless and iconic. *Mumbo Jumbo* opens up the possibility of a counterstory to the Bible.

Although the novel improvises a different story of Moses, the Bible often produces its own theme and structure that are equally improvised and mysterious. The New Testament Book of Revelation, the word of God revealing the second coming of Jesus Christ, is perhaps the best example. Take, for instance, the apostle John's vision of God's throne:

> [John hears a] "voice . . . as it were of a trumpet talking with me . . .
> And immediately I was in the spirit: and, behold, a throne was set in
> heaven, and one sat on the throne. And he that sat was to look upon
> like a jasper and a sardine stone: and there was a rainbow round
> about the throne, in sight like unto an emerald . . . And before the
> throne there was a sea of glass like unto crystal: and in the midst of
> the throne, and round about the throne, were four beasts full of eyes
> before and behind. And the first beast was like a lion, and the second
> beast like a calf, and the third beast had a face as a man, and the
> fourth beast was like a flying eagle. And the four beasts had each of
> them six wings about him; and they were full of eyes within: and they
> rest not day and night, saying, Holy, holy, holy, Lord God Almighty,
> which was, and is, and is to come. (Revelation 4:1–8)

The only distinctive difference between *Mumbo Jumbo's* depiction of Moses and other parts of the text and sections of the Bible like Revelations is that the latter is more phantasmic. Otherwise, theorized as the writer of Revelation, John is improvising just as much as the novel's theoretical artist to create a narrative that is as mysterious. This comparison that I have begun is a difficult one, though.

In fact, the weight of culture is overwhelming; there is no comparison in the context of Western tradition that centers the Bible and Christianity and trivializes a black "novel" like *Mumbo Jumbo*. Conventionalized and naturalized perceptions of a wrathful God and the grave, otherworldly focus of religion and spiritual texts are, at the very least, barriers to consideration of

Mumbo Jumbo's spiritual textuality. Because it is an anti-Christian novel and sets its voodoo creed and practice in the everyday, spiritualized temporal where people express their human desires and human creativity, most would deny that *Mumbo Jumbo* is a spiritual text. However, I take the novel on its own terms, which change the meaning of the spiritual and pose the alternative, and I juxtapose it to the Bible. I use Reed's own words to support my comparison. Responding to an interviewer's statement that he uses his writing to hoodoo people, Reed says: "I think writing can often be prescient . . . I think that's one of the elements in African religion, the seer, the prophet, the necromancer. One almost feels as though one is receiving a vision or revelation in this work. I think the books can be seen as amulets. An amulet, you know, is something you carry around and people say they carry my books around. With *Mumbo Jumbo* I advise if you don't read it, put it over your door! That comes out of the idea of the holy book, the sacred book. There are powers that really influence people in strange ways in these books" (Dick and Singh 185). Reed implies the novel's radically altered African religious view, its potential to create spiritual vision and revelation, and its juxtaposition to the Bible as a holy and sacred book.[19]

The concepts of linguistic and spiritual generation coalesce: as spiritual texts the Bible and *Mumbo Jumbo* purport to be sacred or supernatural revelation from God and the gods, respectively; on the other hand, the Bible is a text that can be theorized as such at the same time that it is a religious work of spiritual revelation, just as *Mumbo Jumbo* is. It is hard to conceptualize the spiritual "writing" of the Bible. John explains his spiritual "writing" of Revelation from the perspective of a vision "in the spirit." According to standard accounts in biblical study guides, the Bible was written as God's law first in nature, then on human conscience, and then on the table of stones that were the Ten Commandments. Later, the scriptures were written and manifested in the life of Jesus Christ, and finally in the human heart and the Christian life. The central principle of this approach is that "it is of the utmost importance that the reader . . . should approach the Bible in a reverent attitude of mind, regarding it as the inspired Word of God, and not as an ordinary literary production." Further, the Bible gives its own theory of the genesis of the Word, which is the spirit of God embodied in Jesus Christ: "In the beginning was the Word, and the Word was with God, and the Word was God. The same was in the beginning with God. All things were made by him;

and without him was not anything made that was made. In him was life; and the life was the light of men. And the light shineth in darkness; and the darkness comprehendeth it not . . . And the Word was made flesh, and dwelt among us (and we beheld his glory, the glory as of the only begotten of the Father,) full of grace and truth" (John 1:1–5, 14). Breaching the great space in the Western tradition that prohibits comparison with the Bible, one can see a generally similar textual explanation of spiritual generation in the novel. About the creative source of Benoit Battraville's story, Black Herman says: "Of course there was the man alternating with the spirit . . . didn't you see him jerk from time to time . . . Next time you go to a so-called Holiness storefront watch the soloist who is backed up by the choir of rattling tambourines; see if he or she doesn't jerk her head at a crucial moment 'when the Spirit hits her'" (138–39). The novel's explanation of spiritual production is more immediate because it manifests the spiritual in bodies and concrete things in line with its emphasis on the spiritualized temporal, but the spirit is ineluctable nonetheless. Overall, the spiritual process of writing and the reality of the spirit manifested in the word are cryptic and unexplainable.

The juxtaposition of texts reveals that it comes down to belief; analytically one cannot preclude comparison and exclude *Mumbo Jumbo*'s spiritual textuality. In spite of what many might initially say, there is no way to prove that either the Bible or *Mumbo Jumbo* is a spiritual text. Arguments become contested by the literary implications of both texts that refute spiritual creation, the reality of the equal lack of evidence of textual spiritual presence, and implicit and explicit areas of theory of textual production that lead to ambiguity. For example, *Mumbo Jumbo* is short, but it also has a larger theoretically imagined form, inspired by the gods and mediated by artists, which is vast and endless, greater than the Bible in fact. The Bible is the Word of God written by many different authors in a process of spiritual inspiration and inscription. It is hard to grasp the reality of *Mumbo Jumbo*'s larger theorized and imagined textuality, while the Bible is visible and thus material, formally and structurally, in spite of its spiritual ambiguity. However, it is also difficult to substantiate the spirit of biblical writing and its production of form and structure by inspired people. The spirit is not present in the writing of either text, and neither is the evidence of the animating force of the writing process. The Bible's spiritual production is more real than *Mumbo Jumbo*'s spiritual and literary production because we believe in God and not voodoo gods. It is somewhat easier to account for the human linguistic production of the spiritual text. Biblical textuality represents racial and cultural viewpoints and a dominant male ethos; it has evolved through versions to develop its past and contemporary forms, which brings to mind the ongoing improvisation of the voodoo text. Human device and desire is behind past biblical productions that all purport to be the word of God, and the same is true of *Mumbo Jumbo,* which takes the thematic and formal guise of improvised mediation between the gods and the human world.

Because God and the gods and the nature of the spiritual are a mystery, mystery is a dominant characteristic of texts that deal with the divine and supernatural to evoke spirituality. The inefficacy of language in demonstrating the spirit notwithstanding, the two works are comparable as spiritual texts because mystery is their general, overarching theme.[20] The Bible foregrounds the idea that the incomprehensible mystery of God will become manifest in Jesus Christ, who, in spite of his birth, life, death, and human legacy throughout the New Testament, only extends the mystery of God. Revelation 22:13 perhaps best sums up the mystery of God in Jesus Christ: "I am Alpha and Omega, the beginning and the end, the first and the last." From the creation in the Old Testament to the miracles of Jesus Christ and the apostles in the New Testament, the overall story of the Bible is mystery. In *Mumbo Jumbo,* the gods reside in a spiritual world, which humans beings can access. Mediators like PaPa LaBas, the incarnation of the Haitian mediator Papa La Bas and others in a line of diasporic mediators, interpret "the will of the gods to man [and] ... [carry] the desires of man to the gods" (Gates 5–6). However, mediation achieves limited solutions in specific instances instead of piercing through to the mystery's inner meaning, and there is no indication that humans can ever penetrate it, as is the case in Brodber's hoodoo novel *Louisiana,* where humans cross over to heaven. Part of the mystery of the gods is whether there is a human afterlife or, if not, what happens to humans when their individual lives end. One is hard-pressed to say which text is more dependent on mystery. The Bible's perspective perhaps promises a conclusion to life that *Mumbo Jumbo*'s does not, but *Mumbo Jumbo*'s reality is a different but equal mystery of the gods who control the never-ending progression of spiritualized temporal, everyday life from their accessible but impenetrable realm.

Form and structure are as important as theme in the voodoo text that expresses spirituality in ways radically redefined in opposition to the Bible.

Talking about Jes Grew, the contemporary form of voodoo/hoodoo, PaPa gives the basis for a discussion of this redefinition: "Jes Grew has no end and no beginning. It even precedes that little ball that exploded 1000000000s of years ago and led to what we are now. Jes Grew may even have caused the ball to explode. We will miss it for a while but it will come back, and when it returns we will see that it never left. You see, life will never end; there is really no end to life, if anything goes it will be death. Jes Grew is life. They comfortably share a single horse like 2 knights. They will try to depress Jes Grew but it will only spring back and prosper. We will make our own future Text. A future generation of artists will accomplish this" (204). As far as the general discussion is concerned, PaPa's statement recalls the spiritual mystery that life has "no end and no beginning," and affirms the point that I made at the beginning of this analysis that the mystery of life/voodoo in all of its diverse expressions and outcomes *is* good and will triumph. In connection with the main point about radical spiritual redefinition constituted by formality, it is textual creation that is pertinent; voodoo will flourish in part because artists in daily life will perform the spiritual act of making their own texts that will carry it and keep it alive.

A salient aspect of the redefinition is the idea that creative writing and other secular creativity is spiritual action that can be a form of mediation with the gods and spirits. In this context, PaPa is talking about the spirituality of the act of improvisational creation of the hoodoo text, which encompasses many individual texts that constantly change as well as a hypothetical Text that has no fixed form. The individual improvisation of PaPa and the artists theoretically creating *Mumbo Jumbo* is congruent with this redefinition. *Mumbo Jumbo*'s creative spirituality is a mixture of oppositional themes and the actual improvised formal diversity of the novel itself, which is syncretic like the practice of voodoo that Reed has related to his writing.[21] As other critics have also said, the novel includes the genre of detective fiction within its syncretic, diverse formal structure.[22] PaPa constructs the story as a detective searching for the missing hoodoo text and answers concerning the overall mystery of voodoo in its struggle with Atonism, and he at the same time tells it as a spiritually inspired mediator between the gods and the human world. PaPa's roles as detective and mediator are functions of the formal artist in which his improvisation redefines spirituality and religious practice as creative endeavors. In the formal construction of his narrative, PaPa performs the same spiritual acts as the theoretical artist of the novel and the artists within the novel who improvise and practice formal diversity. Considering the novel from the outside as a total structure and also from within where the creative process takes place on many different levels, the result is formal artistry that is a kind of gumbo or pastiche of novelistic structure, form, and genre. The creative act and practice of writing have nothing to do with spirituality beyond the boundaries of Reed's individual creation of voodoo, but are very relevant within the system of the novel. This analogy does not work completely because the novel's voodoo tradition is so radical in its opposition that it is incongruous to what we know and believe, but maybe the act of prayer as known in the Christian tradition, which does not exist in *Mumbo Jumbo,* corresponds generally to the formal construction that is the redefined spiritual acts of the artists. PaPa's and the artists' acts are spiritually mediatory like the invocation of prayer.

The substantive difference between the Bible and the voodoo spiritual text theorized and formalized by *Mumbo Jumbo* is the sacred Christian belief in one God as opposed to innumerable voodoo gods who deal with people in terms of the range of their human emotion, action, and creation in the spiritualized temporal world. PaPa's statement of belief in Jes Grew is equivalent to African American faithful vision in the tradition of the characters of most of the other novels that I am studying and the tradition of many African American writers, too. The novel's faithful vision is hardly recognizable as such because it entails spirituality and religious practice that are so different. Everything considered, the novel is atypical among African American texts when it comes to a forthright rejection of dominant traditions. No other text, except possibly *The Color Purple,* is as straightforwardly subversive as *Mumbo Jumbo* is. However, to create a narrative that violates Western and African American novelistic and cultural tradition is Reed's intention.

Its difference notwithstanding, *Mumbo Jumbo* may be a great novel because, among other reasons, it potentially forces readers to suspend traditional belief and consider its epistemological basis. The Bible is universally accepted as a great spiritual text, and others see it as great literature as well. Most importantly, whether certain individuals acknowledge it or not, the Bible undergirds so much of the deepest belief of people of all races who are acculturated in the West. However, consideration of *Mumbo Jumbo*'s overall value as a work that influences critical thinking requires at least a brief additional comparison of the epistemological grounding of the Bible and the reality theorized and actualized by the novel. The text's uses of myth provide examples. The Bible's epic structure is explicit and detailed in mythic formation, and the novel's adumbrated one is implicit, sporadic, and elliptical. Despite this formal dissimilarity, the texts present equivalent overarching myths that support their respective world views and provide a basis to think about epistemology and its relationship to belief.

Although initially the novel's directly and indirectly stated myth seems so unrelated to reality, the difference between the reality prescribed in the novel's myth and the Bible's is cultural perception and valuation as much as substance. We can only believe and have faith in the Bible's consequent Judeo-Christian doctrine and can not ultimately substantiate its defining myth. For example, Genesis initiates its dominant myth that makes God and existence real: "In the beginning God created the heaven and the earth. And the earth was without form, and void; and darkness was upon the face of the deep. And the Spirit of God moved upon the face of the waters" (Genesis 1:1–2). God then creates man and woman in a sin-free state from which they fall and initiate the human journey. The novel develops a creation myth that similarly presents its teleology and story of existence. Voodoo has "no end and no beginning," and "led to what we are now" (204). Although it starts at a certain time and not with the first humans, the novel lays out the terms of its spiritualized temporal life: "A certain young prince who was allergic to thrones attended a university in Nysa, a town in Arabia Felix (now Yemen) . . . At this time in history those who influenced the growth of crops and coaxed the cocks into procreation were seen as sorcerers . . . The processes of blooming were acted out by men and women dancers who imitated the process of fertilization. They would play upon instruments, reeded stringed and percussive, as they acted out the process; open their valves, and allow nature to pour through its libation" (162). Unlike the Bible, which takes a serious tone toward the sacred and divine, the novel adopts a light tone focused on the spiritual that is thoroughly integrated in the secular, emphasizing festive ritual and human sensuality. The novel's stance on reality that is widely divergent from the Bible's and antithetical to the dominant Western belief does not prove that its myth has less grounding in truth. It is our mind set, which is so strong that the novel's perspective does not resonate seriously or at all, that makes it untruthful.

I would conclude that Christian faithful belief is ultimately necessary, and without it life has little promise and stability. However, there may be other ways of seeing the world in terms of the spiritual and supernatural, and epistemologically the Western may not be any more concrete and provable than others. It is almost impossible to escape a reliance on faithful belief, whether it is Christian, voodoo, or otherwise.

Fiction, Life, and Faithful Vision

Final Thoughts on Its Overall Portrayal and Relevance

RELIGIOUS BELIEF AND FAITHFUL vision are fundamental to black culture and black people, and are much more influenced by the African past and voodoo/hoodoo than most people are aware. Some African Americans born before the 1950s know that voodoo/hoodoo has had an influence, while many born later do not. Older black people may simultaneously think of themselves as solely Christian, recognize the hoodoo presence in their family past that has impacted their belief, and talk about family members who were Christians and used hoodoo at the same time. An African American man born in 1938 recently told me that his mother was a staunch Seventh Day Adventist who still practiced hoodoo. The mother remembered her mother, a former slave who professed Christianity and relied on hoodoo as well. The man feels that he does not combine elements of hoodoo with his practice of Christianity, but at the same time he is cognizant that hoodoo is an important religion that deeply informs his past and the African American past and present.

Some black people of this man's generation would disagree and say that hoodoo is a peripheral, occult practice having no religious significance, a sentiment that increases among younger African Americans. The very young have never heard of hoodoo or have heard about it only in the commercialized media. Using my professorial dialogue and interaction with students as a guide, I would quickly add, however, that younger African Americans profess a strong belief in the Christian God, somewhat surprisingly considering the wide range of images and messages to which a global media exposes them. None of this means that African American faithful vision is not Christian as black people claim it is, but there are elements of black Christianity, either ignored, unacknowledged, or unknown, that make African American faithful vision different, just as the cultural past and the historical past are different.

Charles Johnson has consciously set himself apart from the narrative mainstream of African American fiction in most of his writing, but his first novel, *Faith and the Good Thing* (1974), projects this cultural difference among African Americans, not in line with the perception that Christian belief stands alone but with the more inclusive narrative perspective of other novels that specify or imply the dominance of wider influences. The main character Faith Cross sets out on a quest for the "Good Thing." She comes from Hatten County, Georgia, a community in which the preacher is prominent and the Christian tradition is strong, but its main religious belief and practice resides in the hoodoo or conjure tradition represented by the mythical, supernatural Swamp Woman. Through the Swamp Woman, Faith finds more than the Christian salvation figured in her name. She reaches an understanding that the Good Thing is seeking the answer to the unending mystery of life, which is greater than the mystery of God that has a promised revelation and resolution. The Swamp Woman's tale names God but foregrounds mysterious gods who interact with human beings in their search for the Good Thing. According to the tale, the gods decided to torment men by hiding the Good Thing when one human actually saw it: "They hid the Good Thing, child, and the world darkened like a room deprived of its only light. But even the gods could not destroy it. It is a wish, a possibility that can only be deferred; and so, even today, it remains hidden" (30). The most that the Swamp Woman can finally tell Faith is that "there ain't nothin' but searchin' and sufferin,' too! To be human *is* to suffer, child—to feel, to be sentient, y'see?" (189). The novel ends: "There always was and always will be an old Swamp Woman cackling and conjuring in the bogs . . . just like there'll always be the Good Thing for folks willing to hear and hunt for it. But you've got to believe in it. Don't be interrupting to ask if the tale is true." "Was it Good?" "Was it Beautiful?" "All right" (196). As unconventional as Johnson's novel may be with regard to calling its narrative of a black woman's pain and tragedy a good and beautiful story, *Faith and the Good Thing* (as the title would indicate) is, among other things, significantly about faithful vision in the life of an individual and in African American culture, wherein hoodoo forms a syncretism with Christianity and encompasses it.

Johnson's critical enterprise does have a clear connection to the central tradition of faithful vision like those of other writers who focus on the broad scope of the African American cultural tradition. Johnson's later novels take an even more radical stance toward the African American experience, seemingly violating the cultural and writing traditions in which faithful vision substantively mitigates the effects of pain, tragedy, and oppression. But *Faith and the Good Thing* demonstrates that the foundation of important concepts about African American culture in the later work develops from the novel's portrayals that draw heavily from a hoodoo worldview. In *Oxherding Tale* (1982) and *Middle Passage* (1990), two major novels after *Faith and the Good Thing*, the key is trust that means coming to terms with the negative that is part of an intersubjective process that constantly renews. African Americans only have to surrender to the process of intersubjectivity that incorporates everything, good and evil, animate and inanimate, into a positive, ever-evolving Being. Trust in the more recent novels seems to have nothing to do with the heavily hoodoo reliant faith in the first novel. Nevertheless, the idea that one must trust in the constant development of Being is like the Swamp Woman's conviction that "you've got to believe in" the Good Thing, the always-deferred mystery presided over by the gods for which humans always search and evolve into new lives that include suffering. The substance of faith and trust is similar. The ground work of Johnson's later fiction, which incorporates other religions in addition to hoodoo, is in *Faith and the Good Thing*, and the belief systems of the later fiction rest on its highly hoodoo-influenced theme. Johnson tries to rewrite the African American tradition more so than other writers in this study. He succeeds in being unusually subversive but embedded in his work is African American faithful vision that is basic in the culture.

Johnson's work shares the comprehensive viewpoints of other novels that widen the perception that African American faithful vision is only Christian. Unlike Johnson's novels, which are almost polemical in affirming the textual theme of trust that transcends all and leads to renewing wholeness, these texts often give credence to a double focus that legitimizes the cultural point of view as well as a textual one. Most of the novels that I have analyzed reflect African Americans' commitment to a centering faithful vision, which the textual perspective does not subvert. While the narrative viewpoints of the texts do not undercut cultural belief and show the writers' investment in the culture from the culture's standpoint, there are, as I have been saying, a variety of implied critical approaches to faithful vision that almost never parallel the cultural beliefs and practices of the characters. In several cases, the vision of the text is larger and more inclusive than that of the characters. The textual narrative often implicitly or explicitly shows African and diasporic retentions that are greater than the sources of the dominant Western Christian faith (particularly from the early twentieth century to the present), which is especially prevalent in the contemporary perception of African Americans and of other people when they conceptualize African Americans.

In *Go Tell It on the Mountain,* the fundamentalism of the African American religious tradition and of the characters' belief represents the most uniformly Christian portrayal of faithful vision. The characters' interpretation of the Bible in the present, and seemingly in the slavery past portrayed through Gabriel and Florence's mother, is strict, and their adherence to the sovereignty of God is unwavering. The text juxtaposes its social and political viewpoint against this, but *Go Tell It on the Mountain* also implies recognition of the same possibilities of the biblical Word and of faith that the characters see. The novel's social and political critique of the characters and their religious tradition never suggests that the tradition has unrealized sources that are wider than the Christian.

In Randall Kenan's *A Visitation of Spirits* (1989) the textuality of the Bible and associated religious belief also have great power over the characters, even to the point of dictating the suicide of Horace, who violates the biblical prohibition on homosexuality. But *A Visitation of Spirits* sets its own textuality against the biblical as a kind of conjuring reminiscent of hoodoo, although it is not specifically given that name. A counterpart to biblical citation and allusion and the focus on Christianity is the general referencing of the non-Christian supernatural in the section titles: "White Sorcery," "Black Necromancy," "Holy Science," "Old Demonology," and "Old Gods, New Demons." Along with this, Horace practices occult rituals, which are influenced by reading white texts that are not part of his community's tradition, to exorcise himself of the demon of homosexuality. At the end, the biblical, the religious, and the related faith that have been the traditional mooring remain central from the textual perspective and ironically even to Horace, the tragic consequences notwithstanding. If anything, it is the potential counterstory, which does not save Horace, that is destabilized. So the writing of the text and the rituals within it are not explicitly hoodoo supernatural acts, which in other novels are always significantly effectual. However, the supernatural is another major dimension of the narrative—and not the communal tradition—that suggests the desire for hoodoolike possibilities broader than the Christian. This would be particularly true in the context of the mysterious history and tradition of voodoo/hoodoo in Ishmael Reed's *Mumbo Jumbo* (1972) that relates it to the European as well as the African, and to an almost unlimited conception and practice of the supernatural.

In *The Cattle Killing,* the supernatural intrusion of African reality in the vision of the African American Christian preacher, and at least one brief indication of his longing for another god, could imply that he is unconsciously affected by a larger voodoo/hoodoo spirituality. Along with this, the text is, in part, a hoodoo counterstory to oppression like *A Visitation of Spirits.* At the end of *The Cattle Killing,* everything comes back to the hegemony of the biblically inscribed oppressive power of God that the textual narrative seemingly cannot subvert, but when the preacher separates from the white church and takes his African American congregation to the woods, a vision of the African community supernaturally imposes its presence on him. Because of the severity of oppression, he eventually loses Christian faith, which still manifests itself in Bishop Allen's highlighted moment of pain and suffering, and can only pray "not to any god anyone has named" (199). Although he apparently does not realize it or state it directly, his vision suggests supernatural hoodoo realities that are more than the Christianity that he preaches, particularly in light of the reference to the unspecified god and, even more substantively, in the overall context of this analysis of works such as *Mumbo Jumbo.* In the text of *The Cattle Killing,* the hoodoo supernatural is an embedded aspect of many narratives that fail to rewrite oppressive Western textuality, and so on one level the novel is an unsuccessful hoodoo conjuration of oppression.

Although it is not immediately apparent, *The Color Purple* (1982) is another text that has nuances of a supernatural hoodoo incantation against oppression, and unlike *A Visitation of Spirits* and *The Cattle Killing,* its invocation is more in line with the power of hoodoo in *Louisiana* (1994) and *Mumbo Jumbo.* Celie's recreation of God within herself has a lot to do with decentering the patriarchy and centering the black female. However, sometimes the language associated with her destruction of the patriarchal God may indicate that she engages in a hoodoo ritual against him. Shug tells Celie that she should not let God impose his image on her imagination: "*Conjure* up flowers, wind, water, a big rock" (168, italics mine). Celie describes the effectiveness of her conjure: "Every time I *conjure* up a rock, I throw it." The use and repetition of a word could be coincidental, but the larger thematic structure of the novel reinforces the subtle signs of hoodoo presence. The dedication thanks the "Spirit" for assistance in the writing, and a statement at the end calls the author a medium who has invoked the characters and what they have done. In the concluding section of the narrative, God is stars, trees, sky, and people—"Everything" (242). There are overall intimations of the hoodoo supernatural that cannot be separated from the agency that writes the subject of the female self and the story. While the traditional faithful vision is Nettie's, there is still an understated textual affirmation related to hoodoo.

As I already mentioned in the introduction, the folk sources and African nuances that coalesce with the biblical in Toni Morrison's *Beloved* could form a classic portrayal of hoodoo syncretism with Christianity. As is often the case in Morrison's novels, about which it is hard to be conclusive, the complex thematic enriches the text by implying that there is a more universal religion than Christianity. This religion remains ambiguous, perhaps even more than it is in *A Visitation of Spirits, The Cattle Killing,* and *The Color Purple,* where the implications of hoodoo are nascent. The *textual* parody of the Bible is clear, but a specific alternative to biblically based Christianity is not, largely because of the novel's concept of collective consciousness, an all-encompassing racial memory that exists synchronously for individuals and for communities. This consciousness would include Christianity and the life of Jesus Christ, which the text subtly states, and voodoo/hoodoo, which one can infer from the novel. The text critiques the Bible and also makes the sacred, spiritual, and supernatural agency supporting African American faithful vision nondefinitive, the portrayal of which makes it stronger and more substantive in this particular novel.

The various textual treatments of African American religious and faithful belief all reference an identifying feature of black culture. When one sets the novels that significantly negate this cultural aspect against those that exemplify it, the worlds of the former texts are flat and artificial in the specific terms of their failure to project the full scope of the African American cultural tradition as it relates to the group and the individual. *Invisible Man* (1952) is without a doubt one of the great novels of the twentieth century, and it is an African American novel that had an all-important role in shaping the tradition of fiction. However, I would argue that it would be an even more powerful work if it did not end by at least symbolically negating the importance of the African American cultural tradition, a central part of which is the sacred, spiritual, and supernatural tradition that the text earlier reveals. Brief episodes dealing with religious ritual in John Edgar Wideman's early fiction lead to stronger representations of religious belief and tradition in the later years, *The Cattle Killing* being the most complex and provocative. African American cultural and religious tradition becomes an increasingly prominent feature of his work, contributing to progressively rich, diverse, and penetrating exploration. Like *Invisible Man,* Richard Wright's *Native Son* (1940) is a great and important novel in the literary tradition. However, its denial of the importance of the black perception of existence and of faithful vision leaves a great void. The depiction of a hollow, hopeless, and desolate universe, where African American faith based on belief in the sacred, spiritual, and supernatural is irrelevant, does not coincide with the truth of lived experience as many, and perhaps most, people perceive it, or with reality as it is constructed in different creative forms and media, particularly by black artists. In this context, *Native Son* seems shortsighted and inadequate.

My focus on Christianity and voodoo/hoodoo in the preceding chapters obviously does not mean that these are the only religions that have had an impact on African American life, but because of historical and social forces, these are the two that are set deeply as foundations in the African American tradition. For example, the Black Muslim religion led by Elijah Muhammad had and still has a significant influence. However, the religion has had its greatest effect on African Americans since the middle of the twentieth century, and it has never had as many believers as Christianity. Some African Americans would perhaps more readily acknowledge the Muslim religion as culturally significant while denying the importance of hoodoo, but research and analysis confirms the opposite. Voodoo/hoodoo and Christianity have such a strong presence because they are connected to the African cultural past and to the tradition of white Westerners who enslaved Africans, respectively, and they are consequently the subjects of African American writers who write about black people, especially those who explore the African American tradition in depth. The Muslim religion is sometimes a peripheral topic in the fiction, as it is in *Mumbo Jumbo.*

I would only accept the religious beliefs, either Christian centered or broadly conceived in hoodoo syncretism, as they are. What resonates most deeply in my life though is my aunt speaking to me when we discuss our trials and tribulations: "The Lord didn't bring us this far to leave us." She is talking about God bringing the whole race through slavery and its racist aftermath and bringing our family and the two of us as individuals through all of our past and present hardships. The very same words of a good friend, a professor of English at a major university, vibrate in unison with my aunt's when we discuss our personal lives and our endeavors in the profession. As I really focus and listen to African American voices from the media and random moments in life, I hear these words spoken across the boundaries of class, gender, and age by members of so-called religious sects, conventional church denominations, and those who do not associate with any group. Although a different perspective may come from the world beyond family and friends, my personal references are to a specifically and solely God-oriented view of faith that is, in my assessment at least, typical of a dominant cultural perspective that does not include the heterogeneity of voodoo/hoodoo. This is what sustains me from my own vantage point, and from there faithful vision is very real and very necessary.

NOTES

INTRODUCTION

1. As far as recent theoretical and philosophical texts that deal with religion are concerned, Jacques Derrida alone has written many volumes. Not many critical texts dealing with novels analyze African American cultural tradition related to the religious and biblical and thus to the black faith that I am concerned with here, though. Dolan Hubbard's *The Sermon and the African American Literary Imagination* (1994) is one of the few that does. With regard to the treatment of the Christian and biblical in James Baldwin's *Go Tell It on the Mountain,* see, e.g., Nancy V. Burt and Fred L. Standley, eds., *Critical Essays on James Baldwin* (1988) and Trudier Harris, ed., *New Essays on Go Tell It on the Mountain* (1996). Only a few scholars contributing to these volumes talk about the novel's serious spiritual quest, and some reject the idea that there is one.

2. In connection with the assertion that faithful vision very much applies to life, I make the following argument relating to the Bible's theology and empowerment of people. It is important to remember that, as well as being a statement of the law, the Bible is a text that embodies all of the contradictions and complexities of life and that emphasizes people living and displaying human shortcomings. The word and plan of God are incontrovertible in the long and short terms. But in the course of the evolution of God's plan, people have a wide range of opportunity in their actions. Oftentimes, treachery, deceit, and even murder constitute the acts of many people, including those favored by God. His chosen instruments often do bad things, before and after they are chosen. From a larger perspective, human beings are not totally in control, and so no one can determine what will happen. It is impossible to know where human endeavors will lead. God sometimes does not seem to judge or punish evil and uses evil for his own good purposes. One can only say that everything must be part of an ultimately benevolent plan that we do not understand. Nothing is clear in the Bible, however, and analysis only leads to contradiction. But the Bible empowers people in spite of, and in the very terms of, its complexities and contradictions, especially in light of the complex and contradictory doctrine of grace. It empowers them to do good and bad in the process of what they see as necessary, as well as empowers them to see that evil perpetrated against them historically may not serve the intentions of its perpetrators.

3. Basically the word *hoodoo* is the African American version of the diasporic term *voodoo.* I deal with the derivation of the word and its uses in later chapters.

4. Among the writers expressing agnosticism or atheistic frustration and doubt are poets Countee Cullen (Benjamin Mays, *The Negro's God as Reflected in His Literature* [1938], 219–20, 227–29) and Langston Hughes (238–39), and novelists Nella Larsen in *Quicksand* (1928; Mays 220–24), Walter White in *Fire in the Flint* (1924; Mays 225), and Jessie Fauset in *Plum Bun* (1929; Mays 225–26). Other notable writers who have expressed negative conceptions of God are W. E. B. Du Bois (Mays 231–34) and James Weldon Johnson (234–36). Hughes, Du Bois, and Johnson also wrote works that conceptualize God positively or that reflect the important role that God plays in black life.

5. Ishmael Reed's *Mumbo Jumbo* (1972) is the only novel I discuss where voodoo/hoodoo is highly oppositional to Christianity. It is, however, still not possible to say that there is not some form of syncretism with Christianity in this text.

6. Ellease Southerland's *Let the Lion Eat Straw* (1979) is a structurally straightforward novel that nevertheless reveals the great depth of a black woman's life. *Let the Lion Eat Straw* was published during a time when black women's texts had already begun to appear with revolutionary literary perspectives that were reshaping the black and American literary canons. In many ways *Let the Lion Eat Straw*'s depiction of a woman of great strength and creativity who largely accepts her place in society does not fit the expectations created by the other new, exciting depictions of women. Alice Walker's popular and successful *The Color Purple* did not appear until 1982, but Walker's *The Third Life of Grange Copeland* (1970) had been published and Ntozake Shange's *for colored girls who have considered suicide/when the rainbow is enuf* had been performed in 1975, opening the way for a powerful new tradition in black women's writing that Walker's later novel only enhanced. The emphasis on the creativity of black women is an important part of this tradition. Abeba in *Let the Lion Eat Straw* is a creative woman, but she spends her life in the traditional patriarchally imposed role of child bearer, and fails to resist oppression in the way that black women characters resisted in the developing literary tradition of the time.

Along with its simple structure and being out of step with seminal black women's texts of the time, this surprisingly rich novel may seem simplistic because its faith is not intellectually mediated by the political and social to the extent that faith is in texts such as *Go Tell It on the Mountain.* Because of its structure and some aspects of its theme, maybe *Let the Lion Eat Straw* could only be a popular novel, although it is not. It seems to fall somewhere between the popular and serious categories and is not taken seriously in the academy or in the audience for black women's texts. However, we should at least revisit the novel to ask if its failure to bracket the African American cultural view of the sacred, spiritual, and supernatural in the accepted political and social terms, which trivialize the cultural, is a problem as far as its reception is concerned. If it is, then we should further ask if these standards should dictate the neglect of a work that penetrates substantively into African American life and cultural tradition beyond the isolated academic and intellectual world.

7. Generally, the Bible, like the novel, also portrays evil as part of the benevolent plan and, at places, clearly implies that faith is tantamount to accepting evil: "The Lord hath made all things for himself: yea, even the wicked for the day of evil" (Proverbs 16:4). What is different in *Let the Lion Eat Straw* is that someone apparently evil, Angela, lives by her own faithful vision as well as representing the evil that the faithful must accept. Although mystery constitutes voodoo/hoodoo and Christianity, in the case of the novel, hoodoo has another dimension of mystery with regard to Angela being both faithful and evil.

8. An important novel that deals with healing and salvation from an alternative spiritual perspective influenced more by hoodoo than by Christianity is Toni Cade Bambara's *The Salt Eaters* (1980). Minnie Ransom is a modern healer reminiscent of a hoodoo woman who helps political activist Velma Henry to achieve wholeness through a syncretism of various traditions and beliefs. Another text oriented toward hoodoo is Don Belton's *Almost Midnight* (1986). W. Lawrence Hogue describes Belton's novel and its theme: Hoodoo or voodoo "wants to ruin, exceed, or decode the majority, middle-class Christian language. It wants to give history, validity, and existence to Voodoo as a way of life that has been excluded, repressed, or subordinated by the majority language" (*The African American Male, Writing, and Difference: A Polycentric Approach to African American Literature, Criticism, and History* [2003], 227). Among the other texts informed by hoodoo that Hogue lists (250–51) are Rudolph Fisher's *The Conjure Man Dies* (1932), Jewell Parker Rhodes's *Voodoo Dreams* (1993), Mary Monroe's *The Upper Room* (1985), Ntozake Shange's *Sassafras, Cypress and Indigo* (1982), Gayl Jones's *The Healing* (1998), and Rainelle Burton's *The Root Worker* (2001).

CHAPTER 1 *African American Faithful Belief*

1. The King James Bible, which I am using throughout this analysis, reads, "Even today is my complaint bitter: my stroke is heavier than my groaning" (Job 23:2).

2. At least one critic, Jerold Savory in "Bigger Thomas and the Book of Job: The Epigraph to *Native Son*" (1975), sees the aptness in the appropriation of Job. I would argue, however, that he reads the epigraph's significance and Job from Wright's own limited viewpoint instead of from African American culture's broader and more meaningful one.

3. In "Voodoo Parallels in *Native Son*" (1972) Eugene E. Miller says that while voodoo culture was not part of Wright's upbringing, he could have picked up knowledge of its rituals from what was unstated in black church practices that he did know,

or perhaps the influence came from black southern folklore. Further, it is possible that the voodoo influences and belief/faith in the novel are carryovers from African culture that Wright somehow incorporated. While Miller's essay is provocative and potentially illuminating, it does not go far enough in making its conclusions clear or in showing why the voodoo elements in the novel are possibilities about which one cannot reach clear conclusions.

4. As Robert L. Douglas points out, Wright did show the positive potential of black religious songs if not the clear value of Christianity to black people in the context of African American tradition in a work before *Native Son*. "Wright's waxing and waning between religious orthodoxy and skepticism [in *Uncle Tom's Children* (1938) and *Native Son*] signifies his continuing attempt to come to grips with Christian doctrine . . . Perplexed about the values of Christianity as a means of salvation and liberation, not knowing how it can be of value to black people or if it can be, Wright is torn between orthodoxy and skepticism" ("Religious Orthodoxy and Skepticism in Richard Wright's *Uncle Tom's Children* and *Native Son*" [1988], 87–88).

I would say that Wright was perplexed about what others saw as the value of Christianity, but unperplexed in his own negative feelings about it. Whereas Christianity may have some value for others in *Uncle Tom's Children*, it has little, if any, for the characters in *Native Son* and for the character Richard in Wright's autobiography *Black Boy* (1945). If Wright himself had any traces of positive feelings about Christianity and the black religious tradition, and one can by no means be certain that he did, he had changed his mind by the time he wrote *Native Son*.

5. In "Black Boys and Native Sons" (1963), Irving Howe says "the day *Native Son* appeared, American culture was changed forever. No matter how much qualifying the book might later need, it made impossible a repetition of the old lies. In all its crudeness, melodrama and claustrophobia of vision, Richard Wright's novel brought out into the open, as no one ever had before, the hatred, fear and violence that have crippled and may yet destroy our culture" (100–101). Howe also criticizes James Baldwin's negative assessment of Wright in "Everybody's Protest Novel" (98–100); he places the essay among all of Baldwin's early essays whose "rifts in logic" are obscured by "the brilliance of the language" (100). Further, according to Howe, Baldwin has never written "the kind of novel he counterposed to the work of Richard Wright," and even *Invisible Man* by Ralph Ellison, who also criticized Wright, does not surpass *Native Son*: "*Invisible Man* is a brilliant though flawed achievement, standing with *Native Son* as the major fiction thus far composed by American Negroes" (112). (Ellison responds to Howe in "The World and the Jug" in *Shadow and Act* [1964].)

6. Critics have analyzed the perplexing epilogue and its meaning in the overall context of the narrative. A good analysis is Per Winther's "The Ending of Ralph Ellison's *Invisible Man*" (1981). Winther concludes: "It is the Invisible Man's ill fortune that the various pressures that rest upon him are so strong that only through a series of defeats

is he able to arrive at a position which can satisfy his needs as a moral and social being. But in the end those defeats *are* turned to victory. Through various reversals of fortune, much boomeranging of his expectations, and a number of large and small epiphanies, he is led to an acceptance of the value of tradition and his Negro heritage" (286–87). Winther makes some worthwhile comments. However, it seems to me that contrary to what Winther claims, the narrator accepts "the value of tradition and his Negro heritage" to a limited extent at most.

It is clear from my critical perspective that the narrator makes choices that foreground modernism, allow Ellison to position himself as a modernist writer, and push the African American to the background in the process. I am not saying that this is a flaw in this great and important novel. I only assert that this is what Ellison did in the literary milieu of his times, and it turned the emphasis of the novel away from African American culture to serve his purposes. Later African American writers, and apparently also Ellison himself, moved in a different direction in another time with different influences and pressures.

7. John F. Callahan says that he did not rewrite Ellison's work: "Now, the editor of a posthumously published novel should not use his own words to finish what the author left unfinished or unsaid. The state of the latest manuscripts should determine editorial decisions" (366). Callahan used what Ellison had already done to determine his arrangement and sequencing of the narrative sections that constitute *Juneteenth*. He minimizes the actual changes that he makes in Ellison's writing within the sections (*Juneteenth* [1999], 366–68).

8. Ellison left a note (Callahan included it at the end of the text) that is helpful in reading *Juneteenth*: "Bliss realizes [the] political and social weaknesses of Hickman and other Negroes when he's taken from his coffin, and this becomes mixed with his yearning for a mother—whom he now identifies with the redheaded woman who tried to snatch him from his coffin" (357). Further, he "is a man who sees the weaknesses in the way social hierarchy has dealt with race and it is through the chink that he enters white society and exploits it" (358).

9. Wideman has talked about Ellison being one of his influences. See, e.g., John O'Brien's interview with Wideman in *Interviews with Black Writers* (1973) and Wilfred Samuel's in *Callaloo* 6, no. 1 (1983). For an analysis of the relationship between Ellison and Wideman's writing, see pp. 136–39 of James W. Coleman's *Black Male Fiction and the Legacy of Caliban* (2001).

10. Eliot is the modernist who takes an intellectual approach to the world that encompasses religious as well as secular traditions. In his early work, Wideman alludes often to Eliot. In *Hurry Home* (1970), Cecil invokes the personages in Eliot's poems, and is a modernist intellectual looking at and analyzing religious tradition in ways reminiscent of them. Cecil strongly opposes African American religious ritual and faithful belief but deals with religion in abstract intellectual terms, particularly those

of the modernist texts of Eliot and other writers. Among the religious texts that *Hurry Home* refers to and paraphrases is the Koran (178–79).

11. The novel was published in 1970 before the heightened social attention to misogyny in African American culture and the awareness of oppressive patriarchal doctrines of Christianity and other religions generated by academic debate and critique. The text reveals sensitivity toward issues of gender, patriarchal religious doctrine, and the treatment of women but does not share today's full cognizance of the abuse of women and the male centeredness of religions. The central point in *Hurry Home* is about African American Christianity: Esther's religious beliefs make no sense but, paradoxically, are empowering. And, implicitly, Cecil stands apart from an entire black community that is potentially empowered in ways similar to Esther's empowerment.

12. Gospel singing and, to a lesser extent, prayer are recurring motifs in the characters' memories that seem to remind them that they have the black religious tradition to draw on for support, but these references are fragmentary and fleeting and provide no substantive counterpoint to hopelessness and gloom. Desperate for answers, Bernice Wilkerson generates pathos in the jail scene near the end when she reminds herself that she must pray for her husband who is charged with murder (258), but her general bitterness and negativity underlie her desperation at the jail. Much more than in *A Glance Away* and *Hurry Home,* the characters in this text have occasional perceptions of the positive relationship of black secular music to their lives. Jazz, including the "jazz life" of the musician, and the blues are the main contrapuntal symbols to chaos and destruction. The secular musical tradition may have a stronger presence than the religious, but the characters do not move beyond sporadic reminiscence to incorporate jazz and blues music into their lives for sustenance.

CHAPTER 2   *The Centrality of Religious Faith*

1. *Go Tell It on the Mountain* establishes its connection to the (King James) Bible through the epigraphs to the novel's three major sections. Part one's epigraph is from Revelation 22:17, part two's is from Revelation 6:10, and part three's is from Isaiah 6:5.

The text foregrounds the religious fundamentalism that Baldwin experienced growing up and generally connects its role in the characters' lives to the central role that Christianity has played in African American tradition. Shirley S. Allen says that the "unity of Old Testament and New Testament faith . . . is characteristic of the Christian belief described in the novel—the teachings of a sect formed from Baptist practices and Calvinist doctrines, grounded in frequent reading of the King James translation of the Bible, and influenced by the needs, hopes, and artistic expression of Negro slaves" ("Religious Symbolism and Psychic Reality in Baldwin's *Go Tell It on the Mountain*" [1988], 168).

2. In *The Fire Next Time* (1963), Baldwin says repeatedly that life and people are inexplicable. (*Conundrum* is the word that he uses often.) "It seems to me that one ought to rejoice in the *fact* of death—ought to decide, indeed, to *earn* one's death by confronting with passion the conundrum of life. One is responsible to life: It is the small beacon in that terrifying darkness from which we come and to which we shall return. One must negotiate this passage as nobly as possible, for the sake of those who are coming after us" (105–6). We cannot ultimately understand life; we can only realize our potential by committing to it, which, as his novels show, means committing to exploring and defining the self by dealing with other people. This commitment is all that defines life and all one has to live for.

Implicitly, this is agnostic if not atheistic; however, reality as portrayed in *Go Tell It on the Mountain* represents more than Baldwin's personal views. Fundamentalism and the tradition of African American Christianity are juxtaposed to Baldwin's ideas and to implied moral and social standards generally. The novel does not totally privilege African American religion, but it by no means subverts it, either. As it turns out, the characters' religious beliefs that ground them in life and reality are as substantive as the opposing ideas of Baldwin and the secular standards.

3. As Trudier Harris points out, *Go Tell It on the Mountain* "was in many ways an extended rite of exorcism. [Baldwin] was trying in part to rid himself of the demons of hatred his stepfather had instilled in him" (2). As she says further, Baldwin's religious experience was also central (3). I am not so much interested in the autobiographical aspect of the novel as I am in its conflicted perspectives of the moral, social, and sacred that relate to religious belief. Michael F. Lynch finds fault with critics who see in Baldwin's work the dichotomy of the "individual and/or spiritual over against the political, an opposition Baldwin attempts to reconcile" ("A Glimpse of the Hidden God" [1996], 31). I agree that there is no unreconciled dichotomy in *Go Tell It on the Mountain*. For me, the reconciliation is a dynamic tension created by the conflicting perspectives. Lynch sees a similar reconciliation in Baldwin's own life: "Although Baldwin bitterly attacks Christianity over the course of his career for what he sees as its condoning of racism and injustice toward blacks, he developed a theology based on Christian ideals and on his individual quest for a loving God" (32). In the novel, the tension that reconciles is not a flaw but a powerful artistic paradox.

Further, Lynch says that "many critics ignore, minimize, or deny Baldwin's spirituality. But among the few who address the issue in *Go Tell It on the Mountain*, most find the novel an absolute denial of the possibility of belief." According to Lynch, the novel's best critics are Donald Gibson, Sondra O. O'Neale, and Shirley Allen because they "identify the affirmative treatment of Christian belief in the novel" (34–36). I agree with many of Lynch's assessments; however, my analysis reaches different conclusions because I strongly emphasize the novel's intertextual relationship with the Bible.

4. Baldwin does not address a final cause, such as the big bang theory, that falls within the perspective of science. It is interesting to speculate whether Baldwin was interested in science and whether he thought scientific theories lead in the direction of exploration of human interaction, which so much concerned him.

5. In criticizing the narrow perspective of protest fiction in "Everybody's Protest Novel" (1949), Baldwin said that a major limitation of protest was human categorization and thus limitation of the possibility of thought and action. Contrary to what protest shows, human beings strive for "freedom which cannot be legislated, fulfillment which cannot be charted" (15).

6. Sondra A. O'Neale reaches conclusions about Baldwin's works that largely fit my analyses in this chapter: "Baldwin . . . attempts to separate the visible history of black America's experience with [oppressive white] Christianity from the spiritual, visionary experience that both he and the race may have internalized. The reality of that unseen spiritual truth, codified in his novels by the suffering blues and tarrying spiritual motifs, enables him to keep advocating that the demonstrable love of Christ will bring to earth that paradise revealed on the threshing floor . . . The totality of his theme is a cosmologically oxymoronic statement in both language and philosophy that sensible faith in an unseen God cannot transcend experience in self, race, or society" (140–41). O'Neale finds in Baldwin's oeuvre the paradoxical portrayal of a powerful religious belief that I will analyze in *Go Tell It on the Mountain*.

7. It is not totally clear, but apparently David was married to two of the six women he had children by, Bathsheba and Eglah (1 Chronicles 3:1–9), and of course he was not married to the concubines. He was also married to Michal, the daughter of his predecessor King Saul (1 Samuel 18:17–30) but they had no children (2 Samuel 6:16–23).

8. In the context of the Bible, who has the right to think that he can claim David's title of the "Lord's anointed"? Does Gabriel have the right to think this? There is, of course, no definitive answer. But it would certainly seem that in the contexts of the Old and New Testaments and of the African American religious tradition, Gabriel and any other black person (or at least black man from the traditions' patriarchal perspectives) can justly aspire to the title. David is a powerful figure, but he is also "the shepherd boy, raised by God's power to be the king of Israel" (*Go Tell It on the Mountain*, 136). (And as I have said, from a moral and social viewpoint he does horrible things.) In the New Testament, the promise of the potential of holiness extends even further to the most wretched of sinners, such as the apostle Paul, and to the lowest in social standing through the Word and example of Jesus Christ, a descendent of the line of David. The black religious tradition has appropriated the most democratic biblical examples and ideals that apply to men and applied them to black life.

9. Esther is an enigma because the novel only presents her from the perspective of Gabriel and others. (This is also how it portrays Deborah and Elisha, whose strong

religious beliefs contrast them to Esther.) She carries the imprint of her biblical namesake in a complex, ambiguous way, as biblically named people in life and novels sometimes reflect the reality of those in the Bible for whom they are named. She is rebellious and haughty like Queen Vashti in Esther 1, but then her characterization is ambiguous when compared to the biblical Esther, whose internal motivations the Bible also never shows. Esther in the Bible becomes queen because she is the "fairest young virgin" (Esther 2) who pleases the king, and she ends up saving the remnant of the Jews in captivity (Esther 4–10). This story coincides with the novel only if one sees the possibility of the biblical story being "real" and having a substantive relationship to the secular world, which is what the novel poses. In this context, she plays a role with the "king," Gabriel, the "Lord's anointed," and, in ironic, contradictory ways, works toward the good of all, the potential of which manifests itself in John. In the novel the Bible's inscrutable divine plan substantively works itself out with characters who are often more than vaguely reminiscent of biblical counterparts.

There are many different ways of seeing Esther, however. As Gabriel's antagonist in the secular setting, Esther's characterization implies questions that juxtapose the text's secular and sacred views. She thinks that life is simple and that Gabriel makes it too complicated. She will not listen when he tells her that the Lord will punish them for their sin; she says that he has a right to enjoy himself even though he is a reverend (127). On one hand, Esther is the most human of characters who wants to live life by fully engaging it without any limiting ideology. This makes her similar to John's biological father Richard and to Florence's husband Frank, the other characters who totally disavow religion or blaspheme God. All of these characters die young, however, and while they are important alternatives to the characters governed by religious ideology, their view of the world may not give them the same strength to endure. This possible conclusion does not lead to any definitive judgment about either the secular or the sacred in the novel, but it does emphasize the multiple perspectives that, in the end, do not undercut the religious.

10. Trudier Harris says that Gabriel acts to save Deborah and his second wife Elizabeth because they are "fallen" women sexually, and therefore it is his male pride and not selfless motivation that guides him (*Black Women in the Fiction of James Baldwin* [1985], 12–14). Psychologically and socially, this is certainly true, but Gabriel and the text itself are so grounded in the Bible and the tradition of black religion that an opposing perspective is just as relevant.

11. In *The Fire Next Time*, Baldwin describes a similar conversion experience that he had as a boy: "All I really remember is the pain, the unspeakable pain; it was as though I were yelling up to Heaven and Heaven would not hear me. And if Heaven would not hear me, if love could not descend from heaven—to wash me, to make me clean—then utter disaster was my portion. Yes, it does indeed mean something—something unspeakable—to be born, in a white country, an Anglo-Teutonic,

antisexual country, black. You very soon, without knowing it, give up all hope of communion" (44). In *The Fire Next Time,* Baldwin looks back on his experience with knowledge and intellectual distance that John Grimes does not have, and he emphasizes the political, dominating oppressiveness of Western Christianity that undercuts the importance of African American religious experience. In the novel, African American religious belief has equal importance as a perspective that presents an unresolvable opposition to the political.

12. My analysis here mostly focuses on the vision of the apostle John in Revelation, but I point out that the vision of John Grimes in "The Threshing-Floor" is also reminiscent of those of the prophets Isaiah and Ezekiel. Elisha demonstrates his heavenly vision to others in 2 Kings 6:17. John Grimes's first name obviously recalls John the Baptist, the New Testament prophet whose birth and life were a prophecy of the life of Jesus Christ. (However, the last name Grimes is a clear reminder that the novel has its secular setting in Harlem, where John and his family live an impoverished existence.) Further, the mother of John the Baptist in Luke 1:5, 24, 36, and 57 is named Elisabeth, just as John Grimes's mother is.

13. The public life of Royal, Esther and Gabriel's unacknowledged "bad" son who is eventually murdered, is a punishment to Gabriel in the privacy of his heart for what he did in secret, just as some of what Absalom does "before the sun" (2 Samuel 12:12) punishes David for his secret acts. The stories, of course, do not specifically replicate each other, but there is at least a resonance of the biblical story in *Go Tell It on the Mountain* that is part of a strong overall intertextual relationship.

14. First Corinthians 5–8 says, "Charity suffereth long, and is kind; charity envieth not; charity vaunteth not itelf, is not puffed up, Doth not behave itself unseemly, seeketh not her own, is not easily provoked, thinketh no evil; Rejoiceth not in iniquity, but rejoiceth in the truth; Beareth all things, believeth all things, hopeth all things, endureth all things. Charity never faileth." Charity in the Bible means selfless love, and this is Deborah in *Go Tell It on the Mountain.*

15. In 2 Samuel 11–12, the prophet Nathan forces David to acknowledge his sin with Bathsheba, whereas in the novel Gabriel sins with Esther while married to Deborah, who plays a prophetlike role in detecting and presenting to Gabriel what he has done. *Go Tell It on the Mountain* implies a depth of textuality that goes beyond the physical and concrete and provides a compelling spiritual and religious reality that the secular text cannot subvert.

16. It is important to say, however, that the very flawed David is not the same as or the equal of Jesus Christ, but Jesus does descend directly from the line of David (Matthew 1). Even more importantly, the text of the Bible associates the two through their words and actions and through similar scenes. For example, David in great affliction and distress anticipates Jesus' words during the crucifixion: "My God, my God, why hast thou forsaken me?" (Psalm 22:1, Matthew 27:46, Mark 15:34). David

also figuratively describes the acts of his enemies in the terms of the mob's abuse of Jesus: "they pierced my hands and my feet" (Psalm 22:16, Matthew 27:35); and "They part my garments among them, and cast lots upon my vesture" (Psalm 22:18; Matthew 27:35). So in *Go Tell It on the Mountain,* the association of the humanly flawed John with Jesus and other holy prophets is similar to what the Bible does in relating David and Jesus.

17. In V. Hunt's "A Conversation with Randall Kenan" (1995), Kenan paired himself with Baldwin because they are both gay African American males, although Kenan is Southern and Baldwin is Northern and urban in many ways (415). Concerning writing about the gay experience, Kenan says that Japanese writer Yukio Mishima has influenced his work. He talks again about Mishima in Charles Rowell, "An Interview with Randall Kenan" (1998), 139−40, 142.

18. Kenan states that both Judeo-Christian and apparently less rigid humanistic values inform his writing. "It would be very difficult for me to create something that violated my sense of morality, which is not necessary [*sic*] Judeo-Christian all the time. It's much more humanistic" (Hunt 417). One can see how Kenan's work would reveal ambivalence about the Bible's strictures on homosexuality and its influence on Horace's fate. Kenan's comments about having a significantly Judeo-Christian moral sense may further indicate a struggle with biblical doctrine as it impacts the issue of his own homosexuality. He concedes to V. Hunt's statement that "Horace is, in some ways, a younger [Kenan]" (Hunt 416).

19. Kenan says about the parts of the novel that are written in the form of drama: "It was the best form to accomplish what I wanted the reader to see at that moment. When you read a play, you try to visualize it in another way than you do when you read a well-written scene in prose. There are associations that you get along with it. So it was ... something about the reader's relationship to the text that I wanted to exploit, the expectations that are brought to it, the appearance of the text" (Hunt 414). I would emphasize that Kenan's remark connects with my point about *A Visitation of Spirits* looking for its form in the supposedly more objective dramatic structure.

20. Kenan's comments about the title story in *Let the Dead Bury Their Dead* (1992) support what I say about the writing of history in *A Visitation of Spirits:* "I was playing with academic history as opposed to oral history as opposed to personal history, and memory, and plain old gossip. And how at once they are all very different and disparate, and all very much alike. How often do we look back at something that was written in stone, and not only that, but other people have written about it, you know, and secondary sources have become very influential, and then we see that this former person made all these mistakes ... looking back on it, it's all sort of subjective, the way we view history. The idea of historiography points out that there are limitations. You may be able to approximate the facts, but there is only one real event, and even that some people would question" (Hunt 414). As I have said, *A Visitation of Spirits*

shows that the truth of reality is as elusive as the truth of history: "Reality in some ways is like [history]. We can do all sorts of things to approach it, but we can never actually attain it" (Hunt 414).

CHAPTER 3 *Critiquing Christian Belief*

1. Robert L. Broad also compares Paul's words to those of Hosea (Hosea 3:1–3), who was the source for Paul's prophecy. Broad talks about Paul's misuse of Hosea's words and suggests that Morrison may have been using Paul's distortion of history for her own narrative purposes. "In puzzling out the poly-generational identities of the character Beloved and tracking down the full story of the novel's epigraph, we emulate and participate in the spiritual, historical, and political work of Morrison's book: dragging the history of 'Not-my-people' from the mire of the past" ("Giving Blood to the Scraps: Haints, History, and Hosea in *Beloved*" [1994], 195). Broad says earlier that "Morrison's fiction demands that her readers adopt new strategies of comprehension and interpretation" (189), and I emphasize what he says about the spiritual work of the book in this context. The book has a spiritual job as well as a historical and political one, but we must interpret Morrison's portrayal of the sacred, spiritual, and supernatural in light of her thoroughly revised portrayal of African American traditions.

2. Obviously, Solomon's song on another level is about his relationship with his lover. Solomon is the son of David, whom the Bible links directly to Jesus. Solomon loved many women, seemingly many more than David (I Kings 11:1–3). The conflation of the physical lusts of Solomon and the character of Jesus in Song of Solomon makes it atypical in its treatment of spirituality, and this is perhaps part of the reason that Morrison juxtaposes it to the reality of slavery in *Beloved,* which required a spiritual commitment quite different from that typically portrayed in the Bible. See Peggy Ochoa's "Morrison's *Beloved:* Allegorically Othering 'White' Christianity" (1999).

3. Deborah Guth describes the inversion of biblical tradition: "The Christian model becomes the story of motherhood from a new vantage point: instead of historic and personal suffering being a temporal repetition of a transcendent model, the world of the motherbody becomes the prototype of which the male-centered Christological story is a sublimated abstraction" ("'Wonder What God Had in Mind': *Beloved*'s Dialogue with Christianity" [1994], 91–92).

4. The words of the text invoke biblical comparison to the "cup of trembling" in Isaiah 51:17 and 22, which through association recalls Jesus' cry to God to "let this cup pass from me" (Matthew 26:39). The resonance of language and associative reference are subtle but significant because Sethe's redefinition of the Christian example makes her a Christ figure.

5. See also Mark 9:2–10 and Luke 9:28–36. *Beloved*'s intertextual reference includes the three slightly different biblical accounts of the transfiguration, but clearly the text critically engages the general story of the transfiguration in its narrative. The novel may focus more on the version in Matthew that I have quoted. However, some words and images recall Mark and Luke. For example, in Matthew 17:2 "his raiment was white as the light," in Mark 9:3 "his raiment became shining, exceeding white as snow," and in Luke 9:29 "his raiment was white and glistering." In this instance, Luke is the direct influence for the novel's image. *Beloved*'s "thunderblack and glistening" nakedness shockingly contrasts the biblical and highlights the text's method of juxtaposing textual descriptions and realities. The idealized image and the powerfully realistic symbol loudly clash in this comparison.

6. Paul D. is not "Saul [renamed] Paul" (Acts 13:9), but he is a new Paul D by the end of the novel and by intertextual comparison a more realistic Paul for African Americans than the biblical one. Also, at least somewhat like Paul in Acts, Paul D goes on a long journey between the time at Sweet Home when he knew Sethe and when he reunites with her.

7. In Revelation 10:9–11, an angel also gives the apostle John a book of prophecy: "And he said unto me, Take it, and eat it up; and it shall make thy belly bitter, but it shall be in thy mouth sweet as honey. And I took the little book out of the angel's hand, and ate it up; and it was in my mouth sweet as honey: and as soon as I had eaten it, my belly was bitter. And he said unto me, Thou must prophesy again before many peoples, and nations, and tongues, and kings." Although the New Testament prophecy of John ultimately looks toward the promise and fulfillment of the Second Coming, it too is a conflicted vision of plague, suffering, and horror similar to the Old Testament and *Beloved*'s boldly parodic secular prophecy. The novel's grave vision generally invokes a comparative critique of the Old Testament perspective. However, taking into account its many specific references to the New Testament, I would say that the novel also is a "book" that revises the African American experience in line with its own perspective that is more meaningful than that portrayed in both biblical dispensations.

8. In her essay focusing on Baby Suggs, Emily Griesinger writes, "Is Morrison commenting . . . on the inadequacy of Christianity in the face of the profound evils of slavery [through her portrayal of Baby Suggs and her fate]? Judging from the critical debate on the novel, especially those reviews and articles that focus on religion, this would seem not to be the case—not entirely, at least" ("Why Baby Suggs, Holy, Quit Preaching the Word: Redemption and Holiness in Toni Morrison's *Beloved*" [2001], 690). She argues that while Baby Suggs's theology leaves out "key aspects of Christian doctrine" (692), her characterization and the novel are "not subversive but actually supportive of Christianity" (697). Perhaps this is true, but what Griesinger and the critics she cites do not stress enough is that *Beloved* engages in intertextual

critique of the Bible. The values of Christianity received from the Bible have served African Americans well, but the novel's characters also utilize values, practices, and rituals that are not biblical, particularly folk rituals derived from the African past. Further, the narrative of the novel clearly confronts and subverts what is *written* in the Bible.

Approaching the novel from a different perspective, Mae Henderson makes a point similar to mine: "Engaging the Scriptures as a kind of intertext, Morrison enacts in her novel an opposition between the Law and the Spirit, redeeming her characters from the 'curse of the law' as figured in the master's discourse. In her rewriting of Scripture, Morrison ushers in an ironic new dispensation figured not by the Law of the (white) Father, but the Spirit of the (black and female) child, Beloved. Thus Morrison challenges the hegemonic status of the (primarily male) slave narratives as well as the 'canonical' history embedded in the master('s) narratives" ("Toni Morrison's *Beloved:* Re-Membering the Body as Historical Text" [1991], 64).

Well before *Beloved* was published, Morrison said, "There is so much in Christianity that makes it a very interesting religion, because of its scriptures and its vagueness. It's a theatrical religion. It says something particularly interesting to black people, and I think it's part of why they were so available to it. It was the love things that were psychically very important. Nobody could have endured in constant rage . . . But with the love thing—love your enemies, turn the other cheek—they could sublimate the other things, they transcended them" (Charles Ruas, *Conversations with American Writers* [1985], 241–42). Morrison goes on to talk about how African Americans combined the "vestiges" of African religions with belief in the Christian concept of salvation (242). I would take from this that *Beloved* may not be anti-Christian but an interrogation of the text through which we receive Christianity.

9. The specific language of the biblical quotations is a paraphrase that does not match the King James, New Standard, or New International versions of the Bible, but it gives the same general sense.

10. As Fritz Gysin points out, the cattle killing of the novel is based on an actual historical event in 1856 and 1857. It is not totally clear why the Xhosa killed their cattle, but drawing upon historical analysis, he speculates that it may have been because of European trickery and as a response to bovine disease brought to South Africa by European cattle. Whatever the cause was, the event took on larger-than-life ritual meaning for the Xhosa: "The cattlekilling was performed by a majority of the Xhosa as a great purification rite sparked by several millenialist visions and prophecies" ("'Do Not Fall Asleep in Your Enemy's Dreams': John Edgar Wideman and the Predicament of Prophecy" [1999], 623). A primary propagator of the prophecy was a teenaged girl named Nongqawuse: "She claimed she had been accosted by strangers professing to be her dead relatives who ordered her to inform her people that they should get rid of their herds and avoid planting any crops." Some doubted, but,

probably through the manipulation of a white political official, the cattle were destroyed and the Xhosa nation consequently collapsed (623–24). Nongqawuse speaks the prophecy in the novel.

CHAPTER 4 *Rejecting God and Redefining Faith*

1. Diane Scholl perhaps makes the affirmation of biblical gospel too clearly intentional on Walker's part. She says that Walker's "biblical heritage is one shaping influence on her art in this powerful novel" ("With Ears to Hear and Eyes to See: Alice Walker's Parable *The Color Purple* [1991], 264). I do think that she is generally right about the voice of parable in the novel, particularly in the case of Nettie, but might not necessarily agree that Walker has a "biblical heritage," which suggests to me a close knowledge of and connection to the Bible that causes the writer to affirm and parody the biblical text, as is true for James Baldwin, for example. What I see in *The Color Purple* is Walker's less ambivalent radical attitude and approach to the Bible that nevertheless turns back toward more traditional affirmation, particularly through her portrayal of the novel's overall community of African Americans. Scholl talks about the representation of parable in *The Color Purple* in wider terms of ironic reversal and paradox in the life of Celie that go beyond the specific story by Nettie. I focus on Nettie's story as a parable because it is the main cause of the central change that affects Celie's revolutionary view of God and at the same time the source of an underlying traditional spiritual faith.

2. In "'Trying to Do Without God': The Revision of Epistolary Address in *The Color Purple*" (1989), Carolyn Williams says that "on the level of form as well as explicit content, [the] text performs the work of "'trying to do without God,' and by the end, that work is no longer such a 'strain'" (274). This is true for Celie and perhaps for Shug, but not for others in the text, especially Nettie. Williams states that in relationship to white imperialism toward the Olinkas, Nettie recognizes the powerlessness of her God (280). This point may be accurate in this specific instance in Nettie's life, although I read it differently; however, Nettie never changes her overall worldview to believe that God is powerless as Celie does. The underlying implications of her characterization make a much different point, as do the structural elements of the novel.

3. Walker and other African American writers have utilized the postmodern to portray and critique African American culture much better than academic critics have in analyzing the cultural in writers' works. The writers realize that cultural complexity and mystery are in many ways consistent with postmodern theory and practice, and use the postmodern to reveal the great richness of the culture, which includes the theological. Although the novel's primary postmodern practice critiques the theological tradition and then moves away from it, much as academic criticism

does, this richness is apparent in *The Color Purple* because of its overall creative process. The text focuses on the political redefinition of the theological and rewrites the traditional subtly and perhaps unintentionally because of its underlying sensitivity to cultural demands that balance the radical. Critics, on the other hand, have shied away from and neglected aspects of African American cultural analysis that do not fit a narrow pattern prescribed by the academy.

4. Jeannine Thyreen interprets Nettie and the relationship of her theological transformation to Celie's differently. I agree that "Nettie's revised notion of God reflects Celie's new understanding of God" ("Alice Walker's *The Color Purple*" Redefining God and (Re)Claiming the Spirit Within" [1999], 64). Nevertheless, there are many specific and profound differences in their beliefs that place Nettie within the realm of traditional belief in God. Unlike Thyreen, I start with the idea that traditional notions of the sacred and spiritual as reflected in African American culture are also manifested specifically or subtly in the novel, as they often are in various ways in black texts, and this leads me to look more deeply into Nettie's portrayal.

5. The theological has, of course, historically been the impetus behind political, social, and revolutionary movements such as Nat Turner's nineteenth-century slave rebellion and the twentieth-century civil rights movement led by Martin Luther King. Both Turner and King were "men of God" leading crusades for justice that are easily sanctioned by the Bible, and so there is no conflict with African American tradition here. There are many different political, social, and revolutionary struggles historically and presently in African American life, though, and black people, often women as in *The Color Purple*, can separate the secular where there is a conflict in achieving practical goals and still retain sacred belief as the foundation of existence.

6. The academic and intellectual ideology of Christian feminism is a revolutionary one that well applies to *The Color Purple*. Sandra Friedman and Alec Irwin discuss the relevance of Christian feminism to the novel.

> Through eros, through the sharing of creative power in a just relationship, we receive an experience of joy which will not leave our lives unchanged. Like Celie in Walker's *The Color Purple*, as the unimagined force and depth of authentic erotic connection begin to reveal themselves to us, we find our attitudes toward all areas of our lives transformed. We learn that joy shared and multiplied in mutuality is not a possibility reserved for another world; we are capable of experiencing it here and now. And in this assurance we find the power to "talk back" to those who have tried to deny us joy. Such erotic power is not available only to a select group, or dependent upon a knowledge of abstract theories. It is rooted in nothing more obscure than the simple willingness to take seriously basic human experiences of creative pleasure, mutual care and connectedness, and to acknowledge that it is these experiences which

give meaning to our existence. ("Christian Feminism, Eros, and Power in Right Relation" [1990], 403)

While these comments are good, they reflect no recognition of the novel's manifestation of a powerful cultural belief that complicates and potentially problematizes Christian feminism. The critics speak of the transforming religious/political potential of the Christian feminist erotic in terms of faith that sound almost equal to the powerful belief in the sacred tradition of God in African American culture. Critics are quite aware of the novel's politically and socially revolutionary qualities that coincide with academic and intellectual discourses to which they are committed, such as Christian feminism, but are apparently unaware of the strong traditional cultural aspects of the novel that show a different commitment. The text is more complex than critics reveal if for no other reason than that the cultural creates a tension, which critics do not acknowledge, that underlies the primary narrative theme. Individual critics only have the responsibility to do what they choose and want to do, and are not necessarily concerned about analyzing black writing from the traditional cultural perspective. In fairness to Friedman and Irwin, their essay is about different works by white and black writers, not just *The Color Purple*. Still, their project takes a stand similar to works that deal solely with the novel or with African American fiction, and contributes to a general void in academic criticism at the same time that it may do important political work as an individual project.

7. *Mama Day* revises the Christian tradition through matriarchal mythopoeia and by centering women, as David Cowart says, but at the same time shows the strength and importance of traditional African American Christian practice and belief through the characterization of women, especially Mama Day and Abigail. In "Matriarchal Mythopoesis: Naylor's *Mama Day*" (1998), Cowart states: "The single great source of disharmony [in *Mama Day*, Naylor] intimates, lies in an overturning, centuries ago, of matriarchal authority and its divine counterpart. The world still reels from this displacement of the Goddess, the Great Mother" (444). Cowart is correct that the displacement of the Goddess figure is important in the conception and portrayal of Willow Springs, and his analysis of the novel's reshaping of the Christian tradition around the Goddess is good. However, the displacement and the reinstatement of the Goddess is only one aspect of the novel. As I argue, its self-conceived narrative construction and related thematic structure are eclectic and syncretic. The novel depicts a traditional folk belief in Christian ideals and in the patriarchal God, but its narrative also foregrounds Mama's subconscious knowledge of the Goddess and belief in her power and virtue, at one point adding a clear statement of her feeling that women are generally superior to men in human relationships (240).

Also see Dorothy Perry Thompson's "Africana Womanist Revision in Gloria Naylor's *Mama Day* and *Bailey's Café*" (1999), in which she makes a similar and valid case about the text's revision of Christianity and decentering of the patriarchy: "Naylor's strategy successfully revises/deconstructs Judeo-Christian myth by stripping it of male-centered power. Moreover, she joins to that myth a matricentric African spirituality characteristic of Africana womanism [which identifies woman's origins in specifically African terms]" (92). Reflecting on both essays from the standpoint of my analysis, I cannot stress too much the added dimension of the novel's overall thematic eclecticism and the syncretism of its community's belief system, which the text represents in its dense, complicated formal structure.

8. In "Recovering the Conjure Woman: Texts and Contexts in Gloria Naylor's *Mama Day*" (1997), Lindsey Tucker states that Naylor gives Willow Springs the characteristics of the sea islands that stretch from the coast of South Carolina through Georgia: "Naylor's choice of location has obviously been dictated by the historical relationship of the islands to the perpetuation of African culture, for these Sea islands are, with the exception of New Orleans, the most African of places in America. Always important to the slave trade routes because of their easy access from the ocean as well as their proximity to rivers traveling inland, they also became the places where the least acculturated Africans remained" (149–50). Symbolically, Willow Springs is a primal place that is a connection to the deepest reality of the African past and the past of slavery. Tucker emphasizes the centrality of hoodoo retentions of the past and the consequent importance of hoodoo beliefs and practices in the portrayal of central characters, including Mama Day, and of Willow Springs. Tucker's comments generally coincide with my analysis of hoodoo in the novel.

9. Mama acts negatively toward him in many instances, but most people in Willow Springs affectionately call this character Dr. Buzzard. A shyster as far as his self-proclaimed hoodoo powers are concerned, he, unlike the hoodoo woman, is still a positive figure who contributes to the harmonious life of Willow Springs. As the quotation from the novel shows, his folk belief does seem to empower him in a spiritual and supernatural connection to the world around him. Mama even enlists him in her attempts to prepare her niece's husband George to save his wife. Buzzard admits to George that his hoodoo is a fraud but also tells him about the importance of letting his self-belief go to the extent that he can make room for the folk belief of others to assist him in helping the niece, although he might not share the folk belief (291–93).

10. Mama does go to church (237), but the church is a place of gossip and social ostracism in which negative people like Ruby thrive: "Even Reverend Hooper gets down in the mouth them winters [when no one in Willow Springs has trouble that he can preach about to foment gossip]. All that hell and brimstone in his sermons don't carry the same kinda sparkle when there ain't no likely candidates to feed the fires" (132). An alternative to a common church ritual is the "standing forth" funeral service for Pearl's grandson Little Caesar. The service takes place at the church but minimizes the preacher's role (268) and emphasizes the novel's folk syncretism that

is inclusive of Christian values but not limited to Christian belief and ritual as practiced in the church: "The church, the presence of the minister, were concessions, and
obviously the only ones they were going to make to a Christian ritual that should
have called for a sermon, music, tears—the belief in an earthly finality for the child's
life" (269). The people individually "stand forth" and address the child as if he is still
alive and as if they will reunite with him in a specific situation, and they accordingly
suppress the expression of grief. The service implies a non-Western worldview in
which the dead spiritually carry on their lives among the living, but its assertion of
human values such as love and compassion also represents the Christian ideal.

11. The Day family tradition of naming women is varied and ambiguous. The
mythical, subconsciously known Sapphira is perhaps named to suggest her Goddess-
like qualities that transcended slavery. Because of her magical powers, Miranda
(Mama Day) is not so much like her namesake from Shakespeare's *The Tempest* as
she is like her father Prospero (Cowart, "Matriarchal Mythopoesis," 442). Ophelia is
generally reminiscent of the character from *Hamlet* because of her love relationship
with George. The other names — Grace, Hope, and Peace—stand for New Testament ideals and for religious ideals generally. There is no clear symbolism indicating
one tradition or a clear pattern in the women's naming, as there is in the tradition of
naming the Day family men after Old Testament and New Testament figures. But it
would seem that the naming of all the women suggests broad ideals such as the biblical ones or larger-than-life human dimensions such as those of Shakespearian
tragedy.

12. The illustration of the island of Willow Springs at the beginning of *Mama Day*
reveals that Ruby's house is even closer to "the other place" and its graveyard than
Abigail's house and Mama's trailer. So Ruby is symbolically close to the tradition of
"the other place," and what she represents through her negative practice of hoodoo—
hatred, spite, and destructiveness—is an integral part of its tradition and folk tradition generally, although by no means constituting its central essence, which is good.

13. Besides the supernatural things that she does in dealing with Ruby and the
white deputy sheriff (79–81), Mama has previously practiced what sounds like the
more traditional kind of hoodoo that entails "working roots" and coming up with
powerful concoctions, or at least she has threatened to practice it. When Cocoa was
in high school, the lecherous principal threatened her with his sexual advances.
Mama stopped him with the counterthreat of a hoodoo concoction. She told him
that "I could fix it so the only thing he'd be able to whip out of his pants for the rest
of his life would be pocket change" (68). Mama further confirms to Abigail that she
told the principal this and that she actually had the concoction: "As God is my judge.
And I had it all ready at the other place."

14. In *Workings of the Spirit: The Poetics of Afro-American Women's Writing*
(1991), Houston Baker gives a history of voodoo/hoodoo that parallels the points of

W. Lawrence Hogue's definition. (Also see Hogue, *The African American Male, Writing, and Difference*, 54–55.) Baker says that hoodoo is a belief and practice that is the African American variant of voodoo, a Haitian religion of the masses beginning in the colonial period (80–81). The word *voodoo* comes from Vodun, the name of the West African Yoruba deity. Set above the priest, the priestess was the central figure for the Yoruba that was "oracle to the spirit of Vodun carried in the sacred serpent" (Baker 80). (Yoruba cosmology, then, is generally congruent with *Mama Day*'s project of decentering the patriarchy. Mama is the priestess, the dominant figure of Willow Springs and its "oracle." She uses a walking cane carved with snakes that belonged to her father John-Paul—which associates him with voodoo priesthood in addition to a biblical heritage—to strike and ultimately destroy Ruby's house [269–70]). Belief in the mystery of the forces of life is basic to voodoo; the voodoo woman or man is the instrument of these mysterious life forces through supernatural ritual and her/his habitation by supernatural power, which are additional manifestations of mystery. The "influence and effects of voodoo as a diasporic African religious practice can be traced to the early eighteenth century. And voodoo, or conjure, has been an affective presence among blacks from that time to the present" (80). Further, the practices of voodoo were syncretic: Haitian voodoo combined the Catholic and the African. It follows, then, based on Baker's assessment that this syncretism, which is an aspect of voodoo and ultimately African, would have an important influence along with the Christian on the African American cultural tradition and on *Mama Day*.

Baker cites an image from Ellison's *Invisible Man* that references African Americans combining Christianity and beliefs in supernatural knowing drawn from hoodoo practices of the diaspora. The narrator saw "a window filled with religious articles . . . two brashly painted plaster images of Mary and Jesus surrounded by dream books, love powders, God-Is-Love signs" (80–81). This implies a hoodoo practice that, in fiction as well as in life, African Americans may engage in without calling it hoodoo or realizing that it is, the word meaning something more occult and dangerous such as "working roots." In the context of my analysis, the syncretism portrayed in *Invisible Man* is a diasporic influence sublimated to African American belief.

15. Sapphira in this context is the voodoo woman who relates to the present through her psychic connection from the other world. The text then becomes a supernatural voodoo revelation of the past to Mama, to Cocoa at times, and to the reader. Brodber's *Louisiana* theorizes itself as a text in these terms. From this angle, *Mama Day* also theorizes its textuality from a diasporic voodoo perspective similar to the mythic subconscious revelation of the text that I talk about, and similar to and different from the African American Judeo-Christian view of the spiritual. However, this thematic possibility is hidden in the text's ambiguity and overshadowed by the more dominant Judeo-Christian beliefs of Mama and the people of Willow Springs; it only emerges in light of the clearer portrayal of *Louisiana*.

16. I cannot make the point that setting voodoo aside from the sacred/religious meant its absolute exclusion; the case is more complex than this. Hogue says that after the repression of voodoo in New Orleans at the end of the nineteenth century "certain . . . magical practices remained incorporated in the black Baptist Church and the black Catholic Church throughout North America" (Hogue, *The African American Male, Writing, and Difference,* 55). One reason, among others, is that black people from New Orleans certainly must have moved throughout the country and influenced the practice of voodoo in African American Christian churches. Hogue further states that even today blacks migrate from Haiti and West Africa to the United States, causing a resurgence in voodoo belief. The complexity of analyzing hoodoo influence here resides in the possibilities that African Americans in different parts of the country today, and even before, are unaware of what constitutes hoodoo in church ritual and belief. They may refuse to acknowledge that some rituals are not Judeo-Christian according to doctrine and may indeed be voodoo, or they may just be more tolerant of difference (at least in contemporary times) and therefore not question ritual and practice. And there are other potential factors that make ambiguous the place of voodoo influence in African American religious belief and practice. However, while African Americans have not absolutely excluded voodoo from the church, it is true that the Bible and the Judeo-Christian tradition historically have been the greatest influence and still are. Hogue says that voodoo "remained incorporated in" the black church but does not make the case that black people consciously and knowingly practiced voodoo in the church to any significant extent. He also does not say that the resurgence of voodoo among immigrants has significantly influenced other African Americans.

17. The events that unfold around the lives of Cocoa and George draw the larger urban reality of African Americans into engagement with the folk traditions of Willow Springs, especially the positive ones emphasized in the spiritual communion between them at the end. While they are in New York and after they get to Willow Springs, Cocoa and George's interaction reveals this folk/urban intersection. After George dies, Mama goes to New York with Cocoa to get her things. She sees the good and bad of the city, but by getting to know people, she concludes that "New York was full of right nice folks" (305). She brings home souvenirs to give people during Candle Walk, thus associating New York with the humane values and practices of Willow Springs. The text uses Mama's folk idiom to frame New York in a figure of speech that represents Willow Springs' perspective that makes God the creator and controller of everything: "when you stand on top of [the Empire State Building] . . . you kinda see the world the way God must see it—everything's able to be cupped into the palm of your hand" (306). Willow Springs is the symbolic genesis of African American tradition that still has a connection to and relevance to African American life in radically different urban cultures.

18. Critics correctly point out that the Shakespearian plays *Hamlet, King Lear,* and *The Tempest* have influenced *Mama Day.* In exploring the relationship between the novel and the latter play, David Cowart says, "As a romance, this play includes a number of fantastic elements and departs from a realistic portrayal of scene and character and action" ("Matriarchal Mythopoesis," 441). In the context of my discussion, the fantastic and nonrealistic as portrayed in Shakespearian drama, and especially in *The Tempest,* is an influence on radical narrative invention in *Mama Day.* However, an even stronger influence is the novel's own self-constructed theory and concomitant narrative form that encompasses an African American folk belief system submerged in the mythical subconscious.

19. One could explain the novel's approach in terms of narrative theory in women's writing that is different from my analytical perspective on the novel's theory, but that shares an emphasis on narrative representation. In the context of women's novels, it is an emphasis on fractured spirituality, and in my analysis it is on representation of the conflated mythical/subconscious/spiritual. In *Moorings and Metaphors: Figures of Culture and Gender in Black Women's Literature* (1992), Karla F. C. Holloway talks about "narrative strategies of African-American women's texts [in which] dissonance precipitates the foregrounding of the inner text" (121). She says further that "for women of the diaspora, artifice becomes a far more spiritual than tangible dimension of cultural continuity . . . This way of reconstruction (revision) is a way of shifting an alternative universe into the place that history has poorly served. Because women's cultures of the diaspora are fractured by history, the creative literature of African-American women has revised its form of documentation . . . A spiritual luminescence [replaces] their dimmed physical worlds" (121–22). My point is about the novel's theory and belief system that provide a basis for the reconstruction of African American mythical/subconscious/spiritual reality that is substantive and intangible, abstract, and imperceptible at the same time. Holloway focuses on a spirituality of women that history decimated, necessitating reconstructive strategies that document what is beyond a "tangible dimension of cultural continuity." We are analyzing radical narrative invention of substantively similar essences of myth, consciousness, and spirituality. See Holloway's overall treatment of *Mama Day.*

20. I have not analyzed Abigail to a significant extent although she is an important character. She does not have Mama's power, but she adheres to folk spiritual and supernatural belief just as much. She and Mama are composite characters from one perspective. Abigail has experienced childbirth and the tragedy of losing a child at "the other place," and this has alienated her physically from the house but not the tradition. Abigail's biological reality of motherhood goes along with Mama's representation of the folk essence of Mother, which incorporates everything in the realm of folk belief in the sacred, spiritual, natural, and supernatural tradition. The women

have a spiritual connection which Mama can feel in the natural world, even when Abigail has died. Mama calls her, knowing she is there without having to hear her answer: "Taking up her walking stick, she hobbles out to the front yard and looks over at [Abigail's house]. No need to cross that road anymore, so she turns her face up into the warm air—You there, Sister?—to listen for the rustling of the trees" (312).

CHAPTER 5 *Reshaping and Radicalizing Faith*

1. *Louisiana* and *Mumbo Jumbo* portray an African American hoodoo experience that defines itself in terms of an inextricable relationship to the diasporic, which is specifically African religious belief and practice disseminated through Jamaica and Haiti, respectively. African American hoodoo inherently retains its diasporic roots, and *Louisiana* is set primarily in New Orleans and defines African American hoodoo as inseparably connected to the diaspora. It is thus an African American novel that conforms to the contours of African American hoodoo like *Mumbo Jumbo*, which defines hoodoo in the same way. Reed's American and Brodber's Jamaican nationalities are not the main determinants of the novels' classifications; the settings, subject matter, and definitions of hoodoo are more important. See the discussion of *Louisiana* and *Mumbo Jumbo* in the introduction.

2. In discussing Reed's *Mumbo Jumbo*, I essentially use the words *voodoo* and *hoodoo* interchangeably because of the text's usage. Generally, in the text *voodoo* refers to the religion in the form of its African derivation and diasporic practice, and *hoodoo* indicates the manifestation of the religion in North America in the twentieth century. However, the two words reference the same cosmology applied to different times, places, and historical circumstances.

See Houston Baker, *Workings of the Spirit: The Poetics of Afro-American Women's Writing* (1991), 77–82; and W. Lawrence Hogue, *The African American Male, Writing, and Difference: A Polycentric Approach to African American Literature, Criticism, and History* (2003), 54–55 and 243, for brief histories and concise definitions and discussions of voodoo/hoodoo. Also see Michel S. Laguerre's *Voodoo Heritage* (1980) for an analysis and account of voodoo in Haiti, which is a strong point of dissemination of voodoo as a religion to Louisiana and especially New Orleans, which are the settings of the novel *Louisiana*. Zora Neale Hurston's *Mules and Men* (1935) also presents an exposé of voodoo practices and rituals, and links hoodoo in New Orleans to Haitian voodoo. My analysis of Reed later in this chapter provides further discussions that define voodoo/hoodoo.

3. The main character in Brodber's earlier novel *Myal* (1988) is also named Ella, and like Ella in *Louisiana,* she lives in Jamaica and the United States and comes under the positive influence of African and diasporic supernatural powers. Ella Townsend's naming probably implies a spiritual connection to Ella O'Grady Langley

in *Myal* that is congruent with the conception of the oneness of Ella's being with others in the terms of the novel's hoodoo cosmology.

4. Baker sketches a small portrait of Marie Laveau in *Workings of the Spirit* (78–79), and Hogue in *The African American Male, Writing, and Difference* (55) refers to her death as one factor in the repression of hoodoo in African America at the end of the nineteenth century. In *Mules and Men,* Hurston gives a folkloric account of her (200–206). Ishmael Reed in "Shrovetide in Old New Orleans" (2000) talks about Marie Laveau's legend, syncretic practice that combined voodoo and Catholicism, and vacillation between the two religions. Using conflicting stories of her legendary good and bad deeds and of the times when she lived and died, he speculates that there could have been several people called Marie Laveau who have become one in legend and whom he treats as such (314–15). Based on this, we can see that Ella, who begins her practice in New Orleans in the 1930s and learns from a woman named Madam Marie, is a Laveau-like character constructed from a part of the legendary composite that projects the good. Similarly, it is interesting that *Louisiana* does not clearly associate Ella with the voodoo symbol of the snake, which is negative in Western Christianity. (In comparison, the title character in Gloria Naylor's *Mama Day* is an apostate of hoodoo who practices it as part of a syncretic folk worldview that is highly Christian, but the novel does connect her with the symbolism through the snakes carved on her walking cane.)

5. The text never specifies why people call Sue Ann "Mammy." (Mammy seems to call Louise "Lowly" ironically and affectionately because of her uppity carriage.) In "Shrovetide in Old New Orleans," Reed talks about a hoodoo woman named Mammy Pleasants who knew Marie Laveau and was also a madam: "In New Orleans, one of the forms [hoodoo] took was what we call 'Jazz,' a music possibly performed in whorehouses whose madames were 'HooDoo Queens' like Marie Laveau, and Mammy Pleasants of San Francisco . . . A fearless abolitionist, she was active in the Underground Railroad, and was constantly pursued by the authorities until smuggled out of New Orleans by Marie Laveau" (306).

Speculating on the source of Mammy's name leads me to wonder about the construction of the collective being of the hoodoo women in *Louisiana* and its similarity to the conflated characterization of hoodoo women in Reed's version of legend. Mammy and Lowly are spiritually inseparable from Ella and are political activists like Mammy Pleasants and Marie Laveau in Reed's story, and Ella is important in the life of music and jazz in New Orleans like Mammy Pleasants and Marie Laveau. So Mammy Pleasants, who is like Marie Laveau, is the namesake of Mammy in the novel, and along with Marie Laveau, could be a general model for the characterization of Mammy/Ella/Lowly. Collective being in the novel and conflated characterization in Reed's legendary story produce a general similarity among hoodoo women, which perhaps suggests a "hoodoo" in Reed's telling of the legend like the reality of hoodoo in the novel. However, the continuity between legend and novel breaks down at a point: Ella and her larger being in *Louisiana* as created by Mammy and Lowly do not have the same connections to illicit and illegal sexuality as Marie Laveau and Mammy Pleasants.

6. Part of the quotation—"there are more ways of knowing than are accessible to the five senses"—echoes words from *Mama Day*: "*there is more to be known behind what the eyes can see*" (36). The narrative is generally similar to *Mama Day* in the self-consciousness of its narrative construction and its conception of reality as well as its centering of black women.

7. The language and the general description of the scene is also ambiguous in Leviticus 16:5–10. So the text of *Louisiana* is revising the symbolism of a text that is already richly ambiguous. The point implied in the text of *Louisiana* is that the powerful mystery of hoodoo cosmology deepens the already rich ambiguity of biblical symbolism through its critique.

8. Cynthia James explains the literal meaning of the words which Ella never states. She says that "Ah Who Say Sammy Dead" is a subversive Jamaican folk song that is a "paradigm for immortalizing Garvey and Garveyism" (164). This makes sense in terms of the relationship of the response to the words to Garvey's life, which is a part of the novel, and in the context of the fact that Ella hears the words in Garvey's native Jamaica.

9. In talking about Brodber's earlier novels *Jane and Louisa Will Soon Come Home* (1980) and *Myal* (1988), Helen Tiffin states that the "texts trace the processes of female reembodiment and the retrieval of Caribbean voice and body from its entrapment/erasure within European script and from those Anglo-Victorian middle-class values with which an educated Caribbean middle-class were so deeply imbued" ("Cold Hearts and (Foreign) Tongues: Recitation and the Reclamation of the Female Body in the Works of Erna Brodber and Jamaica Kincaid," 912). There is a similar project in *Louisiana* revealed in the analysis of the church mosaic and the overall text. Obviously, disavowing white middle-class values is important to Ella in reference to the church scene, and generally in the novel women are in a sense reembodied through their redefined roles of importance in the context of hoodoo reality. This redefinition of women is also a process of reembodiment after their erasure in "European script," which in this case is primarily the Judeo-Christian Bible.

10. The title character in Gloria Naylor's *Mama Day* bases her folk belief most substantively in Christianity. However, she practices hoodoo, especially in direct response to its evil, in spite of disavowing it. In doing so, she at one point calls on an ambiguously defined deity in terms similar to those in *Louisiana*. The text describes her invocation for her niece's husband: "She . . . turned her face to the sky that's well beyond the tip of the pines. Hot. Vacant. It ain't a prayer. And it ain't a plea. Whatever Your name is, help him" (299).

11. Baker, *Workings of the Spirit*, 80–81, and Hogue, *The African American Male, Writing, and Difference*, 54–55, provide clear discussions of hoodoo origins, cosmology, and history in the diaspora.

12. It is only clear toward the end of the novel how much the characters are dealing with earthly oppression in the overall scope of their lives dominated by hoodoo spirituality and its consequent faithful belief. Earlier in the narrative, Mammy tells Ella about the slavery past that is part of her family history. But it is much later when the heavenly communication reveals that Mammy's personal life is deeply informed by activist work that almost led to her own death at one point (154–55), and also presents a short story about Mammy and Lowly's work for Marcus Garvey (152–53, 159). The role that Garveyism played in the lives of the two women highlights black people's struggles against oppression in the communities in which the women lived. Also, Ella's main figure of speech that Cynthia James says is a folk reference to Garvey (James 164) and the response to it—*Sammy no dead yah. Sammy gone a.'*"—imply religious faith in Garvey's spiritual transcendence and adherence to the political struggle against oppression that he symbolized.

13. Baker explains that the priestess has prominence over the priest as the oracle of the spirit in the West African Vodun religion from which hoodoo derives (*Workings of the Spirit*, 80).

14. Mark Shadle explains that the Petro rite is warlike and the Rada more gentle, and says that Reed's main characters change their views from Petro in the first two novels, *The Free-Lance Pallbearers* (1967) and *Yellow Back Radio Broke Down* (1969), to PaPa's practice of Rada rites in *Mumbo Jumbo*. This does not make it clear whether Petro is evil because it is warlike; however, it would appear that it is not necessarily evil as PaPa says, since the earlier protagonists' perspectives do not indicate this. The Petro is closely associated with Atonism though, and Atonism is evil whether the Petro rite is solely evil or not. How the rites work and relate to Atonism and voodoo is part of what is unclear in a novel in which just about everything is mystery, except that voodoo *is* good and that Atonism is its opposite.

15. According to *Mumbo Jumbo*, Islam is derived from Christianity and therefore is also Atonist. The main character PaPa LaBas compares Christianity and Islam: One was "derived from the other. Muhammed seems to have wanted to impress Christian critics with his knowledge of the Bible . . . They agree on the ultimate wickedness of woman, even using feminine genders to describe disasters that beset mankind. Terming women cattle, unclean. The Koran was revealed to Muhammed by Gabriel the angel of the Christian apocalypse. Prophets in the Koran: Abraham Isaac and Moses were Christian prophets; each condemns the Jewish people for abandoning the faith; realizing that there has always been a pantheistic contingent among the 'chosen people' not reluctant to revere other gods. The Virgin Mary figures in the Koran as well as in the Bible" (35). Islam shares Christianity's intolerant attitudes,

although the text does not indicate that it has the same destructive cultural legacy and portrays Christianity's intolerance of Islam in spite of their similarity. Islam therefore occupies an ambiguous place beside Christianity since its impact is perhaps less severe culturally and Christians think negatively about it.

16. *VooDoo* and *HooDoo* are the spellings of the words in the text. I use the text's spellings when I refer specifically to its usage of the terms instead of my own. I also basically use the terms interchangeably as the novel does, and put them together as one word—voodoo/hoodoo—when I want to indicate the history and meaning of the religion as it has evolved over time. See note number 2.

17. Similar concepts that apply to *Louisiana* are *spiritualized living* and *spiritualized secular,* which refer to a relationship between the heavenly and earthly. In *Mumbo Jumbo,* heaven as a sacred and spiritual place separated from the earth does not exist; the manifestation of the spiritual is in the temporal. The second words of the concepts have virtually the same or similar meanings, and I change the word to *temporal* in *Mumbo Jumbo* in part to avoid confusion. However, as my definitions reveal, there is also an overall substantive difference between the concept of the *spiritualized temporal* and the other two that I apply to *Louisiana.*

18. Other critics have brought a heavily semiotic approach similar to Gates's to bear on *Mumbo Jumbo.* See, e.g., Robert Elliott Fox's "Blacking the Zero: Toward a Semiotics of Neo-Hoodoo" (1999). These treatments of Reed and of black literary texts in general have changed the study of African American literature by opening up revealing and provocative new approaches. However, all critiques and critical movements have their biases, blind spots, and political agenda, and it is unclear what any one actually shows or proves so definitively that it precludes others. My analysis of the novel focuses on its self-conscious objective of portraying voodoo religious spirituality as it relates to theme, form, and writing, which is a major aspect of the text that has been largely unexplored.

The voodoo religion and aesthetic are central throughout Reed's other works. Reginald Martin is one of the few critics who have dealt with this aspect of the writing in some depth and detail. In "Hoodoo as Literary Method," the concluding chapter of *Ishmael Reed and the New Black Aesthetic Critics* (1988), Martin analyzes Reed's first six novels from this perspective.

19. *Mumbo Jumbo* is not somber and humorless like Western spiritual texts usually are, but Reed has always indicated that he is serious about his belief in the voodoo religion, his practice of it in his writing, and the anti-Christian, antibiblical focus of his work. He makes this clear again and again in *Conversations with Ishmael Reed* (Dick and Singh 1995). "When I say I use a Voodoo aesthetic I'm not just kidding around" (124). "Neo Hoodoo . . . doesn't begin with me. There is much in the art of the Afro-American past to suggest that people have been using this kind of gumbo approach all along . . . hoodoo involved art, people made conjure balls, they made

dolls, they used many techniques that we associate with the artist, in making what they call their grisgris. Hoodoo involved dancing, painting, poetry, it was multimedia, the kind of effect that I try to get in my work and not only to describe what I am doing, but so no one can put me in any other kind of bag. My work is different from that of a Christian novelist ... who is up-dating the Old Testament" (54). What he says about the hoodoo artist and the forms of hoodoo art applies to his portrayal of the artist and forms of textuality in *Mumbo Jumbo*.

20. Reed's comments about religion and mystery coalesce with what I say about mystery being central in spiritual texts in my comparison of *Mumbo Jumbo* and the Bible. Asked why Ralph Ellison's reference to "New Orleans as the home of mystery" makes him a "hoodooist," Reed replies, "Well, anybody that refers to New Orleans as the home of mystery is talking about one thing, you know, and that's African religion. Mystery and religion have very much to do with each other" (Dick and Singh, *Conversations with Ishmael Reed,* 108). Of course, spiritual texts are usually associated with religion, as is the case with *Mumbo Jumbo* and the Bible, and Reed's statements about religion and mystery being inseparable imply that mystery is essential to the spiritual text also.

21. Talking about the syncretic in *Flight to Canada* (1976) and black writing generally, Reed has said the following that also applies to *Mumbo Jumbo*: "I call [black writing] *vodoun,* 'Voo Doo,' because this is what *vodoun* does, it mixes many traditions. It may have an African base, but it's adaptable, eclectic. It's able to blend with Christianity, with Native American forms, and with many others. I try to do the same in my art ... it's syncretic" (Dick and Singh, *Conversations with Ishmael Reed,* 136).

22. See, e.g., Steven R. Carter's essay "Ishmael Reed's Neo-Hoodoo Detection" (1976) and also Richard Swope's "Crossing Western Space, or the Hoodoo Detective on the Boundary in Ishmael Reed's *Mumbo Jumbo*" (2002).

BIBLIOGRAPHY

Allen, Shirley S. "Religious Symbolism and Psychic Reality in Baldwin's *Go Tell It on the Mountain*." In *Critical Essays on James Baldwin*, edited by Nancy Burt and Fred Standley, 166–88. Boston: G. K. Hall, 1988.

Andreas, James R., Sr. "Signifyin' on *The Tempest* in Gloria Naylor's *Mama Day*." In *Shakespeare and Appropriation*, edited by Christy Desmet and Robert Sawyer, 103–118. London: Routledge, 1999.

Baker, Houston A., Jr. *Blues, Ideology, and Afro-American Literature: A Vernacular Theory*. Chicago: University of Chicago Press, 1984.

———. *Modernism and the Harlem Renaissance*. Chicago: University of Chicago Press, 1987.

———. *Workings of the Spirit: The Poetics of Afro-American Women's Writing*. Chicago: University of Chicago Press, 1991.

Baldwin, James. *Another Country*. New York: Dial, 1962.

———. "Everybody's Protest Novel." In *Notes of a Native Son*, 13–22. New York: Dial, 1963.

———. *The Fire Next Time*. New York: Dial, 1963; reprint, New York: Dell, 1964.

———. *Giovanni's Room*. New York: Dell, 1956.

———. *Going to Meet the Man*. New York: Dial Press, 1965.

———. *Go Tell It on the Mountain*. New York: Knopf, 1953; reprint, New York: Dell, 1985.

———. *If Beale Street Could Talk*. New York: Dial, 1974.

———. *Just above My Head*. New York: Dial, 1979.

———. *Tell Me How Long the Train's Been Gone*. New York: Dial, 1968.

Bambara, Toni Cade. *The Salt Eaters*. New York: Random House, 1980.

Bell, Bernard. *The Afro-American Novel and Its Tradition*. Amherst: University of Massachusetts Press, 1987.

Bennett, Michael, and Vanessa D. Dickerson, eds. *Recovering the Black Female Body: Self-representations by African American Women*. New Brunswick, NJ: Rutgers University Press, 2001.

Bennion, John. "The Shape of Memory in Wideman's *Sent for You Yesterday*." *Black American Literature Forum* 20 (Spring-Summer 1986): 143–50.

Berben, Jacqueline. "Beyond Discourse: The Unspoken Versus Words in the Fiction of John Edgar Wideman." *Callaloo* 8 (Fall 1985): 525–34.

————. "Prodigal and Prodigy: Fathers and Sons in Wideman's Work." *Callaloo* 22, no. 3 (1999): 677–84.

Birat, Kathie. "'All Stories are True': Prophecy, History and Story in *The Cattle Killing*." *Callaloo* 22, no. 3 (1999): 629–43.

Bone, Robert A. *The Negro Novel in America*. New Haven: Yale University Press, 1958.

Bowers, Susan. "*Beloved* and the New Apocalypse." In *Toni Morrison's Fiction: Contemporary Criticism*, edited by David L. Middleton, 209–30. New York: Garland Press, 1997.

Bradley, David. *The Chaneysville Incident*. New York: Harper and Row, 1981.

Broad, Robert L. "Giving Blood to the Scraps: Haints, History, and Hosea in *Beloved*." *African American Review* 28, no. 2 (1994), 189–96.

Brodber, Erna. *Jane and Louisa Will Soon Come Home*. London: New Beacon Books, 1988.

————. *Louisiana*. London: New Beacon Books, 1980; reprint, Jackson: University of Mississippi Press, 1997.

————. *Myal*. London: New Beacon Books, 1988.

Brown, Joseph A. "I, John, Saw the Holy Number: Apocalyptic Visions in *Go Tell It on the Mountain* and *Native Son*." *Religion and Literature* 27, no. 1 (Spring 1995): 53–74.

Burt, Nancy V., and Fred L. Standley, eds. *Critical Essays on James Baldwin*. Boston: G. K. Hall, 1988.

Burton, Rainelle. *The Root Worker*. Woodstock, NY: Overlook Press, 2001.

Byerman, Keith. *Fingering the Jagged Grain: Tradition and Form in Recent Black Fiction*. Athens: University of Georgia Press, 1985.

————. *John Edgar Wideman: A Study of the Short Fiction*. New York: Twayne Publishers, 1998.

Carby, Hazel V. *Reconstructing Womanhood: The Emergence of the Afro-American Woman Novelist*. New York: Oxford University Press, 1987.

Carter, Steven R. "Ishmael Reed's Neo-Hoodoo Detection." In *Dimensions of Detective Fiction*, edited by Pat Browne, Ray Browne, and Larry Landrum, 265–74. New York: Popular Press, 1976.

Chambers, Kimberly R. "Right on Time: History and Religion in Alice Walker's *The Color Purple*." *College Language Association Journal* 31, no. 1 (September 1987): 44–62.

Chesnutt, Charles W. *The Conjure Woman*. New York: Houghton, Mifflin, 1899.

Christian, Barbara. *Black Women Novelists: The Development of a Tradition, 1892–1976*. Westport, CT: Greenwood Press, 1980.

Clark, Keith. "Baldwin, Communitas, and the Black Masculinist Tradition." In *New Essays on Go Tell It on the Mountain*, edited by Trudier Harris, 127–56. New York: Cambridge University Press, 1996.

Clemons, Walter. "The Ghosts of 'Sixty Million and More.'" *Newsweek* 110 (September 28, 1987): 75.

Coleman, James W. *Black Male Fiction and the Legacy of Caliban.* Lexington: University of Kentucky Press, 2001.

———. *Blackness and Modernism: The Literary Career of John Edgar Wideman.* Jackson: University Press of Mississippi, 1989.

Corey, Susan. "The Religious Dimensions of the Grotesque in Literature: Toni Morrison's *Beloved.*" In *The Grotesque in Art and Literature: Theological Reflections,* edited by James Luther Adams, 227–42. Grand Rapids, MI: Erdmans, 1997.

Cowart, David. "Matriarchal Mythopoesis: Naylor's *Mama Day.*" *Philological Quarterly* 77, no. 4 (1998), 439–59.

Dick, Bruce, and Amritjit Singh, eds. *Conversations with Ishmael Reed.* Jackson: University of Mississippi Press, 1995.

Dickerson, Vanessa D. "Summoning SomeBody: The Flesh Made Word in Toni Morrison's Fiction." In *Recovering the Black Female Body: Self-Representations by African American Women,* edited by Michael Bennett and Vanessa Dickerson, 195–216. New Brunswick, NJ: Rutgers University Press, 2001.

Douglas, Robert L. "Religious Orthodoxy and Skepticism in Richard Wright's *Uncle Tom's Children* and *Native Son.* In *Richard Wright: Myths and Realities,* edited by C. James Trotman, 79–88. New York: Garland Publishing, 1988.

DuBois, W. E. B. *The Souls of Black Folk: Essays and Sketches.* Chicago: A. C. McClurg, 1903.

Dubey, Madhu. "Literature and Urban Crisis: John Edgar Wideman's *Philadelphia Fire.*" *African American Review* 32, no. 4 (Winter 1998): 579–95.

Dunbar, Paul Laurence. *The Sport of the Gods.* New York: Dodd, Mead, 1902; reprint, New York: New American Library, 1999.

Eckard, Paula Gallant. "The Prismatic Past in Oral History and Mama Day." *Melus* 20, no. 3 (Fall 1995): 121–35.

Eliot, T. S. *Prufrock and Other Investigations.* London: The Egoist, 1917.

———. *The Waste Land.* New York: Boni and Liveright, 1922.

Ellison, Ralph. *Going to the Territory.* New York: Random House, 1986.

———. *Invisible Man.* New York: Random House, 1952.

———. *Juneteenth.* Edited by John F. Callahan. New York: Random House, 1999.

———. *Shadow and Act.* New York: Random House, 1964.

Fabre, Michel. "'The Benefit of the Doubt': Openness and Closure in *Brothers and Keepers.*" *Callaloo* 22, no. 3 (1999): 587–93.

———. "Fathers and Sons in James Baldwin's *Go Tell It on the Mountain.*" In *James Baldwin: A Collection of Critical Essays,* edited by Kenneth Kinnamon, 120–38. Engle Cliffs, NJ: Prentice-Hall, 1974.

Fauset, Jessie. *Plum Bun.* New York: A. Stokes, 1929.

Felton, Sharon, and Michelle C. Loris, eds. *The Critical Response to Gloria Naylor.* Westport, CT: Greenwood Press, 1997.

Fisher, Rudolph. *The Conjure Man Dies.* New York: Convici, Friede, 1932.

Fox, Robert Elliot. "Blacking the Zero: Toward a Semiotics of Neo-Hoodoo." In *The Critical Response to Ishmael Reed,* edited by Bruce Dick, 46–58. Westport, CT: Greenwood Press, 1999.

Frazier, Kermit. "The Novels of John Edgar Wideman." *Black World* 24 (1975): 18–35.

Friedman, Sandra, and Alec Irwin. "Christian Feminism, Eros, and Power in Right Relation." *Crosscurrents* 40, no. 3 (1990), 387–405.

Gaines, Ernest J. *The Autobiography of Miss Jane Pittman.* New York: Dial, 1971.

———. *Bloodline.* New York: Dial, 1968.

———. *Catherine Carmier.* New York: Atheneum, 1964.

———. *A Gathering of Old Men.* New York: Knopf, 1983.

———. *A Lesson before Dying.* New York: Knopf, 1993.

———. *Of Love and Dust.* New York: Dial, 1967.

———. *In My Father's House.* New York: Knopf, 1978.

Gates, Henry Louis, Jr. *Black Literature and Literary Theory.* New York: Methuen, 1984.

———. *The Signifying Monkey: A Theory of Afro-American Literary Criticism.* New York: Oxford University Press, 1988; reprint, New York: Oxford University Press, 1989.

Giles, James R. "Religious Alienation and 'Homosexual Consciousness' in *City of Night* and *Go Tell It on the Mountain.*" *College English* 36 (1974): 369–80.

Grandjeat, Yves-Charles. "Brother Figures: The Rift and Riff in John E. Wideman's Fiction." *Callaloo* 22, no. 3 (1999): 615–22.

———. "These Strange Dizzying Moments: Silence as Common Ground in J. E. Wideman's Texts." *Callaloo* 22, no. 3 (1999): 685–94.

Greene, J. Lee. *Blacks in Eden: The African-American Novel's First Century.* Charlottesville: University of Virginia Press, 1996.

Griesinger, Emily. "Why Baby Suggs, Holy, Quit Preaching the Word: Redemption and Holiness in Toni Morrison's *Beloved.*" *Christianity and Literature* 50, no. 4 (2001): 689–702.

Guth, Deborah. "'Wonder What God Had in Mind': *Beloved*'s Dialogue with Christianity." *The Journal of Narrative Technique* 24, no. 2 (1994): 83–97.

Gysin, Fritz. "'Do Not Fall Asleep in Your Enemy's Dreams': John Edgar Wideman and the Predicament of Prophecy." *Callaloo* 22, no. 3 (1999): 623–28.

Handley, William R. "The House a Ghost Built: Nommo, Allegory, and the Ethics of Reading in Toni Morrison's *Beloved.*" *Contemporary Literature* 36, no. 4 (Winter 1995): 676–701.

Harper, Phillip Brian. "'To Become One and Yet Many': Psychic Fragmentation and

Aesthetic Synthesis in Ralph Ellison's *Invisible Man.*" *Black American Literature Forum* 23, no. 4 (Winter 1989): 681–700.

Harris, Trudier. *Black Women in the Fiction of James Baldwin.* Knoxville: University of Tennessee Press, 1985.

———. *Exorcising Blackness: Historical and Literary Lynching and Burning.* Bloomington: Indiana University Press, 1984.

———, ed. *New Essays on Go Tell It on the Mountain.* New York: Cambridge University Press, 1996.

Henderson, Carol. "Knee Bent, Body Bowed: Re-Memory's Prayer of Spiritual Re(new)al in Baldwin's *Go Tell It on the Mountain. Religion and Literature* 27, no. 1 (Spring 1995): 75–88.

Henderson, Mae. "Toni Morrison's *Beloved:* Re-Membering the Body as Historical Text." In *Comparative American Identities: Race, Sex, and Nationality in the Modern Text,* edited by Hortense Spillers, 62–86. New York: Routledge, 1991.

Hogue, W. Lawrence. *The African American Male, Writing, and Difference: A Polycentric Approach to African American Literature, Criticism, and History.* Albany: State University of New York Press, 2003.

———. *Discourse and the Other: The Production of the Afro-American Text.* Durham: Duke University Press, 1986.

———. *Race, Modernity, Postmodernity: A Look at the History and Literatures of People of Color since the 1960s.* Albany: State University of New York Press, 1996.

Holland, Sharon Patricia. "(Pro)Creating Imaginative Spaces and Other Queer Acts: Randall Kenan's *A Visitation of Spirits* and Its Revival of James Baldwin's Absent Black Gay Man in *Giovanni's Room.*" In *James Baldwin Now,* edited by Dwight A. McBride, 265–88. New York: New York University Press, 1999.

Holloway, Karla F. C. *Moorings and Metaphors: Figures of Culture and Gender in Black Women's Literature.* New Brunswick: Rutgers University Press, 1992.

Howard-Pitney, David. *The Afro-American Jeremiad: Appeals for Justice in America.* Philadelphia: Temple University Press, 1990.

Howe, Irving. "Black Boys and Native Sons." In *A World More Attractive,* 98–122. New York: Horizon, 1963.

Hubbard, Dolan. *The Sermon and the African American Literary Imagination.* Columbia: University of Missouri Press, 1994.

Hughes, Langston. *Not Without Laughter.* New York: Knopf, 1930.

Hunt, V. "A Conversation with Randall Kenan." *African American Review* 29, no. 3 (1995): 411–20.

Hurston, Zora Neale. *Jonah's Gourd Vine.* Philadelphia: J. B. Lippincott, 1934.

———. *Mules and Men.* New York: Lippincott, 1935; reprint, Bloomington: Indiana University Press, 1978.

———. *Their Eyes Were Watching God.* Philadelphia: J. B. Lippincott, 1937.

James, Cynthia. "Reconnecting the Caribbean-American Diaspora in Paule Marshall's *Brown Girl, Brownstones* and Erna Brodber's *Louisiana*." *CLA Journal* 45, no. 2 (December 2001): 151–70.

Johnson, Charles. *Being and Race: Black Writing Since 1970*. Bloomington: Indiana University Press, 1988.

———. *Faith and the Good Thing*. New York: Viking Press, 1974.

———. *Middle Passage*. New York: Atheneum, 1990.

———. *Oxherding Tale*. Bloomington: Indiana University Press, 1982.

Johnson, Joyce. "Fiction and the Interpretation of History: The Fiction of Orlando Patterson and Erna Brodber." *World Literature Written in English* 32, no. 2–33, no. 1 (1992–1993): 72–86.

Jones, Carolyn M. "*Sula* and *Beloved:* Images of Cain in the Novels of Toni Morrison." *African American Review* 27, no. 4 (Winter 1993): 615–26.

Jones, Gayl. *The Healing*. Boston: Beacon Press, 1998.

Joyce, Joyce Ann. *Warriors, Conjurers, and Priests: Defining African-Centered Literary Criticism*. Chicago: Third World Press, 1994.

Kelly, Margot Anne, ed. *Gloria Naylor's Early Novels*. Gainesville: University of Florida Press, 1999.

Kenan, Randall. *Let the Dead Bury Their Dead*. New York: Harcourt Brace Jovanovich, 1992.

———. *A Visitation of Spirits*. New York: Grove Press, 1989; reprint, New York: Random House, 2000.

King James Bible.

Kinnamon, Kenneth, ed. *James Baldwin: A Collection of Critical Essays*. Englewood Cliffs, New Jersey: Prentice-Hall, 1974.

Kubitschek, Missy Dehn. "Toward a New Order: Shakespeare, Morrison, and Gloria Naylor's *Mama Day*." *Melus* 19, no. 3 (Fall 1994): 75–90.

Laguerre, Michel S. *Voodoo Heritage*. Beverly Hills, CA: Sage Publications, 1980.

Larsen, Nella. *Passing*. New York: Knopf, 1929.

———. *Quicksand*. New York: Knopf, 1928.

Lynch, Michael F. "A Glimpse of the Hidden God." In *New Essays on Go Tell It on the Mountain,* edited by Trudier Harris, 29–57. New York: Cambridge University Press, 1996.

Macebuh, Stanley. *James Baldwin: A Critical Study*. New York: The Third Press, 1973.

Margolies, Edward. "The Negro Church: James Baldwin and the Christian Vision." In *Native Sons: A Critical Study of Twentieth-Century Black American Authors,* 102–26. New York: Lippincott, 1968.

Martin, Reginald. *Ishmael Reed and the New Black Aesthetic Critics*. London: Macmillan Press, 1988.

Marvin, Thomas F. "'Preachin' the Blues': Bessie Smith's Secular Religion and Alice Walker's *The Color Purple*. *African American Review* 28, no. 3 (Fall 1994): 411–21.

May, Vivian M. "Ambivalent Narratives, Fragmented Selves: Performative Identities and the Mutability of Roles in James Baldwin's *Go Tell It on the Mountain*." In *New Essays on Go Tell It on the Mountain*, edited by Trudier Harris, 97–126. Cambridge: Cambridge University Press, 1996.

Mays, Benjamin. *The Negro's God as Reflected in His Literature*. New York: Atheneum, 1938.

McBride, Dwight A., ed. *James Baldwin Now*. New York: New York University Press, 1999.

McKnight, Reginald. *He Sleeps*. New York: Henry Holt, 2001.

———. *I Get on the Bus*. Boston: Little, Brown, 1990.

———. *The Kind of Light That Shines on Texas*. Little, Brown, 1992.

———. *Moustapha's Eclipse*. Pittsburgh: University of Pittsburgh Press, 1988.

———. *White Boys*. New York: Henry Holt, 1998.

McRuer, Robert. "A Visitation of Difference: Randall Kenan and Black Queer Theory." In *Critical Essays: Gay and Lesbian Writers of Color*, edited by Emmanuel S. Nelson, 221–32. Binghamton, NY: Haworth Press, 1993.

Miller, Eugene E. "Voodoo Parallels in *Native Son*." *College Language Association Journal* 16 (1972): 81–95.

Misenhelder, Susan. "False Gods and Black Goddesses in Naylor's *Mama Day* and Hurston's *Their Eyes Were Watching God*." *Callaloo* 23, no. 4 (Fall 2000): 1440–48.

Mitchell, Carolyn W. "'I Love to Tell the Story': Biblical Revisions in *Beloved*." In *Understanding Toni Morrison's Beloved and Sula: Selected Essays and Criticisms of the Works by the Nobel Prize-Winning Author*, edited by Solomon O. and Marla W. Iyasere, 173–89. Troy, NY: Whitston, 2000.

Monroe, Mary. *The Upper Room*. New York: St. Martin's Press, 1985.

Morey, Ann Janine. "Margaret Atwood and Toni Morrison: Reflections on Postmodernism and the Study of Religion and Literature." In *Toni Morrison's Fiction: Contemporary Criticism*, edited by David L. Middleton, 247–68. New York: Garland, 1997.

Morrison, Toni. *Beloved*. New York: Knopf, 1987; reprint, New York: New American Library, 1988.

———. *The Bluest Eye*. New York: Holt, Rinehart, and Winston, 1970.

———. *Jazz*. New York: Knopf, 1992.

———. *Paradise*. New York: Knopf, 1998.

———. *Playing in the Dark: Whiteness and the Literary Imagination*. Cambridge, Massachusetts: Harvard University Press, 1992.

————. *Song of Solomon.* New York: Knopf, 1977.

————. *Sula.* New York: Knopf, 1973.

————. *Tar Baby.* New York: Knopf, 1981.

Murray, Albert. *Train Whistle Guitar.* New York: McGraw-Hill, 1974.

Nadel, Alan. *Invisible Criticism: Ralph Ellison and the American Canon.* Iowa City: University of Iowa Press, 1988.

Narain, Denise deCaires. "The Body of the Woman in the Body of the Text: The Novels of Erna Brodber." In *Caribbean Women Writers: Fiction in English,* edited by Mary Conde and Thorunn Lonsdale, 97–116. New York: St Martin's Press, 1999.

Naylor, Gloria. *Bailey's Café.* New York: Harcourt Brace Jovanovich, 1992.

————. *Linden Hills.* New York: Ticknor and Fields, 1985.

————. *Mama Day.* New York: Ticknor and Fields, 1988; reprint, New York: Random House, 1989.

————. *The Women of Brewster Place.* New York: Viking Press, 1982.

O'Brien, John, ed. *Interviews with Black Writers.* New York: Liveright, 1973.

Ochoa, Peggy. "Morrison's *Beloved:* Allegorically Othering 'White' Christianity." *Melus: The Journal of the Society for the Study of the Multi Ethnic Literature of the United States* 24, no. 2 (1999): 107–23.

Odamtten, Vincent O. "Reviewing Gloria Naylor: Toward a Neo-African Critique." In *Of Dreams Deferred, Dead or Alive: African Perspectives on African-American Writers,* edited by Femi Ojo-Ade, 115–28. Westport, CT: Greenwood, 1996.

O'Daniel, Therman B., ed. *James Baldwin: A Critical Evaluation.* Washington: Howard University Press, 1977.

Olson, Barbara K. "'Come to Jesus Stuff' in James Baldwin's *Go Tell It on the Mountain* and *The Amen Corner.*" *African American Review* 31, no. 2 (Summer 1997): 295–301.

O'Meally, Robert G. *The Craft of Ralph Ellison.* Cambridge: Harvard University Press, 1980.

O'Neale, Sondra. "Fathers, Gods, and Religion: Perceptions of Christianity and Ethnic Faith in James Baldwin." In *Critical Essays on James Baldwin,* edited by Nancy Burt and Fred Standley, 125–43. Boston: G. K. Hall, 1988.

Osagie, Iyunolu. "Is Morrison Also Among the Prophets? 'Psychoanalytic' Strategies in *Beloved.*" *African American Review* 28, no. 3 (1994): 423–40.

Petry, Ann. *The Street.* Boston: Houghton Mifflin, 1946.

Porter, Horace. *Stealing the Fire: The Art and Protest of James Baldwin.* Wesleyan, CT: Wesleyan University Press, 1989.

Pratt, Louis. *James Baldwin.* Boston: Twayne, 1978.

Reed, Ishmael. *Conjure: Selected Poems, 1963–1970.* Amherst: University of Massachusetts Press, 1972.

———. *Flight to Canada*. New York: Random House, 1976.

———. *The Free-Lance Pallbearers*. 1967. Chatham, NJ: Chatham Bookseller, 1967.

———. *Japanese by Spring*. New York: Atheneum, 1993.

———. *The Last Days of Louisiana Red*. New York: Random House, 1974.

———. *Mumbo Jumbo*. New York: Doubleday, 1972; reprint, New York: Macmillan, 1988.

———. *Reckless Eyeballing*. New York: St. Martin's Press, 1986.

———. "Shrovetide in Old New Orleans." In *The Ishmael Reed Reader*, 305–26. New York: Basic Books, 2000.

———. *The Terrible Threes*. New York: Atheneum, 1989.

———. *The Terrible Twos*. New York: St. Martin's Press, 1982.

———. *Writin' Is Fightin': Thirty-Seven Years of Boxing on Paper*. New York: Atheneum, 1988.

———. *Yellow Back Radio Broke Down*. New York: Doubleday, 1969.

Rhodes, Jewell Parker. *Voodoo Dreams: A Novel of Marie Laveau*. New York: St. Martin's Press, 1993.

Rowell, Charles. "An Interview with Randall Kenan." *Callaloo* 21, no. 1 (1998): 133–48.

Ruas, Charles. *Conversations with American Writers*. New York: Knopf, 1985.

Ryan, Judylyn S. "Spirituality and/as Ideology in Black Women's Literature: The Preaching of Maria W. Stewart and Baby Suggs, Holy." In *Women Preachers and Prophets through Two Millennia of Christianity*, edited by Beverly Mayne and Pamela J. Walker, 267–87. Berkeley: University of California Press, 1998.

Samuels, Wilfred. "Going Home: A Conversation with John Edgar Wideman." *Callaloo* 6, no. 1 (1983): 40–59.

Savory, Jerold J. "Bigger Thomas and the Book of Job: The Epigraph of *Native Son*." *Negro American Literature Forum* 9 (1975): 55–56.

Scholl, Diane. "With Ears to Hear and Eyes to See: Alice Walker's Parable *The Color Purple*." *Christianity and Literature* 40, no. 3 (1991): 255–66.

Shadle, Mark. "A Bird's-Eye View: Ishmael Reed's Unsettling of the Score by Munching and Mooching on the Mumbo Jumbo Work of History." In *The Critical Response to Ishmael Reed*, edited by Bruce Dick, 59–69. Westport, CT: Greenwood Press, 1999.

Shange, Ntozake. *Sassafras, Cypress, and Indigo*. New York: St. Martin's Press, 1982.

Smith, Theophus H. *Conjuring Culture: Biblical Formations of Black America*. New York: Oxford University Press, 1994.

Southerland, Ellease. *Let the Lion Eat Straw*. New York: Scribner's, 1979.

Sstorhoff, Gary. "'The Only Voice Is Your Own': Gloria Naylor's Revision of *The Tempest*." *African-American Review* 28, no. 2 (Spring 1995): 35–45.

Standley, Fred L. "Go Tell It on the Mountain: Religion as the Indirect Method of Indictment." In *Critical Essays on James Baldwin Literature,* edited by Nancy Burt
and Fred Standley, 188–94. Boston: G. K. Hall, 1988.

Swope, Richard. "Crossing Western Space, or the Hoodoo Detective on the Boundary in Ishmael Reed's *Mumbo Jumbo." African American Review* 36, no. 4 (Winter 2002): 611–28.

Thompson, Dorothy Perry. "Africana Womanist Revision in Gloria Naylor's *Mama
Day* and *Bailey's Café."* In *Gloria Naylor's Early Novels,* edited by Margot Anne
Kelley, 89–111. Gainesville: University of Florida Press, 1999.

Thyreen, Jeannine. "Alice Walker's *The Color Purple:* Redefining God and (Re)Claim-
ing the Spirit Within." *Christianity and Literature* 49, no. 1 (1999): 49–66.

Tiffin, Helen. "Cold Hearts and (Foreign) Tongues: Recitation and the Reclamation
of the Female Body in the Works of Erna Brodber and Jamaica Kincaid." *Callaloo*
16, no. 4 (Fall 1993): 909–21.

Toomer, Jean. *Cane.* New York: Boni and Liveright, 1923.

Tucker, Lindsey. "Recovering the Conjure Woman: Texts and Contexts in Gloria
Naylor's *Mama Day."* In *The Critical Response to Gloria Naylor,* edited by Sharon
Felton and Michelle C. Loris, 143–58. Westport, CT: Greenwood Press, 1997.

Walker, Alice. *The Color Purple.* New York: Harcourt, Brace, 1982.

———. *Meridian.* New York: Harcourt, Brace, Jovanovich, 1976.

———. *In Search of Our Mothers' Gardens: Womanist Prose.* San Diego: Harcourt,
Brace, Jovanovich, 1983.

———. *The Third Life of Grange Copeland.* New York: Harcourt, Brace, Jovanovich,
1970.

Wall, Cheryl. "Extending the Line: From *Sula* to *Mama Day." Callaloo* 23, no. 4 (Fall
2000): 1149–63.

Warren, Nagueyalti. "The Substance of Things Hoped For: Faith in *Go Tell It On The
Mountain* and *Just Above My Head." Obsidian II* 7, no. 1–2 (Spring–Summer
1992): 19–32.

Washington, Bryan R. "Wrestling with 'The Love that Dare Not Speak Its Name':
John, Elisha, and the 'Master.'" In *New Essays on Go Tell It on the Mountain,* edited by Trudier Harris, 77–95. New York: Cambridge University Press, 1996.

White, Walter. *Fire in the Flint.* New York: Knopf, 1924.

Wideman, John Edgar. *Brothers and Keepers.* New York: Holt, Rinehart, and Winston, 1984.

———. *The Cattle Killing.* New York: Houghton Mifflin, 1996.

———. *Damballah.* New York: Avon, 1981.

———. *Fatheralong: A Meditation on Fathers and Sons, Race and Society.* New York:
Pantheon, 1994.

———. *Fever: Twelve Stories.* New York: Henry Holt and Company, 1989.

————. *A Glance Away.* Chatham, NJ: Chatham Bookseller, 1967.

————. *Hiding Place.* New York: Avon, 1981.

————. *Hurry Home.* New York: Harcourt, 1970.

————. *The Lynchers.* New York: Harcourt, 1973.

————. *Philadelphia Fire.* New York: Henry Holt, 1990.

————. *Reuben.* New York: Henry Holt, 1987.

————. *Sent for You Yesterday.* New York: Avon, 1983.

————. *Two Cities.* New York: Houghton Mifflin Company, 1998.

Williams, Carolyn. "'Trying to Do without God': The Revision of Epistolary Address in *The Color Purple.*" In *Writing the Female Voice: Essays on Epistolary Literature,* edited by Elizabeth Goldsmith, 273–285. Boston: Northeastern University Press, 1989.

Williams, Sherley Anne. *Dessa Rose.* New York: William Morrow, 1986.

Winter, Per. "The Ending of Ralph Ellison's *Invisible Man.*" *College Language Association Journal* 25, no. 3 (1981): 267–87.

Wright, Richard. *Black Boy.* New York: Harper and Brothers, 1945.

————. *The Long Dream.* New York: Ace Publishing Corporation, 1958.

————. *Native Son.* New York: Harper and Row, 1940; reprint, New York: Harper and Row, 1966.

————. *The Outsider.* New York: Harper and Brothers, 1953.

————. *Uncle Tom's Children: Four Novellas.* New York: Harper and Brothers, 1938.